What Market, What Society, What Union?

Martinho Lucas Pires · Francisco Pereira Coutinho
Editors

What Market, What Society, What Union?

The Treaty of Amsterdam and the European Thought of Francisco Lucas Pires

ASSER PRESS

Springer

Editors
Martinho Lucas Pires
Faculty of Law
Católica Law School
Lisbon, Portugal

Francisco Pereira Coutinho
Nova Law School, Faculty of Law
Nova University of Lisbon
Lisbon, Portugal

ISBN 978-94-6265-370-2 ISBN 978-94-6265-371-9 (eBook)
https://doi.org/10.1007/978-94-6265-371-9

Published by T.M.C. ASSER PRESS, The Hague, The Netherlands www.asserpress.nl
Produced and distributed for T.M.C. ASSER PRESS by Springer-Verlag Berlin Heidelberg

This T.M.C. ASSER PRESS imprint is published by the registered company Springer-Verlag GmbH, DE part of Springer Nature.
The registered company address is: Heidelberger Platz 3, 14197 Berlin, Germany

Foreword

What Francisco Lucas Pires Can Teach Europe Today

Francisco Lucas Pires was a true European in the most genuine and valuable sense. He was a European in the footsteps of Ortega y Gasset or Georg Steiner. He was a uniquely creative and cultivated intellectual whose thinking was inherently European. Shaped by European ideas and a perspective on reality that was embedded in Europe. He also followed the great European intellectual tradition where knowledge and curiosity know no borders, either of style, scientific disciplines or activities. He was comfortable as a politician as an academic or as an essayist as he was uncomfortable in all of them... His mind was restless and guided only by intellectual curiosity and the need to understand the world around him in a productive way.

That is visible in his legal writings, such as this book, now published in English with a remarkable set of comments that make clear how much of what Lucas Pires thought is still pertinent today and of great value to understand and shape the current challenges faced by the European Union.

Francisco Lucas Pires was a visionary. Perhaps the first to use the expression European Constitutional Law and one of the first to understand that the development of European integration would require a new understanding of democracy and social justice beyond the state. He did not argue against the state, but argued that the future of governance in Europe would also require the development of a European political community founded on democracy and justice.

Many have argued in favour of political integration in Europe, but if Francisco Lucas Pires were here he would tell us that we are already politically integrated, such is the degree of interdependence between our policies. What we need do is to discuss how to legitimate such political integration with the absence of European politics being the biggest of our democratic challenges.

This remains the key issue today, as what followed the recent European Parliament elections made obvious. We ask citizens to be part of a European polity but then allow such polity to be dominated by national politics. It is also clear that overcoming the current crisis entails the enlargement of the fiscal and political responsibilities of the European institutions. This, in turn, requires the emergence of a European political space so as to give to the Union the legitimacy, authority and efficacy necessary for the tasks that is acquiring and will need to acquire. At the centre of this political space must be the citizen, the citizen of both the States and the European Union. As argued by Francisco Lucas Pires, by putting the citizen first we can overcome a zero-sum approach to the relation between the European Union and the Member States. It is possible for State and European political communities to co-exist, precisely because of the primacy of citizenship at the core of any constitutional project.

In fact, for Lucas Pires, national and European constitutional forms and ambitions were different but had to be part of the same project of constitutionalism. They would mutually reinforce and correct each other. This was not absent of problems and challenges, but it was required to achieve the goals of constitutionalism in an increasingly interdependent world. This was the challenge for constitutional scholars and European politicians alike. To build an open model of European integration that would embody both national and European constitutionalism in a broader open constitutional project for the future. As he stated it: "A model of open unity, by definition indefinable, is the only viable and desirable one. But it needs to be inspired by the basic ideas of subsidiarity, solidarity and openness. This is the Europe we can build democratically and in peace".

It was so when he wrote it. It is even more so today.

Miguel Poiares Maduro
Director of the School of Transnational Governance
of the European University Institute in Florence
Florence, Italy

Preface

Twenty-two years have passed since the signing of the Treaty of Amsterdam. At the time, this Treaty was understood as a moment for amending and strengthening some of the bold options taken previously in the Treaty of Maastricht,[1] particularly regarding the social and political dimension of the Union's constitutional order. Important developments were made in Amsterdam regarding mobility and external relations, with the formal introduction of the Schengen agreements into the EU's *acquis* and the granting of legislative power to EU institutions in the area of asylum policies. The capacity to coordinate national employment policies and the possibility of taking some measures in the area of social policy were added to the Union's legal framework. Institutional and procedural reforms were also implemented, such as the spread of the co-decision procedure and qualified majority voting to the majority of policy areas, and the introduction of the mechanism of enhanced cooperation. Constitutional "teeth" were added with Article 6 of the Treaty of the European Union for suspending a Member State's rights under the Treaties for breaching the "ideals" of the EU: no less than democracy, liberty and the rule of law.

Despite the improvements, the perception was that Amsterdam did not amount to the change that was necessary, ending up, as a typical Portuguese saying goes, to "taste very little".[2] The passing of time did not help: shortly after Amsterdam came the Treaty of Nice, followed by a period of an apparent *pouvoir constituant* that ended up in the Treaty of Lisbon, where many of the issues and controversies arising from Maastricht were set (in a good or bad way, it remains to be seen). It therefore seems easy to overlook Amsterdam as just a moment for supranational

[1]Weiler J. H. H. (1999) The Constitution of Europe: 'Do the New Clothes Have an Emperor?' and Other Essays on European Integration, Cambridge University Press.

[2]On the Amsterdam Treaty and its achievements at the time, see Pernice I (1999) Multilevel Constitutionalism and the Treaty of Amsterdam: European Constitution-making Revisited?, Common Market Law Review 36, 703–750. and Moravcsik A and Nicolaidis K (1999) Explaining the Treaty of Amsterdam: Interests, Influence, Institutions, Journal of Common Market Studies Vol. 37, 59–85. For a current opinion, see Craig P (2017) Development of the EU, in Barnard C and Peers S (eds) European Union Law, Oxford.

"housekeeping", to fix certain institutional and normative aspects and lose track of its significance between the two constitutional enterprises of Maastricht and Lisbon.

However, a closer look at Amsterdam's main innovations from the current point of view—in an era where the EU's political credentials are more at stake than before, as demonstrated by the subjects and aftermath of the several post-Lisbon crises (refugees, Euro, rule of law, Brexit…)—shows how this often unheralded Treaty marked a significant step towards a more profound, humanistic stance of European Integration. Building upon the Maastricht steps, it developed a more protective and broader space for the individual in Europe, an individual that stopped being limited to the consumer but included now also the foreigner, the refugee, the worker, the pensioner—the person. More than a mere constitutional re-tuning, it rather confirmed and set out a clear constitutional path to Europe, despite all the shortcomings. The impact of these measures is being widely felt today in Europe, as it can be seen, for example, with the migration crisis and the tensions surrounding application of the Schengen rules, or the enforcement of Article 6 against certain Member States for failure to comply with the respect for the rule of law, or still with the development of differentiation in policy areas such as the EMU and the cuts on social policies coming from the application of austerity policies due to EU macroeconomic supervision rules. The constitutional delivery of Amsterdam may have been modest, but its "promise" was not.

In this sense, a revision of Amsterdam is also, necessarily, a reflection on the current constitutional status of the EU, and an important backdrop in which to assess the merits and pitfalls of such a path, and to consider how to better build upon its achievements to guarantee the fulfilment of its "promise".

If there was someone who would revel in participating, discussing and debating about constitutional moments, constitutional challenges and promises, that person would be Francisco Lucas Pires, my father. Lucas Pires was a Portuguese professor of constitutional law and EU law, and also a politician. As a scholar, Lucas Pires, who graduated and received his Ph.D. in constitutional law from Coimbra Law School (where he was an associated professor), researched and lectured in public law and political science. He started his research in the field of constitutional theory, the subject of both his post-graduate thesis ("*O Problema da Constitutição*") and Ph.D. dissertation ("*Teoria da Constituição de 1976: a Transição Dualista*"), before moving his analytical and critical insights to the legal and political nature of the EU. He published extensively in these fields, becoming one of the most original and known constitutionalists in Portugal. His interventions and books on European Integration—such as *"Introdução ao Direito Constitucional Europeu"* ("Introduction to European Constitutional" *Law*) published in 1997—also made him one of the most known and respected Portuguese thinkers of European law and politics.

Lucas Pires' interest on constitutional law was not only theoretical, but also practical. As a politician, Lucas Pires served as a Member of the Portuguese Parliament, from 1976 to 1985, where he was an active participant in the constitutional reform of 1982. He was Minister of Culture between 1982 and 1983 and leader of the Christian Democratic Party in 1983 to 1985. In 1987, he was elected to the European Parliament, where he served until his untimely death, in 1998. In Brussels, he was no less active than in Lisbon, participating in the drafting of the Maastricht and Amsterdam treaties, coordinating the European People's Party Parliamentary Group and being twice elected vice-president of the European Parliament (in 1987 and 1998).

I will leave more details about his political life and biography to the short note prepared by Edmundo Alves. I will also leave the explanation of the importance and impact and thought of his works to the preface generously prepared by Miguel Poiares Maduro. I would just like to say that Lucas Pires was a cosmopolitan scholar and an active political participant. He had in him the sagacity and creativity of an academic mind, mixed with the desire and fight of a parliamentarian, willing to argue and discuss, with a great degree of knowledge and depth, his ideas and ideals. He was also a strong believer in the European project, an enthusiastic parliamentarian, never shying away from a political debate and participation. He was a civic, public actor *in totem*, willing to defend his ideas for the common good, both in universities and in assemblies. He lived, in the words of Helmut Kohl, "in exemplary fashion, the ideal of comprehension between nations".[3]

His untimely disappearance came 20 years ago, but his readings still show a remarkable and provocative actuality, providing important reflections and many new ways to look at the current political and constitutional challenges that the EU now faces. His swan song was the book "*Amesterdão: do Mercado à Sociedade Civil Europeia*" ("Amsterdam: from the Market to the European Civil Society") published posthumously in 1999. In it, Lucas Pires discusses the drafting and discussions of Amsterdam, and its wider implications, introducing the Treaty and the history of its negotiations with the nous and authority of an active participant in the process, as well as with the critical eye of a distanced analyst.

The result is a profound and original reflection, in the form of a legal-political essay, of an important moment in European Integration history, that had a crucial impact in the time we are now living in. The book looks at the most important issues that Europe is facing today, such as the power of the Union as a community of values and citizens, the importance of social policy, the governance questions arising from institutional and normative changes, the relationship between Member States, the new competences on asylum and Schengen, and of the role of the euro as a catalyst for European Integration.

Francisco Pereira Coutinho and my family devised under this scenario, the perfect homage to the person that the American constitutionalist Bruce Ackerman labelled an "original thinker": a conference on the past, present and future of the EU based on the comment of Lucas Pires' last book. This was possible thanks to the translation of Lucas Pires' book *Amsterdam: from the Market to the European Civil Society* to English, generously supported by the European People's Party, and commented by young European academics that never had contacted with the thought of Lucas Pires before. In this way, it would be possible to offer new and

[3]Citation on the back page of the Portuguese edition of the book, translated by the author.

enriching thoughts and considerations on political and legal challenges of our times and, at the same time, to honour Lucas Pires' legacy. The conference, titled "What market, what society, what Union? The Treaty of Amsterdam and the European thought of Francisco Lucas Pires", took place on 4 October 2018.

This book is the result of that conference. The first part of the book is composed by the translation of *Amsterdam: from the Market to the European Civil Society* to English, made by Luís Tirapicos Nunes, with a revision by Richard Rodgers. The translators successfully managed to adapt the Portuguese text to the English language while maintaining all its depth of content and literary "punch". The second part of the book consists of six short essays written by six EU Law professors, from different European universities, discussing and engaging with a topic of Lucas Pires' manuscript. In the first essay, "Constitutionalism, Federalism and Constitutional Reforms in Francisco Lucas Pires' Thought", Giuseppe Martinico, associate professor of comparative public law at the Scuola Superiore Sant'Anna, Pisa, focuses on the analysis of three points: notions of constitutional terminology, importance of constitutional reforms for the creation of a "federal-like" EU and the importance of the social question at supranational level. In the second essay, "The EU Democratic Governance in Francisco Lucas Pires' Thought and Its Enduring Topicality", Cristina Fasone, assistant professor of comparative public law at LUISS School of Government, Rome, reflects on EU governance and its connection with the many dimensions (representative, participatory) of democracy, and the latter's importance as a more civilizing force on the market. The third essay, "European civil society, rights and non-Europeans: thoughts upon reading Amsterdam—From the Market to the European Society by Francisco Lucas Pires" comes from Samo Bardutzky, assistant professor and head of the constitutional law department of the University of Ljubljana Law School, Ljubljana. In this essay, the author discusses the current status of European citizenship and tensions within European civil society regarding the refugee situation, addressing the importance of the role of rights and of the notion of public sphere. The fourth essay comes from Diane Fromage, assistant professor of European law at Maastricht University, Maastricht, and is entitled "Francisco Lucas Pires' views on the Economic and Monetary Union and the Single Currency: An Assessment Twenty Years Later". Fromage engages with Lucas Pires' view on the Economic and Monetary Union and the euro, critically assessing the evolution of the single currency in the years that followed the publication of the manuscript. Paschalis Paschalidis, former referéndaire at the Court of Justice of the European Union and current senior associate at Shearman Stearling, reflects on the significance of asylum policy in the EU and its critical development, in the fifth essay "Asylum policy: a measure of the EU's fidelity to its history and values". Finally, in the sixth and final essay "A Sisyphean struggle: Portugal's referendum on European integration", Francisco Pereira Coutinho discusses the complexities of the relationship of Lucas Pires' country of birth with European integration.

The best homage that this book could provide to the memory of Lucas Pires can be summoned in three points: first, that it serves as the first English translation of his works to be published for a broad audience of scholars, politicians and alike;

second, that it provides a platform for discussion of the past and present of European Integration by different original voices; and third and final, that it can help in the reflection and subsequent debates and actions for the improvement of EU integration, particularly given the challenges ahead. As Lucas Pires stated at the beginning of his manuscript,

> Indeed, it is actually at moments when one is at a crossroads and the ambiguity is at its greatest, or when, as now, the result seems more dispersedly reactive than coherently propositional, that the integrating contribution of the law can offer a perspective that is simultaneously more consistent and useful than that provided by fickle conjunctural political purposes.

Hopefully, this book will provide such a contribution.

On behalf of Lucas Pires' family, I would like to make some acknowledgements. The first and principal thank goes to Francisco Pereira Coutinho, a true academic and friend who actively proposed and helped develop this book. The second goes to Frank Bakker and Asser Press for accepting to publish this book and for all the patience with the process. Thank you to everyone at Nova Law School who helped organize the conference and this book, with a special thanks, regarding the latter, due to João Azevedo. Thank you to Luís Tirapicos Nunes for the translation of Lucas Pires' manuscript to English and for Richard Rodgers for the revision work for the manuscript to be published in this book. Thank you to Rui Moura Ramos, Nuno Piçarra and Paulo Rangel for their testimonies and statements in the conference at Nova Law School. Thank you to Miguel Poiares Maduro for continuing to honour the legacy of Lucas Pires. Thank you to Henrique Mota and Principia for all the friendship, help and support with the publication of the manuscript in English. Thank you to Miguel Seabra, for just about everything in what relates to keep the memory of Lucas Pires alive. A special thanks to Edmundo Alves for the biographical note. Finally, a great thanks to Cristina, Diane, Giuseppe, Samo and Paschalis for their time and work in reading and critically reflecting on Lucas Pires' work and engaging with his ideas. It was what he liked the most: to discuss, to engage, to act upon the discussion of ideas and, if not change, at least shake the paradigm.

This book would not have been possible without the support of the EPP, of which the family of Lucas Pires in particular thanks the person of Martin Kamp, Secretary-General of the Party, who generously supported the translation of Lucas Pires' manuscript into English. The help of the European Parliament's representation in Portugal in supporting the conference in Lisbon is to be acknowledged also, in the person of Pedro Valente. I would also like to thank, on behalf of the family of Lucas Pires, Jurisnova for making it possible that this oeuvre can see the light of day.

Lisbon, Portugal

Martinho Lucas Pires

Biography of Francisco António Lucas Pires

Francisco António Lucas Pires was born in Coimbra in October 1944.

After finishing his secondary education at Liceu D. João III, Lucas Pires pursued studies at University of Coimbra Law School. Specializing in constitutional studies, obtained a post-graduate degree in Political and Economic Sciences in 1969 and a Ph.D. with the Dissertation *Teoria da Constituição de 1976. A Transição Dualista*, both from University of Coimbra.

In 1967, Lucas Pires started a thirty-year-long teaching career, first at his *alma mater*, as an assistant lecturer, and later at Catholic University of Portugal and Autónoma University of Lisbon, as headmaster of its law department.

As a nationalist right militant in his youth, Lucas Pires took part in movements such as Movimento Jovem Portugal and Cooperativa Livreira Cidadela. After the coup of 25 April 1974, he joined the Christian Democratic Party Centro Democrático Social (CDS), being one of its vice-presidents between 1978 and 1983 and president between 1983 and 1985. As president of CDS, he was elected vice-president of the European Union of Christian Democrats (UECD). Member of the Portuguese parliament—Assembleia da República—between 1976 and 1986, he was nominated, in that capacity, to the Council of Europe Parliamentary Assembly.

At the end of the 1970s, Lucas Pires successfully coordinated the negotiations between the centre-right parties in order to form a coalition, Aliança Democrática (AD) that would lead three successive governments between 1979 and 1983, taking part in the coalition's third government, the VIII Constitutional Government (1981–1983), as Culture and Scientific Coordination Minister.

In 1987, he was elected member of the European Parliament (EP), as CDS candidate, taking seat at the European People's Party (EPP) parliamentary group. Re-elected in 1989, Lucas Pires detached himself from CDS in 1991, mainly as a consequence of the growing influence of its euroskeptical wing, which would soon take over the party's leadership. In 1994, he was elected for a third term in the EP, this time running in Partido Social Democrata's (PSD) list. Despite PSD being at the time a member of European Liberal Democrat and Reform Party (ELDR), Lucas Pires remained, in his own right, as a popular European MEP, thanks to the efforts of Aníbal Cavaco Silva, president of the social-democrats and Wilfried Martens, then chairman of the EPP.

At the EP, Lucas Pires was a very active member, taking part in numerous parliamentary commissions, being its first Portuguese vice-president, between 1986–1987, and again in 1998, when he was also elected vice-chair of the Committee of Institutional Affairs. He was a member of the Committee on the Verification of Credentials, the Committee on Budgets, the Committee on Regional Policy and Regional Planning and the Committee on Legal Affairs and Citizen's Rights, among others.

Lucas Pires was also a member from the European Parliament to the Joint Assembly of the Agreement between the African, Caribbean and Pacific States and the European Economic Community (ACP-EEC), the Delegation for relations with the countries of South Asia and the South Asia Association for Regional Cooperation (SAARC) and the Delegation for relations with Estonia.

As an EPP affiliate, Lucas Pires was spokesman and coordinator of the party's parliamentary group and member of the party's think-tank *Nostradamus*.

His prominent career as MEP and professor came to an abrupt end with his premature demise at the age of 53, in May 1998.

Edmundo Alves
Researcher at the Institute of Contemporary History of the Social and Human Sciences School of Nova University Lisbon and Ph.D. Candidate in institutional history and contemporary politics at Nova University Lisbon
Lisbon, Portugal

Contents

Part I
Amsterdam: From the Market to a European Civil Society

Editor's Note[1]

Francisco Lucas Pires handed us the final version of the work we are now publishing at the Europe Day celebrations at the Belém Cultural Centre early last May. Its publication was one of the things he wanted to achieve in the run-up to and during the campaign for the referendum on the Amsterdam Treaty. Unfortunately, Francisco did not get to experience the vicissitudes the referendum process went through first-hand, and never knew it would be necessary to wait until 1999 for the Treaty to finally be ratified.

Francisco Lucas Pires was one of the most lucid, committed and creative protagonists of the European project. These pages are his last contribution to an "interpretation of the general and essential sense and direction in which this stage of the construction of Europe is taking us forwards"; they are also his last warning about the need to "redefine objectives and commit to collective goals for reform and action on the arduous path that lies ahead of us, at home and abroad, in this second and other post-single-currency and post-enlargement Europe".

In accordance with the express wish of his family, publication of this text has been postponed until today.

---

[1]Note to the 1998 Portuguese Edition (*Amsterdão: do Mercado á Sociedade Europeia?* (ISBN 972-8500-04-1)), published by PRINCIPIA, Cascais, Portugal.

Chapter 1
Introduction

Amsterdam: A New Stage in the Construction of Europe?

Francisco Lucas Pires

This collection of political/legal (above all political) and legal/political (more clearly in the latter sense) studies on the Treaty of Amsterdam[1] seeks to simultaneously be an evaluation of some of its more symptomatic sectoral progresses and—together with the Preface and Postface—an interpretation of the general and essential sense and direction in which this stage of the construction of Europe is taking us forwards.

A lot of the disappointment caused by the agreement that was reached may in fact be linked to a perspective which looks at the wrong side of things—the side where power takes centre stage. However, Amsterdam is actually revealed when we look at it from the other side—as a "cornerstone" of a European civil society that is not only capable of "civilising" the market, but also of underpinning the popular consensus with regard to the single currency at the same time.

A single market that was crowned by a single currency but lacked both sufficient "union" or political solidarity on the one hand and the legal and moral backing of a European civil society on the other would entail a dual risk. The fact is that while

[1]These are very substantially reviewed and expanded versions of previous public papers or talks, namely: Europa, Novas Fronteiras, n.º 2, Galileu (a journal published by Universidade Autónoma de Lisboa), December 1997; and the Colloquium on Inclusion and Exclusion, We and the Others, which was organised by the Jus Gentium Institute of the University of Coimbra Law School (FDUC) on 21 November 1997.

This chapter was originally published in Portuguese by PRINCIPIA, Cascais, Portugal in the book *Amsterdão: do Mercado á Sociedade Europeia?* (ISBN 972-8500-04-1) in 1998, which was translated from the Portuguese by Luís Tirapicos Nunes and Richard Rodgers. For more information, contact the editors of the present book via the following e-mail address: martinholucaspires@fd.lisboa.ucp.pt.

F. Lucas Pires (Deceased) (✉)
Lisbon, Portugal
e-mail: martinholucaspires@fd.lisboa.ucp.pt

M. Lucas Pires and F. Pereira Coutinho (eds.), *What Market, What Society, What Union?* https://doi.org/10.1007/978-94-6265-371-9_1

the *power* with the capacity to overcome the flaws in the market can only be generated on the political and institutional level, it is on the "civil society" level that the *authority* presumed by the ethics of a liberal order which is capable of becoming consensual can be engendered.

Here, we are obviously not talking about a concept of a Hegelian-type civil society, seen as a set of institutions and rights of a homogeneous, uni-national and single-class bourgeois community. By definition, the civil society of a unity that is as extremely pluralist as the European one cannot reproduce the forms of Hegel's "concrete universal", even when it is capable of encompassing part of its meaning at a moment in time which some have already considered to be the "end of History".

However, I also feel that something more than the simple Habermasian "public sphere" is indispensable where the market and the single currency are concerned. Because without a greater community sentiment, a shared moral and cultural willingness, sufficient guarantees of equal rights and an albeit minimally fulfilled notion of the responsibility of one-for-all-and-all-for-one, the market and the currency would at one and the same time be too abstract, too easily manipulated and too random; and also because, "paradoxically, the total triumph of the market system of values would simultaneously be its hecatomb".[2]

It is only by means of such a "civil society" that one can operate a "civic conversion"[3] of the market and at the same time attain an active reality that interiorises the most generic goals and ensures the normality of life—objectives which go beyond the purely economic moment of the new construction. Only then would one be able to talk about a prior common interest with the ability to articulate—albeit implicitly or unconsciously—the tropism of a borderless Europe, and above all to smooth the path towards a true democracy.

The fact is that it is only possible to foresee the existence of such a European democracy if and to the extent that it is simultaneously anticipated and consummated by the notion of "civil society" as an authentic and current "way of life" (John Dewey). Otherwise, as may often already be happening with the aforementioned construction, one can fall into the trap of an illegitimating contradiction between that democracy and the political rhetoric about it.

Indeed, this reconstruction is both facing a challenge and finding a driving force in the paradigm of globalisation, which, as I have already argued in the past,[4] and now that the issue of European disunion is solved and the spectre of war has passed, one could today consider to be the first justification for a renewed perspective in relation to the construction of Europe. At the very least, this globalisation means

---

[2]See Hösle 1998, p. 867.

[3]See the interesting analysis by Perez Diaz 1997.

[4]At a conference during the Calouste Gulbenkian Foundation Seminar on Europe towards a Protective but non-Protectionist Globalisation (May 1996).

that Europeanisation and its transnational constitutionalisation can no longer be conceived solely on their own basis and within themselves.

On the one hand, as André-Jean Arnaud[5] says, the contemporary movement towards the globalisation of exchanges is being accompanied by a return of a civil society, with an increasing role being played by social regulation; on the other, its reconstruction at the level of the new macro-regional platforms like the European one is acting like a necessary regulatory counterweight—with a function that is at least similar to that of floodgates—to the way in which the markets are overflowing across and above borders.

Without the minimum existence of a corresponding "civil society", the European Constitution, which many have already seen as the best framework for the Treaties establishing the Union and the Communities,[6] will also continue to be distant from what some (Judge Black) call "faith" and others (Habermas) "constitutional patriotism". It is only in that Constitution that it is possible to lastingly imbue that notion, in such a way that its subjectivation is both natural and deep-rooted.

The need for the reconstruction of this concept of a "social society" at the European level may prove even more decisive at a time when the State/Market polarisation is threatening to empty the middle ground which that concept has been occupying[7] and has thereby been ensuring minimum degrees of cohesion and solidarity among political units.

It is precisely on this level that Amsterdam's contribution can be seen as helping to achieve a more democratic and less economics-based culture of European construction—taking advantage of Lincoln's definition of democracy, one could say a culture that seeks a "government" that is more *for* the people (social and employment policies), more *of* the people (substantial strengthening of the European Parliament's powers of co-decision and assent), and more *by* the people (new rights in relation to non-discrimination, equality and participation).

On the one hand the new Treaty outlines the recognition of volunteer work, the public status of churches and the right of sports organisations to be consulted in advance, while on the other it proclaims and guarantees the principles that will govern the life of this new civil society, subordinating the Member States themselves (Democracy, Rule of Law, Social Justice…). What one might call the "citizen's unique space" is thus enlarged.

It is true that solidarity mechanisms are still lacking. However, at least there are more and more legal ones. The essential question that remains in this respect actually lies outside the Treaty. Inasmuch as no true "financial constitution" of the Union has been structured yet, and with the existence of such a constitution dependent on the multiannual budget regime, the question is the extent to which Agenda 2000 will be substantively capable of underpinning the cohesion needed for that "European civil society" project. The fact is that a superstructure of integration

---

[5]Arnaud 1998, p. 32.

[6]See Lucas Pires 1997.

[7]See Barber 1996, pp. 147 *et seq.*

through the law would not achieve much without an infrastructure which provided for any risks of economic disintegration.

It is also within this context of the end of a cycle that the opportunity offered by the following texts may also have to do with a revaluation of the European project in our country. If the idea underlying the minimalist design of Agenda 2000 is—perfectly in line with the Amsterdam Treaty in this respect—one whereby *the Member State that wants more must pay for it*, then the race to achieve *greater flexibility* is indeed underway. That race can already be glimpsed in the new Treaty and, even though it cannot be mistaken for a "*Europe à la carte*", may bring about the formation of avant-garde regroupings at a moment when the enlargement itself will tend to delay the peloton.

There is thus no guarantee that after Amsterdam it will still be possible for the construction of Europe to continue in the same way as it has so far. Having said that, nor is it impossible that, if the euro manages to bring the whole together, it may become the essential integrating cement with the ability to exponentially and lastingly enhance the "ever-closer union among the peoples of Europe" which Maastricht offered us as a motto.

It is true that the enlargement seems on the contrary to be opening the way for centrifugal forces, but the euro's centripetal force is both stronger and was formed earlier than them. What is more, by posing the question of the final frontier (Turkey? Ukraine?), the enlargement itself calls for a more common, stable and solid direction in relation to the future of Europe. The final frontier is the one which, so to speak, makes it possible to start looking within ourselves and thus also concluding the question of purpose.

The attempt that I am making to reconstruct a common purpose in the midst of the myriad of changes made in Amsterdam preserves the last of the hypotheses I have alluded to. Indeed, it is actually at moments when one is at a crossroads and the ambiguity is at its greatest, or when, as now, the result seems more dispersedly reactive than coherently propositional,[8] that the integrating contribution of the law can offer a perspective that is simultaneously more consistent and useful than that provided by fickle conjunctural political purposes.

Is all this enough to enable us to talk about a "new stage in the process of creating an ever closer union among the peoples of Europe" (former Article A, TEU and new Article 1 of the Consolidated Treaties)? As Maastricht said about itself, within the gradualist constitutional development scheme that had indeed already been implicit, I believe the answer is yes, albeit with two provisos: on the one hand, that that phase will not be comparable in importance to the one initiated with the Treaty on European Union (TEU) negotiated in Maastricht; and on the other, it will proceed alongside, and in the short term will certainly be subordinated to, the advent of the common currency, from which it cannot be separated.

It only remains to add that the language and type of analysis I adopt in the following essays attempt to interpret the law in context, in such a way as to help

[8]Expressed in other terms but with the same sense, see Bieber 1997, p. 245.

both reveal and legitimise its meaning. Indeed, I hope that taking this stance will also serve to go beyond the so-called "community of interpreters" and reach the public debate that will precede the first referendum on the Portuguese participation in the construction of Europe.

At a moment when, thanks above all to the prospects of stabilised and inflation-free growth, but also to the fact that the threshold of irreversibility and necessity has now been attained, Europe once again appears to be a construct that is consensual and happy, but also daring and uncertain as to the future, the important thing is no longer even the choice between a "yes" and a "no" to what already exists. What this means is that, as we approach the first Portuguese referendum on Europe, raising people's awareness along the lines of "Yes, but which Europe?" and doing so in a way that is able to help reach a long-term and certain answer, could well be the most suitable and useful contribution anyone can make.

References

Arnaud A-J (1998) Entre Modernité et Mondialisation. Paris

Barber B R (1996) Three Challenges to Reinventing Democracy. In: Hirst P and Khilmani S (eds) The Political Quarterly

Bieber (1997) Reformen der Institutionen und Verfahren - Amsterdam Kein Meisterstück. Integration 4/97, p. 245

Hösle V (1998) Ethik und Politik. Munich

Lucas Pires F (1997) Introdução ao Direito Constitucional Europeu. Coimbra

Perez Diaz V (1997) La Esfera Pública y la Sociedad Civil. Madrid

Chapter 2
Amsterdam: From the Single Market to a European Civil Society

Francisco Lucas Pires

Disproportion Between the Size of the Challenges and the Not Very "Fertile" Revision Method

The "pregnancy" of the Amsterdam Intergovernmental Conference dragged on for a long time—one could say for twice the normal gestation period. It crossed four presidencies of the European Union. Even so, the birth was extremely painful and the child was born half-rickety. Of course, none of this prevents it from being "our baby". However, the immediate underlying problem is the awareness that a European adaptation to an increasingly faster and challenging world is becoming ever slower and more timid.

As we come to the end of the century and the millennium, Europe has been facing at least three historic challenges of a great magnitude:

(a) European enlargement to the east.
(b) Globalisation and its negotiation on terms that are as equal as possible with the United States.
(c) The political/social/institutional accommodation of the arrival of the single currency.

The extent of these challenges was probably going to require a change of both rate and paradigm. The simple natural tropism of the Communities was incapable of forging an adequate calibre of answer to a simultaneously post-communist,

---

This chapter was originally published in Portuguese by PRINCIPIA, Cascais, Portugal in the book *Amsterdão: do Mercado á Sociedade Europeia?* (ISBN 972-8500-04-1) in 1998, which was translated from the Portuguese by Luís Tirapicos Nunes and Richard Rodgers. For more information, contact the editors of the present book via the following e-mail address: martinholucaspires@fd.lisboa.ucp.pt.

F. Lucas Pires (Deceased) (✉)
Lisbon, Portugal
e-mail: martinholucaspires@fd.lisboa.ucp.pt

M. Lucas Pires and F. Pereira Coutinho (eds.), *What Market, What Society, What Union?* https://doi.org/10.1007/978-94-6265-371-9_2

post-modern and post-industrial agenda… We were facing the need for a revision—one that had, moreover, been calculated beforehand (Article N, TEU), but was dependent on the unanimity of fifteen members in a Europe that was even more heterogeneous that that with twelve, and all this in order to govern a third Europe that may come to have twice the current number of Member States.

The Intergovernmental Conference that was concluded in Amsterdam made a real effort, above all thanks to the acceleration provided by the last locomotive—the Dutch presidency. Moreover, its work proceeded more openly than in the past, partly due to the participation of two Members of the European Parliament (Brok and Guigou) as observers. One could say, as a consolation prize, that the "baby's" ultrasound scan was more perfect, but the fact is that this did not reduce the feeling of despair caused by the slowness of the gestation.

At the Limits of the Current Revision Process? The Less the Revision, the Greater the Flexibility!

It is well known, however, that a political Constitution whose revision was dependent on unanimity—as in the case of the Treaties—would, in principle, be rigid, which is to say unchangeable. We also know that globalisation is by definition the opposite of models based on mere intergovernmental cooperation, which globalisation itself renders dysfunctional.

Lastly, it is a no less well-known fact that the integration policy was going through a morbid phase, with governments re-centred on domestic issues, namely unemployment, and absorbed by the desire to reach the single-currency finishing line on time. The conditions could thus hardly have been worse.

What all this means is that not only is the methodology for intergovernmental conferences within a Community that was born with six states getting close to the limit in terms of the number and heterogeneity of the participants, but also that the context and the matters it had to address did not really favour it either. In general, one could even reach the following conclusions about the progressive reduction in the "fertility" of IGCs:

(a) *IGCs are becoming too frequent*: after a break of almost thirty years since the Treaty of Rome, the rate at which IGCs are held has accelerated since the Single European Act, which entered into force in 1987, and each new treaty has subsequently corresponded to an increasingly short cycle.
(b) *IGCs are lasting longer and longer*: as I have already mentioned, it took eighteen months and four presidencies to get to the Treaty of Amsterdam.
(c) *IGCs decide less and less and progresses tend to be more quantitative than qualitative*: the "distance" covered between Maastricht and Amsterdam is small, and people have seemingly forgotten that a lot of water has passed under the bridge in the meantime and that in practice the process was about building a bridge from one century (the 20th) to another (the 21st).

(d) *IGCs are becoming more and more complex*: each new treaty adds new twists to the inherited labyrinth, notwithstanding the fact that Amsterdam has also simplified some aspects by reducing both the separation between Maastricht's three pillars and the number of legislative procedures (from five to three), and by ending the third reading of the co-decision procedure, for instance.
(e) *One of the main decisions taken by each IGC becomes when to schedule the following one, or whether to put the hot topics off until then in a kind of "we'll deal with it next time"*: now, after three IGCs in the last ten years, a new one has already been announced for when the enlargement reaches 20 states (stipulated in the Enlargement Protocol). The issues regarding the number of commissioners and the weighting of votes in the Council should be the primary foci of that prior agenda.

If this descending seriation of results of the European constitutional revision process proves to be true, as seems to be the case, the next question will be: *Will it be worth calling another IGC in the hope of a positive outcome?* If one were to choose to look backwards, prewarned by this set of tendencies determined by the requirement for unanimity, one would not be surprised by Amsterdam's modest results.

The Treaty of Amsterdam thus seems to be too much like a kind of acrobatics with a scattering of reflections that "enshrine environmental conservatism" and, with the exception of the reaffirmation of the single currency, lack a will, goals and a common vision that are sufficiently clear.[1] This is indeed what the postponement of the hardest question—institutional reform—demonstrates. In a sense, at the end of the day Amsterdam could be said to reflect the most eminent exercise of a "reflexive law" that is in fact characteristic of the postmodern law which "Community law" is said to be.[2]

With the enlargement to the other half of Europe—or simply to the "other" Europe, which is itself different in qualitative terms[3] and in relation to which the instrument of mere derogation is no longer enough to serve as an integrative safety valve—the results of that revision method and the extreme inflexibility of the law produced in that way can only get worse.

It was probably also thoughts about the exhaustion[4] and sterility of the ongoing revision procedures that led to a half-opening of the door to flexibility in Amsterdam. At this point one could even postulate the following equation: the less effective revisions become, the more people will resort to flexibility. This now makes both the proposals and the threats of the most integrationist countries in

[1]See Dehousse 1997, pp. 265 *et seq.*

[2]See Lucas Pires 1997, p. 82.

[3]See Mendras 1997, pp. 12 *et seq.* The author particularly highlights both the centrality of the individual in Western Europe as opposed to the prominence of the group in the Eastern part of the continent, and the greater autonomy and laicism of the State in relation to the Church in the West, in contrast to the practices in the East.

[4]See Janning 1997, p. 285.

general and the Franco-German duo in particular more credible, above all at moments of crisis, when that increased flexibility may attain the peak of its effectiveness as a kind of "reserve clause".

The risks of a "Carolingian Europe" or a European Directorate are thus more obvious. The path to the alternative of a more democratic constituent will, based on a broader participation of the European Parliament in the constitutional development process, has not yet opened up. In some respects, it has even seemed as though we have been going back to the policy of "small steps"—literally, that of "lost steps"—with the risk of allowing the construction process to get stuck.

When Portugal reconsiders its positions at the dawn of this new cycle, it should guard against those risks. One might say that a "football metaphor" would be appropriate here—that we were already given advance warning when, in the recent draw for the European Football Championships, we were included in a group made up of Eastern European teams.

On the one hand, it seems that we should continue to bet on the "premier league", as we did with the "single currency". On the other, however, we must ask ourselves whether we should not now invest more deliberately in a democratic and parliamentary Europe. Only the latter can ensure a lasting cohesion of a simultaneously constitutional and popular kind. This is exactly why only such a Europe can ensure that it is proofed against both attacks by major states seeking a more directorial or flexible system and the paralysis brought about by greater intergovernmental complexity, in a Europe enlarged to more than twenty members, most of which carry even less weight and are smaller than us.

In any case, *there now begins a new critical debate, which is now no longer, or at least not mainly, about the Portuguese economy's capacity to coexist in a more developed market with a single currency—problem solved and no turning back—but about the European model which serves Portugal's interests and in which we are not only able to defend and profit from our commitment to the euro, but also to express our interests and our identity in a forceful enough fashion.* This in parallel with the awareness that, although we are being left a bit more to our own devices, there is also an ever more pressing need to speed up the necessary internal reforms—above all with a view to once again sustaining the conquests that have been achieved at a monetary level.

A Return to Consensus! But What Is There to Put to a Referendum?

The fact that Europe is facing a crossroads is thus no reason to stand still with a wait-and-see attitude. Our contribution as a country to a "new vision" of the construction of Europe could even be an essential contribution to the realignment of the role of the small countries. It is no accident that, disconnected as they are from a re-founding vision, the small advances that are still being made in terms of the revision of the Treaties are now also tending to go more sideways than forwards.

Indeed, *the paradox or vicious cycle also consists of this: boxed in between globalisation, Europeanisation and rising domestic pluralism (territorial and corporative), states increasingly need to delegate authority both upwards and downwards, but the truth is that the weaker they feel, the more they resist delegating.*

It is thus no wonder that, as the process advances, it is the pro-Europeans who are becoming more sceptical.[5] With regard to Amsterdam, a few have already gone so far as to ask whether it would be worth ratifying such an outcome at all. Others are beginning to call for a new IGC "now", even before any enlargement—something which, if one believes in the prediction contained in the conclusions I outlined earlier, would only lead to further disappointment.

Symptomatically, in Portugal it was the parties that are most opposed to the construction of Europe which allowed the conclusion of Amsterdam to pass by practically without saying a word. Privately, they must have seen it as "the lesser of two evils". The People's Party (PP) initially appeared to be divided about the single currency, and then even signed up for some, albeit restricted, forms of political union. In the meantime, during a public debate (with Mário Soares and moderated by Gomes Canotilho) the former Secretary-General of the Portuguese Communist Party (Álvaro Cunhal) said that he was not in favour of a Portuguese exit from the European Union… The very loss of ground by both "Eurosceptic" parties in the subsequent local elections may reflect a loss of relative weight in the dispute about Europe and explain the subsequent ongoing reconversion.

Conversely, it was the most pro-European parties that here and there expressed deception with regard to Amsterdam. Quite apart from anything else, this suggests that the Heads of State and Government may have tried to use the pendulum idea, avoiding a repetition of the storm that battered Maastricht in favour of an upturn in the consensus on the construction of Europe, which was broken in the hangover that followed Maastricht.

National leaders must also have intended to thereby avoid obstacles to ratification—which have tended to grow continuously, not least due to the increasing number of national constitutional processes they have to face (fifteen now, instead of twelve) and the factually greater rigidity of the old national Constitutions in relation to the revising dynamic of the Treaties. A political storm identical to that regarding Maastricht would shake the stability of the path towards the single currency and, despite the fact that it is already ratified and in force, would also leave that Treaty in limbo, as if it were a virtual project.

To appease the anti-Europeans thus appeared to be an act of realism, even when—as in the Portuguese case—it meant running the risk of no longer having anything very mobilising—a concept that also signifies debatable—to put to a

[5]However, on a perspective that is more optimistic than the average among self-confessed pro-Europeans, see Ludlow 1997.

referendum. Apart from the general question of the continuity or otherwise of the process of integration itself, which is now political, social and Pan-European and not just economic and occidental, what else of substance is there in the Amsterdam Treaty, in fact, to vote on in a referendum? This is one more reason why I also consider that a referendum under those conditions will serve above all to complete the appeasement process and move forwards.

And can one ignore the dissatisfaction of the Euro-optimists? In the long run they are not even dangerous... They know they are unable to organise so much as a mini-demonstration against the Amsterdam Treaty! And for them it is also better to move forwards to Amsterdam than to go back to Maastricht. The relevant comparison is with the latter, not with some ideal model of the construction of Europe. Questioning Amsterdam would also mean questioning the sole "masterpiece" of Maastricht—the single currency.

Besides, the pro-Europeans have had long enough to understand that many of their previous deceptions have in the end proven to be much less disappointing than they were predicted to be. Pierre Pescatore, one of the most respected former Judges of the Court of Justice of the European Communities, actually went so far as to say that the Single European Act had been a backwards move, but today it is commonly considered that, on the contrary, it was a substantial step forward.

Quickly and Decisively Towards the Post-Amsterdam Era...

This time, the confidence that the Treaty will be ratified is so great that both the Luxembourg Presidency and then the UK Presidency began to execute it right away, before the ratification processes had even begun. Within the framework of the CFSP, the analysis and early warning unit created in Amsterdam began to be set up immediately; and the implementation of the procedures for the Schengen integration then got underway as well. The employment policy has already had an extraordinary summit, on 20 November 1997. In answer to a question I asked at the meeting between Jacques Poos (the Foreign Minister of Luxembourg and former President of the Council) and the chairmen of the European Parliamentary Committees, Mr. Poos argued that it was possible to implement such policies even though they had not been approved in Amsterdam...

What is more, the draft Treaty—concluded in the city whose harbour provided the title and the theme for one of Jacques Brel's most beautiful and best-known songs—deliberately adopted open concepts in the expectation that they would be especially developed later on. *That development includes the* "generalissima *clause", which goes by the name of the "area of freedom, justice and security". A "public area" is a new type of political and legal construction site and one which, incorporating Schengen as it now does, may prove to be extremely productive.* It is no accident that there is already talk of a "95 Package" or "Monti Package" (named after the commissioner with responsibility for freedom of movement), in a sort of equivalent for this area, albeit on a smaller scale than the famous "Single Market White Paper".

The concept of "flexibility" was also introduced. Although highly conditioned and policed, it opens up the possibility of new forward-traction models for the construction of Europe. It is the outline of a new method for moving forwards. It is not an exception or a mere way of negatively opting-out, but instead represents the possibility of a collective headlong flight into the future. *Both cases ("area" and "flexibility") presuppose possibilities, restricted though they may be, of an evolution into uncharted waters.*

In turn, the employment and social policies have ceased to be subsidiary or supplementary and have acquired almost the same status as that of the economic policies. At the same time, certain fundamental principles, such as non-discrimination between men and women, have taken on a more positive and global formulation, to the extent that ensuring this principle of equality is now considered to be one of the Community's central tasks (Article 2, TEC).[6]

In any case, treaties are not the only source of the constitutional development of the Communities. We have already witnessed the signature of a Stability Pact between the Finance Ministries of the Fifteen—at the end of the day, a kind of "enhanced cooperation" *avant la lettre*—and an Interinstitutional Agreement on Provisions regarding the Financing of the Common Foreign and Security Policy (16 July 1997). Both created *praeter tractatuum* norms and (especially the former) lasting restrictions on the exercise and scope of national sovereignties.

What is more, in an emergency it will be possible for the treaties themselves to be modified as the enlargement takes place, taking advantage of the fact that the entry of each new Member State requires the ratification of the applicable accession agreement by all fifteen existing Members; albeit it may be felt that compliance with the TEU revision rules would include having to both consult the European Parliament and allow the Commission to intervene, thereby effectively presupposing a virtual IGC.

It is worth adding that the Court of Justice's case law, the principle of the primacy of EU law, Article 235, the concept of effectiveness and the various implicit powers will all still be there to make it possible to fill in the gaps, as they have in the past. Community law is moreover the favourite ground for "hermeneutics", at least in the sense that everything in that law is about interpretation, and the whole of that interpretation revolves around both the norm itself and the event that allows us to unravel its meaning.

Beyond the current procedures, the incrementalism derived from the mere necessity and contiguity of the various different aspects of Community life will

[6]On these points, see Amsterdam: the first Social Constitution of a Liberal Europe, also published in this set of essays (note from the original manuscript).

continue to operate, even more so after the introduction of the single currency, which will simultaneously be "the great step forward", the jet engine and the primary anchor of the irreversibility of the construction process.

Ratifying Amsterdam Will also Mean Ratifying the Single Currency and the Continuity of the Integration Process

Indeed, this is where we find the practical reason that even Europhiles cannot fail to take into consideration. *From the standpoint of the main objective—the single currency—Amsterdam, Agenda 2000 and the Extraordinary Council meeting on Employment (20 November 1997) are mainly "maintenance exercises" or "respiratory gymnastics".* Seen from a different perspective, they are also rituals for "calming" the wrath of external elements towards the single currency, whose arrival people are waiting for and hope to protect and legitimise by any means, now that it has been cut down to its weakest version: the more who are in it the better, even if that means flexibly interpreting the convergence criteria.

It is dangerous to piggy-back successive revolutions; and this time the revolution is that of the single currency and is still ongoing. This is perhaps the biggest European revolution since Russia in 1917—perhaps even bigger, now that the latter has consumed itself. The efforts which are being made in parallel to that involved in the creation of the euro thus generically match the classic Lampedusa saying whereby we have to change something if we want everything to stay as it is, albeit in this case with a small improvement. The thing is that while the single currency does not countenance spending a single extra euro, let alone from European funds (see Agenda 2000), at the same time it requires the continued possibility of movement, which in this case is like that of a two-wheeler for which stopping is equivalent to crashing.

Understanding this point is absolutely essential. *To ratify Amsterdam is also to ratify both the single currency, and over and above that, the continuity of the social and political integration of Europe. It also represents the authorisation to move on to the next stage. Hence the dual strategy—i.e. criticising and approving at the same time—is the ideal one.* The criticism is effectively a demand for what people want next, and not just protest for its own sake. It serves to clarify goals, which are even more obscured than they used to be by the complexity of additional normative provisions and may cause voters in a referendum to be discouraged in a variety of ways.

In fact, there is another advantage to the general question that will be asked in the referendum—whether people are willing to subscribe to the continued Portuguese participation in the social and political integration of Europe or not: not only does it transfer the problem, for the first time, from the political class, elites and groups with access to power, to the people, but it also lifts the curtain on the potential adversaries of integration as a whole, at a time when the mirrors offered by political parties no longer sufficiently reflect those images of rejection. "Yes" supporters, on the other hand, must be clear about their choice, because the post-single currency period will not be a walk in the park either. Without that clarity, the European referendum could actually be the victim of too much consensus and end up not even mobilising the fifty per cent of voters needed to legitimise it.

Consequences: A Cut-Down Version of Enlargement or 15+5

The single currency instrumentalises and reduces everything around it in order to better sustain itself. *Amsterdam began by reducing the enlargement. The fact that it says that once five new Members have joined and there is one commissioner per Member State, the Commission's format should be redefined and in parallel the weighting of votes should be re-evaluated, means that this Treaty seems to only be for five new members (see Article 2 of the Protocol on the Institutions with the Prospect of Enlargement of the European Union).* In the countdown to another enlargement, institutional reform—like the one decided in Lisbon in June 1992—would be put off until afterwards.

Some people think that Amsterdam does not even work for those first five candidates and that the situation is very different to the one that was preconfigured at the aforementioned Lisbon Summit.[7] Moreover, this time, such opinionators are more numerous than those who already believed that not even Maastricht would be capable of accommodating the former Nordic EFTAs and Austria; and just imagine what would happen if they were joined by those who, unhappy with Agenda 2000, then added that they did not want enlargement without prior financial reform either! On top of all this, by proposing a first round of negotiations with six enlargement candidates—albeit in the 5+1 version—the Commission also seems to be asking for a strategy of "a new IGC now".

In the long run the integration logics are inclusive and it will not be possible to turn anyone down, but in the short term, the truth is that the number of "constitutional" and "political" conditions to which enlargement is subject has constantly been growing. And the probability that something equivalent will occur in financial terms is equally great. After all, according to the Treaty of Maastricht, being European is supposed to suffice to apply for accession; but under the Treaty of Amsterdam, it is now necessary to observe the principles of liberty, democracy, fundamental rights and the rule of law.

---

[7]One example is Victor Louis 1997, p. 18. From a political standpoint, the European Parliament is also predominantly in favour of the idea that there should be no enlargement without prior institutional reform.

The 1993 Copenhagen Summit was to underline three criteria: respect for minorities and the ability to deal with competitive pressures within the Union and to attain its monetary objectives. From 1995 onwards, the Commission was to add the requirements to match the fundamental legislation in terms of the internal market and to adopt a consistent pre-accession programme in areas ranging from the institutional to the legal and economic fields. The fact that the single currency is taking the lead is, moreover, making the train that people want to catch go too fast, and could cause risks for those who put their foot on the carriage step too soon… Now the single currency is simultaneously making the Union more magnetically attractive and—and once again—a more distant goal for external countries to reach.

The Small Countries Have Won the First Round, but the Big Ones Are Gearing up for the Second and Final One

Be that as it may, one of the consequences of Amsterdam is that if it does lead to enlargement, the latter could be narrow; as narrow as Agenda 2000 is in financial terms, seeking as it does to fund everything—cohesion, enlargement, revision of the CAP, and a new social policy—from the very benefits it is expected to produce. Just as it is necessary to convince the taxpayers in the rich countries that no one will pay a penny more for the enlargement, it was also necessary to reassure the small countries that they would not lose seats on decision-making bodies such as the Council and the Commission, despite the overcrowding which that same enlargement will cause.

Even if melancholically realist, a realistic interpretation of Amsterdam suits us. It allows us to gain time. The people in a hurry who are asking for a "*revision of the revision, now*" are primarily looking for a reweighting of the votes in the Council. I ask some of my colleagues at the European Parliament who call themselves federalists solely because they confuse federalism with speed and who strive so arduously for that reweighting, why they are more concerned with the "effectiveness" of the Council than with that of "their" Parliament, when on top of everything else the former is going in the same direction as the worst intergovernmental anti-federalisms—the one that ranks Member States according to a population-based criterion and by means of a body that cannot possibly be expected to possess a representative nature like that of the Council.

A period of waiting and reflection thus appears appropriate, and not just because of the single currency. *The issues of the number of commissioners and the weighting of votes are, at one and the same time, too little to solve the problems of the passage to an enlarged Europe and too much in the sense that they alter the model of European construction in its entirety, without sufficient debate or express authorisation by voters, as if they were sneaking in through the back door.*

Is What Is at Stake the Enlargement or the Pan-European Model of the Union?

At this point in time, the fact is that the big and correct question is whether what is at stake is primarily the enlargement, or rather the model for a Union of a political and enlarged Europe that is capable of unity in the face of the problems of globalisation. In one sense, the debate has already started up again, albeit in a way that is partly hidden, if not entirely obscured.

For the first time at the table of this IGC, there were proposals that sought to row back the EU *acquis*, namely with regard to the powers of the Court of Justice. One explanation for this could be the fact that *we are, in part, and as was the case at the beginning of the construction of Europe, now facing the most essential choices, albeit in a context that may not permit the same syncretic answer: intergovernmentalism, federalism, or the combination of both that was recently called the "Community method"?*

Ideally, the third solution is still the best. What is more, it once again includes the path of a tiebreaker between the centripetal force of the *euro* and the centrifugal force of the *enlargement*. The problem, however, is whether it will withstand a 30-Member Europe—i.e. whether the tension between, on the one hand, an intergovernmentalism that is now multiplied by five times the initial number of members (of the Council), which are not only more numerous but also much more heterogeneous, and on the other the proportional federalism which the European Parliament is now assuming with the increase in the co-decision process, means that the two are incompatible with one another.

So far, those plans have been segmented by different thresholds (e.g. monetary union was pro-federal, while political union was intergovernmental). From now on, however, the level of monetary integration that has already been attained seems to itself call for other forms of political integration—not mere cooperation—without which the former may fail. Which is why the latter has already started to spread, namely within the scope of the third pillar.

Meanwhile, given that no one—neither the big countries, nor the small ones—is daring to take the federalist path, the solution attempted by the large states is to make themselves more "equal" than their smaller counterparts—something they are achieving by means of the ranking of their votes and the selection of commissioners. This clearly suggests the introduction of a "Directory-type" factor and tears up the "social contract" on which the current European constitution is based, to such an extent that it requires another basis for its legitimation.

While the questions that need resolving are linked to institutional efficacy and democracy, one must nonetheless realise that some people may want to solve them as if they were about a redistribution of power. The temptation is all the greater when, in a Europe enlarged by Agenda 2000, the resources are scarcer and the possible dividends can only be attained by winning positions on the starting grid. From there it is but a step to a split between a leading peloton and a political/geographical "Club Med"—a step that becomes all the shorter, the more the single currency (which, with eleven members from every corner of Europe, no longer serves to perform the desired selection function) is "democratic" or inclusive.

This reordering of power could be achieved in two ways: either between states, or between states and citizens. Besides being regressive, the former could only favour the big countries; whereas in addition to being the only coherent line along which to pursue the Community project, which is now increasingly closer to citizens but enjoys less legitimacy through them, the latter is the only way to preserve equality of the Member States, which are themselves "legal persons" that all possess an identical degree of "dignity".

The question at this point is thus whether, in the absence of another alternative, the time has come for the small countries to prefer a more federalist model which, although reducing their power as states, would also decrease the power of the big countries. Unlike the alternative offered so far, such a solution would also continue to guarantee the smaller nations a formal principle of equality.

Incapable as they are of affirming a more federative logic, the last line of defence available to the small countries in the negotiations will end up being a minimalist reweighting of votes, with or without a rotation of commissioners. However, not only would intergovernmentalism and a lack of cohesion be strengthened in both cases, but an additional nuance would be that the reweighting would be restricted to areas such as defence policy, in which the current relative equality is more unrealistic and counterproductive.

One must bear in mind that although the Commission is neutral, it has historically worked as a substitute for the states where the organisation of the common economic area among them is concerned. The representation of the states within the Commission was thus functional from the standpoint of a set of Communities that were designed to be an Economic State. With the transformation of the Communities into a Union, with greater autonomy in relation to the states, the question could pose itself in a different way. In that case it would, however, be more coherent to take the new logic all the way, transforming the Commission into a sort of Government legitimised by the European Parliament and constituted within it. This, however, appears to both lack consensus and fail to correspond to the state of political state development attained in Amsterdam.

In the meantime, and unlike the last point, separating the question of the number of commissioners from the weighting of votes in the Council would be an important plus. The thing is that the first of these two questions is probably easier to solve in a way that satisfies the small countries, which are happy with the principle of one commissioner per state;[8] whereas, by contrast, it is more difficult for them to get

[8]In the comments on an article by the journalist Teresa de Sousa in the *Público* newspaper on 7 May 1997 that I made in a subsequent issue of the same daily, I took the opportunity to argue against the possible reduction of the number of commissioners at the IGC that was concluded in Amsterdam. I based my position on the following:

their way in relation to the question of the weighting of votes, which in the worst-case scenario is expected to be the object of a minimalist arrangement.

Institutional Reform: The Tasks at Hand Are More About Democratisation than About Reweighting the Power of the States

At this point, the small states should not restrict themselves to merely side-stepping the big states' game. The fact is that a political, enlarged Europe needs real institutional reform. This is why Europe cannot limit itself to adjusting weightings

---

(a) "The number of commissioners has grown with the rise in the number of Member States, but also due to the parallel increase in the Community's competences, either as a result of the revision of the Treaties, or by means of Article 235. Some consider that the range of competences pertaining to the Union is now comparable to that of the national states, none of which however has a government with less than twenty members. It is now expected that, by the end of the IGC, those competences will be further extended to areas such as the third pillar and the CFSP and will correspond to an equivalent increase in the Commission's other functions.

(b) Invoking the "nationalisation" of the Commission is a shaky argument, especially because that body's decisions do not require unanimity, and commissioners—like ECJ judges—cannot be replaced by national states before the end of their term of office. In any case, that kind of nationalisation is less dangerous than the constant transaction of interests in which five thousand "lobbyists" engage as they swarm around the Commission, at a time when its control by the Parliament is still embryonic. In that regard, the designation of commissioners by the Member States serves as a lightning conductor in relation to the untamed neo-corporativism that is spreading in that environment.

(c) To my knowledge, only France has argued in favour of a reduction in the number of members of the Commission, whereas the German Foreign Minister recently restated in Lisbon the principle that every Member State should, for now, continue to designate a commissioner. Why should we be more papist that the Pope when, on top of it all, the Gallic position is subject to an electoral outcome.

(d) I am not sure that using rotation to reduce the number of commissioners would strengthen the Commission. For the moment, it seems to combine the worst of both worlds. On the one hand, rotation officialises the nationalisation of the commissioners, which has thus far been, if anything, informal. On the other, it worsens the distrust that countries without a commissioner feel about the Commission's initiatives in relation to both the Council and public opinion, at a time when the authority of the European Parliament is still insufficient to compensate for those losses.

(e) If an alternative criterion to that of designation by the Member States exists, it is designation by the European Parliament. When and if the EU becomes a parliamentary democracy with a Commission that answers, like a government, to the Members of the European Parliament, then the format of the Commission and the number of its members could depend on its President, who would decide them in accordance with such criteria in terms of organisation and distribution of competences as he deemed appropriate.

(f) It is true that, as I already admitted long ago, a Commission with thirty members might prove excessively large. However, it is also true that we have a long time to go until we reach that point, which will come after the single currency. Moreover, for as long as cohesion levels require a strong leverage, representation of the peripheral states in Europe's central institutions is even more necessary than that of the central states."

between states, and should therefore start with a proposal from Jacques Delors, if it were possible to go ahead with the idea that has already been mooted of appointing him as "*rapporteur*" for this question. What is at stake here is the decision-making method in its entirety, all the way from the initiative pertaining to the Commission, whose autonomy and transparency need strengthening, to the implementation, which needs to be distanced from the Council, which must increasingly become a body that serves to establish political and regulatory directions.

Reducing comitology and extending the European Parliament's co-decision powers to cover one hundred per cent of legislative matters are parallel movements that need to be undertaken and foundations that are inseparable from and preeminent elements of the construction of a democratic Europe. Identifying responsibilities is no less crucial, namely in terms of attaching greater value to the role and democratic nature of the President of the Commission, apart from anything else in order to compensate for the increase in the number of commissioners—and even to stop Kissinger from continuing to ask: "Who do I call if I want to speak to Europe?"

The General Affairs Council increasingly seems to be the superstructure of COREPER (the meeting of the permanent representatives of the Member States) and the shadow of ECOFIN the (Economic and Financial Affairs Council)—a body which, once the single currency has been introduced, will tend to gain new privileges and promote the economic argument over the political one. The simultaneous revalorisation of the Council and of politics should lead to the reformulation of both its membership (appointment of the first vice-presidents?)—and its competences, which should possess a more general nature.

It is necessary to reinforce the political decision and the democratic accountability inherent in its legitimation. Without such an increase in political authority, instead of becoming the undisputed and glorious arbitrator, the European Central Bank would on the contrary end up being turned into the go-to scapegoat. At the same time, it is important to strengthen the control/review, transparency and subsidiarity mechanisms by awarding true powers of inquiry to the European Parliament and possibly creating a Constitutional Court alongside the Court of Justice. In other words, the tasks at hand are more about democratisation than a reweighting of the Member States' powers within the Council.

Priority to European Society via the European Parliament/ Commission Axis, or to the European State(s) via the Council/Commission Axis?

For now, the European Parliament has won a greater share of the co-decision-making in the legislative process, and this foreshadows the trend towards democratisation—a trend which corresponds to the increased centrality of citizens in that process. The co-decision powers pertaining to the Parliament—a body that promotes political cohesion, without which the cohesion in the economic and social field would be precarious—have gone from encompassing forty percent of legislation to covering about sixty/sixty-five percent, which is a great feat. The closer this co-decision gets to one hundred percent, the more the reweighting of votes in the Council can be relativised.[9]

If that threshold—i.e. full co-decision—were to be attained, the European Parliament could truly take on its role as the authorised legislative representative of the EU's populations, while the Council would just represent the Member States. *The western constitutional profile based on the balance between the nation (*à la Française*) or society (the English way) on the one hand, and the state (the German* staatsrecht*) on the other, would thus also be appropriately reflected in the Community architecture.*

The alternative on the table is a different one, however. It consists of turning the Council into another parliament with votes weighted according to population—which would ultimately make both the European Parliament and the concept of equality between states superfluous. For now, what we do know is that the existing deadlock in relation to these options must be broken and the choice must be made, because in the current model there is an obvious connection between the necessary increase in the number of cases in which the Council takes decisions by a qualified majority on the one hand and the weighting of votes on the other.

The big countries do not accept a move to more decisions by qualified majority unless the votes are reweighted. However, this means the starting point continues to be the hegemony of the Council, not that of the European Parliament—i.e. the hegemony of national states, not of European civil societies or Democracy. A number of specialists[10] who tested the various models for getting out of this impasse concluded that, in that case, the double qualified majority rule would actually be preferable for the small states, for the simple reason that it would entail an increase in the minimum number of states, while the minimum population would remain the same.

The Idea of European Civil Society Has Progressed More than the Idea of European Power

Luckily, besides the Parliament's co-decision powers, and with them, the idea of democracy, what progressed most in Amsterdam was also the idea of a European civil society. *In logical terms, and just as in Europe the nation preceded (and has*

---

[9]In the reports from Amsterdam, however, Portugal does not seem to be one of the most enthusiastic supporters of this line, unlike Germany, Italy, the three Benelux States, Greece and Austria (see Arbeitskreis Europäische Integration, Der Amsterdamer Vertrag—Eine vorläufige Bewertung. Integration, 4/97, p. 307). Having said that, this fact can be discounted as yet another form of the repeated mirroring of the traditional anti-parliamentarism that exists within our institutional idiosyncrasy.

[10]See Peters 1996, p. 260.

survived) the state, it is more urgent to think about the idea of a European society and its democratic organisation than about that of a European (federal) state.

There is already a single market, but there is a shortfall in European society from both the standpoint of common values and the perspective of the mobility and internal communication within that society. Where this aspect is concerned, one could probably say that *Amsterdam put the questions of society and democracy before that of European power.*

After all, the idea of a European constitution supposes the possibility of the self-constitution of that society, which underlies it. Not only is any true democratic constitution a self-constitutive process, but since Maastricht, one can see that the time of the prophets (Spinelli) or the illuminist leaders (Monnet, Delors) may partly have passed.

That which is asked of the Treaties nowadays is the possibility of asserting and organising social citizenship and associationism, together with the recognition and protection of European society as such—with regard to this aspect of the question, albeit crude, the Commission's decision on the Boeing/McDonnell Douglas merger was effectively more meaningful than most of the decisions about the Treaty.

Besides, what the situation may suggest is that the question is not so much or solely about the increase in the Union's competences and the balance with those of the state, but the democratic organisation of the power of this European society within the Union. The Community's competences have been expanding, first during the 1970s and 80s outside the direct scope of the Treaties (implicit competences, Article 235, effectiveness, teleological interpretation etc.), and then after the Single Act, primarily by means of three revisions of the Treaties.

Perhaps it is now possible to start to reduce the field in which those "competences" can be expanded—or at least to make it more democratic and controlled. In return, it is time for the Union to grow as a democratic "power", capable of legitimating competences which in fact are more demanding in nature—i.e. increasingly political. What would be paradoxical would be to broaden the power of the big states instead of that pertaining to citizens.

Improvements: Guarantees of a "Legal Community", More Inter-parliamentarism (European Parliament and National Parliaments), Employment and Social Politics and Citizenship

There are in fact signs of an ambition that goes beyond the mere market,[11] probably reflecting the recognition or emergence of a true "European civil society". In this respect, a series of new contradictions are going in the right direction, although all

[11]See Dehousse 1997, p. 267, who sees that same idea of a horizon which goes "beyond the market" as the "only desire for change" brought by Amsterdam.

of them represent cautious steps forward and none of them can be interpreted in generalising or maximalist ways.

Apart from the growing democratisation brought about by the introduction of a democratic principle and above all by the European Parliament's broader powers of assent and co-decision, the guarantee of the fundamental rights and status of individuals has been improved and aspects of a European social citizenship have been hinted at, once Maastricht had brought with it a draft form of political citizenship.

It is worth emphasising that, in addition to the European Parliament's co-decision powers, COSAC's status as a form of intermediation between national parliaments on the European question has also been strengthened. Along with the European Parliament, national parliaments are thus among the winners of Amsterdam.

My experience as representative of the European Parliament's Institutional Committee at COSAC meetings is also that there is a tendency to reinforce the role of the Conference, which, although far from being institutionalised, is itself calling for increasing participation, based apart from anything else on the prospects which the Amsterdam Protocol on the subject have opened up. The most optimistic even consider that *the door has been half-opened to a kind of inter-parliamentarism, alongside the old inter-governmentalism.*

Another curious sign of this is the new wording of Article 138, which has put the European Parliament in the position of defining the "common principles" of the electoral legislation governing the Parliament itself, and thus, for the first time, in that of an entity that substantively delegates matters to its national counterparts, which will then approve the final configuration of such legislation at the national level.

In turn, the "principles of liberty, democracy, respect for human rights and fundamental freedoms, and the rule of law" are now not only raised to the status of one of the foundations of the Union (Article 6 of the consolidated version, former Article F), but also guaranteed in terms which may imply the suspension of rights of the Member States that have breached them (Article 7, former Article F-1).[12] Those principles are now conditions for the accession of new members (Article 10) and undoubtedly form part of the essential and immovable core of the "substantive constitution" and the "substantive limits" on the revision of the Treaties.

At the same time, the scope of the various social rights has been increased, namely by means of the albeit incidental and exemplificative referral to the Charter of the Fundamental Social Rights of Workers and the fact that the Social Protocol has become consensual and the right to employment has been rendered viable, to the point at which it can be seen as a first step in a European "civil society";[13] and

[12]The introduction of this principle was probably due to a suggestion that André Gonçalves Pereira made as a member of the Group of Wise Men who cleared the path for the preparation of the IGC-96.

[13]See my *Amsterdão: A Primeira Constituição Social da Europa Liberal*, also published in this collection of texts.

all of this at the same time as the beginning of the communitisation process linked to the third pillar and the extension of the latter's review by the Court of Justice, with all the positive consequences that this step forward will have for the protection of the rights of individuals.[14]

Also significant are: the expansion of the bases on which it is possible to invoke the principle of non-discrimination, whose scope can now be considered to be generic, albeit still without direct effect (new wording of Article 6-A, TEC); the right of European citizens to communicate directly with any Community body or institution in their own language (new wording of Article 8-D, TEC); and the immunisation of European citizenship against possible forms of "closer cooperation" [Article 5-A(c), TEC].

On another, albeit related, level, the specific recognition of volunteering as an important contribution to the development of social solidarity and the strengthening of the principle of transparency—"decisions are taken as openly as possible" (new wording of Article A, TEU)—and access to documents [new wordings of Articles 191-A and 151(3), TEC] both go in the same direction.

Particularly significant for us, the Portuguese, is the declaration on the abolition of the death penalty—something we pioneered almost a century and a half ago. Legally defining Europe as effectively the continent where the death penalty is no longer applied sends an important message of a common identity and at the same time generalises a particular conception of the right to life as one of the values that specifically characterise this European society.

These progresses form part of a continuous development of the bond between the Community and the Union and the various fundamental rights. They come on top of those made in the ECJ's case law since the 1970s, the creation of a catalogue of Fundamental Rights by the European Parliament, the added efficacy which the "direct effect" doctrine has brought to the implementation and protection of same rights, and more directly, the referral in the TEU to the European Convention on Human Rights and the common constitutional traditions in this field. The foundations that underpin the architraves on which the idea of the autonomy of both individuals and European civil society rests in terms of legal principles are now even more solid.

There are also: new clauses on non-discrimination between Europeans and on favouring policies for equal treatment and opportunities for men and women; the important progresses in the fields of common "liberty, security and justice", including the incorporation of Schengen; the new legal basis for data protection, accompanied by the creation of a body to oversee executive acts regarding the protection of individuals in these matters (new Article 213-A and B, TEC); and the upgrade of the policies on consumer protection (new Article 129A, TEC), the

---

[14]See my *O Direito e a Política de Asilo na União Europeia antes e para lá de Amsterdão*, also published in this collection of texts.

environment (new Article 100-A, TEC), and the protection of public health (new Article 129-A, TEC). Once again it is the new pre-eminence of the citizen that is apparent in all these measures.

Institutions and Political Authority (Europe as a Power) in the Freezer

In contrast, the questions of power, or of Europe as a power, were given the roughest ride. This is why parliamentarian Europe won out over Bonapartist Europe, and it may come as no surprise the that Germans and even the British were relatively happier than the French, when the truth is that consciously or unconsciously, everybody uses European integration as a mirror for their own domestic constitutional idiosyncrasy.

The countries with a strong state but a dependent society are not betting on the European Parliament, in a tendency that is a sort of transference of their domestic reflexes. And yet it is within a parliamentary Europe that the dialectic of the old nation states could be more respected and compensated for at the same time. *Additionally, Europe wants first and foremost to be a strong society, more than a super-alter-ego of strong national states—something which, moreover, would risk becoming more dangerous than such states themselves were in the past.*

Less still is it possible to think that the democratisation process has already gone far enough. The truth is very different, especially if we anticipate the weakness of the legitimation of political institutions in relation to the future strength of the euro and the European Central Bank, based as they will be on the most powerful market in the world.

On the one hand, a politically blocked or piecemeal Europe would be both an unbearable burden and a dangerous flaw at the stage in which it already found itself in economic and financial terms, with the ideal of parity with the US dollar and the United States still to be achieved by means of the euro and the ECB. On the other hand, *in a Europe with a strong monetary power and a weak political power, citizens would partly be turned into subjects of their own currency.*

Taken as a whole, and together with the strengthening of the second and third pillars (CFSP and internal security), the institutional reform had been seen as the main goal of the IGC. Where the reform is concerned, and setting aside the significant extension of the co-decision-making process, the fact is that the most important thing was the attribution to the European Parliament of a true power of veto (the assent procedure) over the appointment of the President of the Commission—a move that moreover possesses positive consequences in terms of the legitimation of the Parliament and its internal leadership.

In favour of the European Parliament and against comitology, one can thus ask how it is that the Commission's executive powers continue to be seen as merely delegated to it by the Council, when the majority of the legislation that is to be implemented is now approved in accordance with a co-decision principle in which the Parliament is the said Council's peer. The European Parliament should therefore now become able to review the implementation of a legislation of which is a co-author. It may well be a good idea, in the future, to ask the CJEC for a decision that would clarify this point.

One might thus say that within the plan described above there was not only a rebalancing of the institutions that favours the European Parliament and the Commission in relation to the most powerful of them all—the Council—but also progress in the process of democratisation with regard to the technocratic and "enlightened despotism" that has dominated the previous phases of the Community.

By comparison, a major failure was the broadening of the processes whereby the Council takes decisions by a qualified majority, with a sole relevant exception being that regarding research policy. The one that suffered most was thus Europe as a political power. One example in this respect (as was predicted beforehand) was the absence of a position of its own and the disparity of the positions taken by the Member States[15]—namely those with seats on the UN Security Council (the UK and France), regarding the observance of that body's decisions on Iraq. One could say for now, and at best, that the European "power" is more of a "civil power" than a "political power"—a sort of *soft power*—although having said that, this is a type of power that is increasingly more significant on the new international stage.[16]

A qualified majority in terms of the CFSP would in fact get stuck both upstream and downstream, on the one hand due to the unanimity required for the definition of strategic goals—including the definition of "means" itself—by the European Council, and on the other, due to a complex type of veto available to the Member States.

Mention is made of the progressive integration of the WEU into the EU, but the setting of a calendar for that purpose is side-stepped. The status of the EU's High Representative for Foreign Policy still seems unclear, albeit in the background the analysis and early warning unit will make it possible to form a diplomatic culture of its own. The inclusion of the competence to take decisions on humanitarian missions (Petersberg) is positive, but the experience of those missions indicates that they are problematic if proportionate diplomatic and military capabilities do not exist.

On the other hand, *the reform of Article 113 with regard to matters concerning external economic relationships falls far short of the requirements of a powerful Community bloc within the context of globalisation, and the refusal to attribute legal personality to the EU is symptomatic of the incomplete and uncertain profile this entity will have to go on maintaining in the sphere of international relationships.*

---

[15]Both Lamego 1998 (in *Público*) and Barroso 1998 (in *Expresso*) underlined this point in connection with the difficulties of a future CFSP.

[16]See Vasconcelos 1998, pp. 44 *et seq.*

It was also expected that the path towards the communitisation of the third pillar would be faster and more complete. Above all if it could be consummated automatically, without having to rely on a unanimous decision following the end of the planned transition period (five years). One must also regret the lack of adequate parliamentary and judicial review. It is true that in some cases that review has been broadened, but in others it seems to have left the purview of the national parliaments without entering that of the European Parliament. Not to mention the fact that the planned procedures for the welcome integration of Schengen into the Treaties constitute an additional puzzle.

Conclusions Looking Forwards

In general, one might say that we are seeing a worsening of the inherited complexity, rather than the imposition of a new coherence that would be the specific reflection of a true "constitutional" spirit. There may even be a certain obfuscation of the ultimate meaning of European construction, which is in fact automatically challenged by enlargement. At least, this is the conclusion I feel like reaching in relation to what is, essentially, the first Treaty in the history of the construction of Europe without a Preamble.

It is that "beyond-Amsterdam" that cannot be adequately "glimpsed", despite the new principles and values (democracy, liberty, rule of law) that are emphasised right from the beginning of the new Treaty. It is as if the European Sisyphus not only had to go on climbing the mountain, but also had a boulder that was becoming increasingly harder to roll.

Luckily, Amsterdam is now nearly in the past, and following the single currency there will be new conditions and other demands. Even from an economic standpoint, the euro will not be the end of the path, but the beginning of a new stance, in a Europe whose main problem may well also have been one of having lost touch with both the vanguard of the world economic revolution and the new information technologies and biotechnology.

Until we have come out of the other end of the final tunnel of the euro, on the route between the financial system and our pockets, it will however be necessary to think primarily about a new political and institutional model—one that will be consensual and capable of fitting large and small alike, overcoming the extreme and undigested tension that seems to have been attained by the Gordian Knot which ties the opposing directions of intergovernmentalism and federalism together.

Be that as it may, one might calmly conclude that, although it falls short of the historic challenges of this end of century and worsens the regulatory and structural complexity of the construction of Europe, Amsterdam:

(a) Represents progress in relation to Maastricht, even on the level of political and institutional capacity and efficiency.

(b) May render an albeit restricted enlargement—i.e. one that is limited to the first five candidates—viable.
(c) Improves the conditions for the democratic exercise of power and its legitimation within the various institutions.
(d) Strengthens both the status of European civil society and the rights of European citizens, and the paths along which their quality of life and social citizenship are promoted and guaranteed.
(e) Opens up an "area" of liberty, justice and security, which in time will be "communitasable", and will be capable of turning Europe into an area of greater protection and common responsibility.

The overall balance sheet thus appears to be sufficient. *At first, people promised at least a Maastricht 2. Perhaps it is just a Maastricht 1.5. If even so the glass is still half empty, what anyone who is thirsty has to do is drink it straight away, so that it fills up again.* It is also for that reason that Amsterdam certainly deserves ratifying, and the sooner the better.

References

Dehousse F (1997) Le Traité d'Amsterdam, Reflet de la Nouvelle Europe. Cahiers de Droit Européen Nos. 3–4.
Janning J (1997) Dynamik in der Zwangsjacke - Flexibilität in der Europäischen Union nach Amsterdam. Integration 4/97, p. 285.
Lucas Pires F (1997) Introdução ao Direito Constitucional Europeu. Coimbra.
Ludlow P (1997) Preparing Europe for the 21st Century. Brussels.
Peters T (1996) Decision-Making after the EU Intergovernmental Conference. European Law Journal, Vol. 2, No. 3, p. 260.
Vasconcelos A (1998) La Politique Extérieure d'Une Europe Ouverte. In: Duraud M F and Vasconcelos A (eds) La PESC, Ouvrir l'Europe au monde. Paris, pp. 44 *et seq.*
Victor Louis J (1997) Le Traité d'Amsterdam, Une Occasion Perdue? Revue du Marché Unique Européen, 2-1997, p. 18.

Chapter 3
Amsterdam: The First Social Constitution of a Liberal Europe

Francisco Lucas Pires

For a Revised and Active European Social Model Within the Globalisation Process

The Crisis in the Social State and the European Social Model: The National State Is No Longer the Framework for Reconciling the Social and the Economic

The crisis in the social state is now unquestionable and universally acknowledged. It reciprocally conjugates and multiplies itself, as a crisis of both the Welfare State and the Sovereign State. The social has also ceased to correspond to a functional unity with the political and the economic.[1] The causes are multiple.[2] Some internal ones are primarily based on reasons linked to fiscal issues and inefficiency[3] and generate forms of *stress and entropy*, causing distortion and irrationality in the social system, which is thus rendered intrinsically unsafe. Others are external.

[1]For a discussion on the breakdown in the "theoretical-practical" unity of these three elements, see Bercusson 1997, p. 190.

[2]See, e.g., a list in George 1997, pp. 22–27.

[3]See Archibugi 1996, p. 217.

This chapter was originally published in Portuguese by PRINCIPIA, Cascais, Portugal in the book *Amsterdão: do Mercado á Sociedade Europeia?* (ISBN 972-8500-04-1) in 1998, which was translated from the Portuguese by Luís Tirapicos Nunes and Richard Rodgers. For more information, contact the editors of the present book via the following e-mail address: martinholucaspires@fd.lisboa.ucp.pt.

F. Lucas Pires (Deceased) (✉)
Lisbon, Portugal
e-mail: martinholucaspires@fd.lisboa.ucp.pt

M. Lucas Pires and F. Pereira Coutinho (eds.), *What Market, What Society, What Union?* https://doi.org/10.1007/978-94-6265-371-9_3

The fact is that it is globalisation which is depriving the state of means of absolute control that it used to have at its disposal in order to play a part in the shaping of society; globalisation is corroding the prior social homogeneity that was a premise for that ability to intervene. Processes are interlinked on what is sometimes a planetary scale, and the spatial outlines of national political power are vanishing. One example of what this means is that external decisions on the currency or on investment, which arise in political or corporate centres that are external to and independent from the state, are becoming socially more relevant than those taken by the latter. In fact, every social agent now has access to an alternative arena to those of the national state and markets.

In general terms, the biggest concern is the fact that by moving the axis of reflection about Europe to its relationship with non-Europe, globalisation is posing the problem of whether *it is possible to both enter the world economy and maintain one's own social model.* Here, I am talking about a "social model", but the question can be extended to other aspects of the European model, such as the public health model—this is clear, for example, in the conflict between the European Community and both the United States and the WTO itself, with regard to the use of hormones in animal production.

The question is thus whether one should not immediately adopt the American "model" (which, despite everything, is preferable to the Asian or Singaporean ones) with lower wages, broader flexibility and lower public spending compared to Europe—a model which, while producing much less unemployment (4.5% in August 1997), also generates poorer quality of life and more criminality?

Or one could also ask whether, at the other end of the scale, one should not instead rethink the European model of a Social State with its Bismarckian-Beveridgian[4] roots? A model which, albeit relatively recent, shares historical values of both Christian and secular solidarity that are considered co-essential to the idea of Europe and had legitimised the Welfare State in the post-war period as the ultimate superlative form of a national democratic state.

While it is good to pose these questions in an incisive and dilemmatic manner that reveals the choice between opposing "models", the solutions reached by using "good reasoning" in a situation which is complex and transitional cannot be that grotesquely extreme. It is no accident that there is a fashionable idea of a third way, lying somewhere between the reaffirmation of traditional rigidity, as recently re-endorsed by Jospin and accompanied solely by a reduction in working hours (thirty-five hours a week, paid as though they were thirty-nine), and an American-style flexibilisation, which is more tempting to young right-wing liberals,

[4]The move from assistance to security was made with Bismarck. The model was "built on the foundation of a system of mandatory social insurance (1881–1889) that was financed by earnings-related contributions and was co-managed". The famous 1942 Beveridge Report then presented a complete programme based on universality (the whole population), unicity (a single regime) and uniformity (of income supplements)—See Chalmin 1997, p. 10.

but which imposes a choice between unemployment and inequality[5] and puts an end to any faint desire for a European social identity.

The Impossibility of Returning to the Solutions of the 1930s: Globalisation Has Come to Stay, and the State and Society Are Different to What They Once Were

Consensus can only be achieved around the fact that it would be difficult for the solutions of the 1990s to be those of the 1930s, when the cycle of trade wars, unemployment, public spending and nationalism began its march in ways that even included the military sense of the term—a memory that single-handedly generates more nightmares than hopes. Quite apart from anything else, the framework is now totally different.

The radically new fact is a globalisation which "is here to stay", unlike the one at the turn of the 19th century which, "conveyed" by the locomotive, the telegraph, the steamship, the convertibility of currencies and the liberal trade regimes, served as a backcloth to the analyses of Marx and others.[6] The crisis in the Welfare State has been showing its face since the 1970s, but after seemingly being reabsorbed in the '80s, is now being confirmed in the '90s.[7] It is now being caused by the consistency and violence of that new phenomenon of a borderless economy, and is forcing us to engage in a long-term revision of the system.

On the one hand, globalisation will surface in an inextricable connection to deregulation; on the other, it will transform international institutional capital into the largest pressure group in the world. From an external structural constraint, it is turning into the "ideology" of the economy itself,[8] probably going beyond what it would really signify, and in contrast, also helping to ideologise economism.

It is at this point that the sometimes dreamt-of return to the solutions of the 1930s seems to be automatically excluded in a world where the idea of national borders has not only dimmed in today's material life, but also lost its original *forma mentis* nature in the fields of education, information, communications and trade. Neither the transformation of solidarity into a Welfare State, nor that of commercial competition into military war are tolerable or even conceivable nowadays.

---

[5]Despite everything, Paul Krugman is one of the American economists whose view of this question is more moderate. As he recently said, "I don't believe that Europe is able to solve its unemployment problem without accepting a worsening of the inequalities in the distribution of income, but it doesn't need to be as brutal as in the USA" (interview given to the *Público* newspaper of 13 October 1997).

[6]See my *Europe in the Face of Globalisation*, Conference at the Calouste Gulbenkian Foundation seminar on Europe-96, Lisbon, 6 May 1996.

[7]See Rhodes 1996, p. 306.

[8]Ibid., p. 309.

One might say that taxpayers in the first case, and citizens in the second, guarantee that—as the poet and writer José Régio famously cried out—they will not go down that path… This supposition is even more valid on the European scale, where there are insufficient fiscal resources to be able to imagine a second welfare-based metamorphosis of the state, or enough military resources to provide for defence, let alone war… Besides, it is the very "myth" of the state, as an entelechy kneaded by the dramatic memory of a history, that dilutes itself or fades away on the far shore of the ocean, moved by successive waves of privatisation and decentralisation and others of globalisation and continentalisation.

In open economies and with a view to the structural competitiveness of the national economy, the state is seeing the privileges of its role removed in favour of governance mechanisms that operate on multiple levels.[9] The loss of autonomy caused by the international context is instead generating a need for greater supranational coordination and for a space in which subnational structures can rise again. The powers of the national state are being limited by a complex "upward, downward and outward" movement of power (Bob Jessop).[10]

Society is also "another", which is referred to precisely as "post-industrial" (Daniel Bell). Its economy is now the main arena in which to achieve and exercise power, and its instruments of war (or guerrilla warfare?) are information technologies, the media, and financial resources.[11] In this new so-called "post-Fordist" cycle, both the labour process and the type of macroeconomic growth and the model for regulating the economy are being revised in accordance with the new paradigm of flexibility and constant innovation.[12]

The society that is currently forming attains a much greater autonomy there, and some people go so far as to imagine that this process will enable it to achieve such a degree of "affluence" that there will be no need to "redistribute" wealth via the state, but simply for society to "distribute" wealth within itself and by its own means[13]—something that would, however, suppose a large degree of consensus, balance and social levelling, and is therefore frankly utopic.

Nor Can Europe Shut Its Doors and Choose Solutions Against the World—A Fact that Calls for an Effort at Self-reform Before Anything Else

We are therefore far from the industrial-society state that used to direct and control standardised production, which is now seen as a job-killer with hierarchised and

[9]See Greve 1996, p. 126.

[10]Ibid., p. 178.

[11]Murray 1999, pp. 38–47.

[12]Ibid., pp. 170–171.

[13]Archibugi 1996, p. 217.

rigid structures that are enemies of the flexibility brought about by modern development. Within this framework, *the first sensible remedy thus seems to be to resituate Europe in the world and not above it.*

The fact is that what usually needs curing is a patient, not a healthy person. And just like charity, sacrifices should also begin with ourselves. On condition that we do not give up our own nature, which is a sort of historical/political/cultural DNA without which Jameson's "inverted millenarianism" would be right about the end of everything—history, ideologies, identities—without any prospect for the future. In that case, we would not be talking about a cure, but rather an immolation pure and simple.

But how to revert the situation, if it is true that we are faced with the scandal of a differential that can reach forty to one between the higher wages paid in developed Europe and the lower ones paid in the Third World for the same productive activities in the world market? Having said that, despite that reality there are also two other, no less evident facts: *that the balances within each economy cannot be imposed from outside and determined by others; and that it is due first and foremost to questions of internal economic, political and social degeneracy that the European social model must be revised.*

At least no one would dare to claim that non-Europeans are responsible for our demographic crisis or the increase in average life expectancy, which are undermining our social security systems; *and how can we hold the Third World responsible for the crisis in our industry if European imports represent a mere nine per cent of Europe's production and more than two thirds of those nine per cent come from the United States and Japan?*

It seems even more reasonable to hold ourselves accountable when we look at the panorama that lies ahead of us. *Not only is the weight of some countries' social-security-based obligations already approaching the value of their domestic product, but the latter has in turn grown less than less half as much as the increase which is getting underway in the health field. The thing is that when people can expect to work thirty years and live eighty while simultaneously maintaining a negative demographic balance, the clouds on the horizon are not likely to lift.*

And all this while the bond between effort and remuneration is dissolving, and the moral result of the more radical and extensive socialising operation in the west has ended up in the civic anomy of individualism—a "mortal degeneration of the European personalist vision of Mankind".[14] As Meinhard Miegel, one of the greatest Germen thinkers on the social question, recently asked: *how can one re-ensure a social system when men only think of themselves and the immediate?*[15] In fact, according to the results of several well-known surveys, individualism and laicism are the fastest-growing background trends in the sociological area of the fifteen countries of the Union, and it is not easy to imagine that reformist values and a will to reform will take root in that kind of soil…

[14]See L'Épée 1993, p. 163.

[15]See Miegel and Wahl 1994.

We must therefore begin by refusing the logic of the good old world. The question lies in reforming it, before we so much as start looking at how the rest of the planet should be governed—something that could be likened to an unfeasible colonising ghost peeking out from behind the curtain. Otherwise, it would be like returning to the Titanic, only this time we wouldn't be hitting an iceberg, but the polar ice cap itself.

Europe may no longer be the world economy's sanctuary, but it must at least be an insider. Apart from anything else, this was precisely one of the reasons for the genesis of European integration, which was born in order to favour that insertion, re-establishing the link with the new revolutions like those in the biotechnology and information fields, which we have increasingly ignored in the meantime.

The Failure and Frustration of the European Commission's First Attempts at Reform: Delors and Santer's Proposals for Fighting Unemployment

Another vision would lead to the idleness of a sort of premature reform. What would really be worthwhile would be not to lose any more time. In order for Europe to even reach the point which Japan and the United States have already been faster and nimbler at leaving behind them, it would be necessary to start straight away by rapidly forming the new trans-European networks that can create *immediate employment*, and decisively getting into the new information and education technologies for competitiveness that will create the jobs of the future. This is moreover the path that was taken by both Santer's Pact of Confidence for Employment and the policy set out in Jacques Delors' forgotten White Paper on Growth, Competitiveness and Employment.

The starting point for the Commission's structural analysis lay in unemployment and its causes. Among the latter, it exposed both the imperfections and differences within the labour market and its lack of flexibility. These were worsened by disincentives for job creation resulting from mandatory contributions to social security systems and a pervading trade-union philosophy that was more directed towards protecting employment than fighting unemployment.

There were even some who interpreted the White Paper on Growth, Competitiveness and Employment as a call for an employment-market reform with the capacity to encourage a more flexible organisation of the market itself, a better division of working hours, lower wage costs, improved occupational qualifications and a more active employment policy.[16] Implied in some interpretations was even the dismantling of the traditional forms of protection of the labour-related world.[17]

[16]Whiteford 1995, p. 126.

[17]Ibid.

I do not think the White Paper went that far. However, a certain ambiguity and paralysis have prevailed. Certain contributions from the Commission, such as that regarding investment in trans-European networks or in research and development were in turn criticised for the fact that the best known of their immediate consequences were based more on the idea of fighting unemployment than on that of creating jobs. People began by wanting to attack the symptoms more than the causes. At the state level there was still insufficient awareness that the problem had already partly gone beyond the available means. At the level of the Communities too, people failed to understand that it was already necessary to reorder the respective overall priorities, starting with the budgetary ones.

Many of the suggestions in Delors and Santer's proposals were positive, however, namely that regarding a lessening of the fiscal burden on unqualified labour[18] (at present there are already discussions about subsidising it), to be offset by a green tax on carbon-based gas and nuclear energy.[19] Their orientation in relation to some points could be revised, but their idea of self-reform and their anti-immobilism seen through the prism of the construction of Europe were positive signs. However, they became a dead letter, despite the billions of ECUs that were left over from the CAP at the time.

The surprising contradiction is that the Member States considered that the scale on which the new or 21st-century policies (such as the research policy, in which the United States and Japan invest 2.5% of their GNPs) should be resolved continued to be the national one (in the case of the research policy, this was true at least until Amsterdam, when it became subject to decision by qualified majority), whereas the old "Common Agricultural Policy" survives at the top of both the agenda and the list of areas of expenditure, as the Union's main budgetary "item". As if the future had stagnated behind our backs…

The CAP is still capable of aspiring to engender a productivity which results in surpluses and which, solely in order to secure more funds, has already gone so far as to affect the cycle of life, as we saw in the "mad cows" affair, while the new policies lack the minimum responses they need. It is as if, for the first time, Europe has got stuck in defence of its hunting trophies, rather than assuming its stance as the vanguard or new frontier of its old nation states.

Simple logic in the competitive world should prevent us from privileging overproduction in the sectors that are losing out due to a lack of demand, seeking to fix things that were already fixed a long time ago or can no longer be fixed. The solution instead lies in policies that can open the way for the new social concerns

[18]According to Maarek, one "consequence of the rise in unemployment is the increase in social contributions and labour costs. That was how the fiscal burden on labour in France went from 38.4% in 1982 to 43.8% in 1992". A parallel phenomenon was to occur in all the European countries. Between 1981 and 1995 the fiscal burden on labour constantly worsened in that respect, going from 34.9% to over 42%, while dropping from 45.5% to less than 35% for the remaining production factors—capital, energy and raw materials (*apud* Albert 1997, p. 15).

[19]See Toulemon 1996, pp. 485 *et seq.*

and demands which, on this level, moreover include regional and rural development, which should rightly receive redoubled attention.

More Flexibilisation of Structures, but More All-for-One Responsibility in the Rediscovery of a Social Identity Which Ensures that Mankind and Its Organisations and Groups Are at the Centre of Concerns

Will this adaptation not mean jeopardising everything, yielding to the logic of total flexibility? Not necessarily. *After all, Japan is surviving globalisation with modest unemployment rates of around three per cent, while over the same period—the last twenty-five years—the unemployment rate of the Fifteen has multiplied fourfold;*[20] *and Japan has managed to achieve all this while preserving high levels of job security, seniority-based criteria in corporate promotions, high salaries and acceptable social protection.*

The question is that in Japan, the policies on research and new technologies went further, capabilities in terms of innovation, productivity and quality were preserved, and commercial aggressiveness was developed, all of which helped offset the difference in costs. When more backward economies advance to intermediate positions, the opportunity for those that were already in those positions is to move on into cutting-edge areas.

The lesson is that Europe needs to reform its model in terms of both priorities and methods. This is not a question of giving up its identity, but rather of thinking that the more it uses others—especially the most competitive among them—as a mirror for itself, the stronger an identity becomes. A comparison with those others also serves to show that Europe cannot be a Super-Welfare State, nor can it slash its wrists and open the veins of a super-breach in society between it and itself, along the lines of a new human "Berlin wall" and one that would paradoxically be cross-border in nature.

One of the limits on the need for a European adaptation to globalisation is in fact the idea that the centrality of Mankind and the concern for Man in the economy constitute the essential feature of the social policy and the famous European model with regard to it. This is at least the case if we are going to respect the parameter for action postulated by one of the fathers of the so-called "German miracle" during the post-war era, Ludwig Erhard, who said that: the "measure and judge of good and evil in economic policy are not dogmas or positions taken by groups, but solely Man, the consumer and the people".[21]

---

[20]See Sorz 1996, p. 14.

[21]*Apud* Horst Afheldt, *Austieg aus dem Sozialstaat?* In: Aus Politk und Zeitgeschichte, B-25-26/95, 16 June 1995, p. 3.

Pope John XXIII spoke of that which is "owed to Man" due to the simple fact of his dignity, in the tradition of the biblical man conceived in the "image and likeness of God" and the "measure of all things". Beyond the great "macro" liberal revolution, this man cannot be seen as a Kantian man, lacking identity and ties with the community, or as Rawls' man is suspected of being—i.e. the subject of an excessively schematic relationship with justice. Without joining in the polemic between "liberals" and "communitarians", I would say that if the "macro" world is increasingly more liberalised, the successively lower thresholds—starting with the still very liberal threshold of the European Union—should become increasingly communitarian.

If the value of labour is currently falling, it is because its function has become almost exclusively economic and separated from its social function.[22] The "human" quality in the production process has thus ended up being split. Taken together, the growing heterogeneity, individualisation and economism of labour relationships is probably responsible for generating this "bill" or "account payable" within society—and going a step further, within each person. In this sense, dehumanisation can be said to begin with the separation of the economy and the social field, and reconciling the two of them should start at the bottom.

This does not preclude the probable need for a greater degree of flexibilisation at the national level, albeit both a limit and other dimensions that would help overcome this trend should be defined at the same time. Another reason why more flexibility is needed at the national level is that that threshold was simultaneously exclusive and super-rigid. What is more, in a dynamic society it is necessary to avoid the bureaucratisation of both labour and social security. As Bill Clinton said, welfare should be a second chance, not a way of life.

By contrast, the European level which was almost the liberal clean slate remains virgin enough that it can still become a field for creating frameworks and forms of compensation. The growing internal liberalisation may thus even presuppose a *subsidiary employment policy or the rehabilitation of services that are of general economic interest* (see Article 16, former Article 7-D, of the new Treaty), albeit on a less statist basis, at the European level—i.e. on a scale that matches the new single market.

Even Liberals Are More Popperian than Hayekian Nowadays

As we shall see, those solutions have also now been enshrined in the Treaty of Amsterdam. It seems logical to admit, for example, that if the Union had gone ahead with the construction of the trans-European networks, that would have created a counterbalance which would also have enabled the Member States to more rapidly move forwards with the flexibilisation of their own social structures.

---

[22]See Bercusson et al. 1997, p. 194.

After all, even European liberals want less Hayek[23] *and more Popper:*[24] *fewer solutions recommended by the* vademecum *and greater consideration for the diversity of "patients" and "illnesses".* For instance, reducing working hours even when it is a bad policy in overall terms can prove to be a good sectoral or corporate policy; and while there are services that should come to be paid for at a fair price, at the same time some of the rules in the multilateral trading system should be improved, especially if Europe goes into the negotiations united.

On this last point, it is just a pity that Amsterdam hesitated at the external trade level. Article 113 of the European Union Treaties does not yet include services and copyright, whose delegation to the EU requires a unanimous vote, when the truth is that states acting alone are becoming less and less relevant in global negotiations.

There is a minimum social safety net that has to be rebuilt on a global scale, at least in terms of protection against exclusion—a direction in which Amsterdam also appears to be pointing [see Article 118(2)]. Failing which we might have to ask what level of inequality could be acceptable to democracy, or whether the social divide will not end up jeopardising growth itself, as seems to happening in developed countries that have reached excessive levels of social differentiation and insecurity, albeit new technologies are probably[25] more to blame than globalisation.

While it is true that mass unemployment is costing the EU-15 more than two hundred billion euros in benefits—money that could theoretically circulate in the economy to productive ends—and while it is still true that that kind of substitution has turned potential assets into people who are automatically excluded, it is also true that unemployment benefits facilitate mobility and are unsurpassably fast in the way in which they circulate as an instrument that fosters consumption. Even looking at them solely from the economic standpoint, things are not so bad after all!

New paths to job stability, or at least employability, will have to be rediscovered, because we know that no one—neither the worker him/herself, nor the entrepreneur—invests in a company's accidental "passenger", at a time when

[23]Given that he is considered more of a libertarian than a liberal, one can thus ask whether Hayek should not be positioned half-way towards conservatism instead. In any case, his philosophy does not contain any remnant of the idea/value of "sociability"—one that many authors include in the central core of the liberal tradition—let alone that of the "social". According to him, these days the latter would include global planning and would be linked to a community's undefined generic goals, thus falling outside the liberal notion of society (see Hayek 1967, pp. 236–247). His model is thus more rigid in this respect, probably constituting the most perfect and symmetrical alternative to Marxism, with the idea of individual liberty occupying the position of "supreme and absolute value" and not just that of a foremost value that co-constitutes the human and the social, within the framework of which it would, however, be tempered by others. A true liberal supposes the definition of the "rules of the game", even on the social level, as well as an openness to the problems of society as it presents itself. At the very least, the notion of order implied by liberalism certainly requires strong guarantees of "sociability"; and in this respect, we can say that the "single market" also postulates at least the existence of guarantees of sociability on the same scale.

[24]As we know, Popper believed that it is more important to know which theories are refutable than which ones are correct. For a Popperian notion of social justice based on that assumption, see the liberal standpoint of Ackerman 1993.

[25]See Lucena, p. 8.

continuous training is, however, becoming more and more necessary. If not enterprises, it will be up to an Educational State (the new successor of the Social State?)—and preferably both of them—to permanently insure and protect assets from falling out of the system, or at the very least to preserve their aptitude to re-join it.

In the social security field, on the other hand, although the situation is urgent, there is no reason to panic. After all, while there are more and more people working less hours for an increasing number of pensioners with a longer life expectancy, as João César das Neves[26] recently reminded us it is also true that we are producing much more than before and there is therefore much more to distribute. What does make sense and is increasingly widely accepted is that there is an ideal mix between the existence of a minimum safety net and additional voluntary contribution systems, with a cap on the total amount that benefits can attain; and although no one wants or is able to Europeanise these policies—decisions on which continue moreover to be subject to the unanimity rule after Amsterdam—the common nature of the causes and effects of the problem and the need to coordinate and harmonise policies in this regard are patently clear.

On the other hand, while the European Union does not need to entrench itself in a fortress on the external front, it does not have to lie down like a doormat either. It should remain alert and activate GATT's social clause. When South Korea considers the recent introduction of the fifty-two-hour week with no holidays to be progress and nonetheless competes in the automobile market with the most developed economies, the existence of an imbalance seems evident.

Europe should also be capable of reacting faster and with greater authority, namely in crisis situations. To that end it must have an *active trade policy*, both for fighting dumping, contraband and counterfeiting and for promoting European and a "Made in Europe" label—a policy which simultaneously defends and brandishes the seal of quality that will also allow it to preserve jobs and higher wages at the same time.

A Global but Pragmatic and Progressive Revision of European and National Social Policies: Revising the Socialist Paradigm also Involves Revising the Liberal Paradigm

As we have seen, it does not seem as though the challenge can be met by small adjustments or tip-toeing… The time for caution has passed… Even the German and Rhenish strain of *social market economy*, which was deemed impregnable and

[26]*Do livro branco ao cheque em branco* (From the White Paper to the blank cheque). In the *Diário de Notícias* newspaper of 30 March 1998.

was until recently the supermodel for the European model, is currently facing a debate about the need to revise its social contract.[27] However, this fact has also had a positive reflex effect in Germany: that of making people understand that the future of their model also involves the hidden outsider that is globalisation, and can now only be negotiated with the intervention of Europe, as the only possible representative of the same single market, in which Germany is just the biggest seller and therefore the party with the largest vested interest.

While not everything is clear, we do at least know that, as things stand and unless we act collectively and with a view to reform in the sense of a re-identification of the European social model, this Asian promontory that is the "Original West" will paradoxically turn into the Far West to come; either inertia or a sudden dismantling of the system would have tragic consequences for the security of the social fabric, enterprises, families and people.[28]

Looking at a symmetrical aspect of the question, we also know that whether one sees it as fiscal statism or as "welfarism", the old Welfare State cannot go on being the stronghold/taboo of European identity. Perhaps post-socialist Europe is also post-liberal; or in any case, perhaps the liberal paradigm has to adapt to the end of the socialist paradigm. That path to qualitative mutation ranges from new business ethics to placing the educational before the social in the qualification and revalorisation of certain public policies; but in parallel it also entails more responsible forms of funding for education, health and social security.

Social Policy: A Shared Responsibility from the European to the Local Levels

Entities on different levels like the state and the European Union—but also local authorities—do not have to just sit and do nothing and watch things happen. While observing the vertical division of competences between them, they should act in such a way as to make a subsidiary social policy, a coordinated employment policy, an active commercial policy and a harmonised emigration policy—policies which moreover correspond to the necessary regulation of an economic area that is not merely "common" but also "unique"—all viable. Once that is the case, the use of antidumping policies in self-defence could form part of the general provisions in this respect, while enjoying greater authority and being more efficient.

[27]See Smith 1997. The author ends up concluding that this is mainly an adaptation process. Via its leader Gerhard Schröder, the SPD itself recently presented a set of twelve theses aimed at the model's revision, pointing towards greater competition, corporate vitality, a smaller state and subsidised wages (see the *Die Zeit* newspaper, No. 39, 19 September 97, p. 29).

[28]Jordan 1997, p. 48.

The European level is fundamental, and in a sense is the point at which everything comes together and the final link in the chain that resolves the problem is established.

Albeit decisive, the national dimension is no longer enough to achieve the mastery of the various economic factors that is indispensable to making them socially compatible. From the external perspective of globalisation and as has already occurred on the monetary level, it is only with the European contribution that we can stop the whole thing falling apart.[29]

However, the European Union's responsibility lies above all in ensuring that which is no longer possible on a state-by-state basis: the re-adaptation of the essentials of a specific social model—i.e. a notion of a minimum degree of all-for-one responsibility,[30] *now in terms that are simultaneously broader (single market), but also less divorced from competitive capacity at the world level. Neither a self-exclusion of Europe from the world, nor an individual hetero-exclusion from the common society brought by the single market.*

This is what we could call a protective but non-protectionist Europe. A Europe that is not a simple "decompression chamber for the effects of globalisation",[31] *but also shows that it is capable of playing the new game on its new board.* Amsterdam seems to cautiously go in this direction, albeit with huge ramparts that allow us to say "yes" to the European social and employment policies, but with the notion that it is only slowly—perhaps too slowly—that we will go far.

A Social Europe After Amsterdam? Many Limits, Obvious Need, Some Possibilities

With the Extraordinary Summit of Heads of State and Government on Employment (20 November), the European Community's social and employment policies have moved onto the "front shelf" of the Community agenda.[32] Despite the fact that individual countries display some important differences in relative terms, the record percentage of unemployed shows there is an unsolved common and structural social problem within the Union that could create a new division of classes or "social fracture" at the level of the whole single market. Indeed, this was why, when looking at this problem from the widest possible perspective, an international mega-seminar on Social Europe at the Gulbenkian Foundation (5–7 May 1997)

[29]To quote Delors, "regional organisations are a way to handle certain consequences of globalisation" (see *Visão* of 4 December 1997).

[30]L'Épée 1993, p. 165.

[31]Cohen 1996, p. 153.

[32]According to De Sousa, they are even likely to be at the top of that agenda (see *O Próximo Desafio*. In the *Público* newspaper of 22 October 1987).

presented an "image of doctors conferring beside the bed of a critically ill patient".[33]

It is thus no wonder that the Amsterdam Treaty has incorporated the social topic into the Union's constitutional programme, postponing questions like institutional reform, which had previously seemed to need solving first and more urgently. Even before any country ratified the Treaty on which this new line of normative action is based, the Extraordinary Summit then tried to lay the first brick in its implementation, bringing the Member States together—with a degree of epic commotion that was subsequently contradicted by the conclusions—around a new employment pact.

Difficulties and Limits

However, two facts suggest that the seriousness of intents in this regard may be suspect. On the one hand, there is the experience of past failures, first in the 1970s and '80s (Social Action Programme), and subsequently with the successive proposals by Delors (White Paper) and Santer (Confidence Pact) on competitiveness and employment. On the other, there is the idea that Amsterdam was primarily about accommodating Jospin's electoral promises in order to save the summit and the last stage on the road to the single currency.

The truth is that even if the Member States are now more aware that the very viability of the single market involves a minimum degree of social regulation on the same scale, without which any cross-border mobility would be impracticable and the whole of the labour world's faith in the project itself would be precarious, the difficulties of and limits on a communitarian social policy have not faded away.

They begin with the absence of a European civil society that is sufficiently homogeneous and minimally integrated. The combination of the shortage of associative structures and the inability of those that do exist to work together on the one hand, and the heterogeneity of national social institutions on the other, suffices to warn us that any centralising and all-embracing social policy will be inefficient. Besides which, the future European society will never exist as such in the sense presupposed by the old idea of a social policy, although having said that it may serve as an advance prototype of Giddens' notion of a society seen more as a set of procedures and mechanisms for representing and organising social relationships than as an organic entity which is delimited in time and space.

There also remains another related shortcoming—the deficit in European democracy. The fact is that the history of social politics is one of a permanent bond with democracy. It is through the latter that the essential trade-off between efficacy and redistribution (G. Majone) operates in Europe. Social Justice and Democracy mutually feed and condition each other, expanding and retracting together.

---

[33]Nadal 1997, p. 230.

Amsterdam symptomatically reduced this kind of democratic deficit by increasing the proportion of legislative competences that are subject to the co-decision process in which the European Parliament acts as the Council's equal from forty to sixty per cent. However, European democracy still lacks a true public space, public-opinion movements of its own, proportional party-political instruments and a vigorous political citizenship, as well as the full complement of powers that is still escaping the European Parliament.

A European social policy also faces the resistance of a nation state that strengthened its position by being a welfare state and is now afraid that the transfer of political instruments in the social domain may amount to an automatic loss of legitimacy. On the day the nation state stops being the official protector of the weak, the probability that it will no longer be obeyed becomes much greater. No matter how much it may admit that the efficiency with which it solves social problems has diminished, the nation state wants to avoid a worsening of the erosion of authority that could be especially serious on this level, quite apart from anything else because it does not yet have any forms of compensation from the European Union in this regard.

On the other hand, a real social policy would amount to a definitive passage from market-building to state-building and would possess an obvious federalist connotation[34] that few would openly assume for now. In the constitutional history of the United States, it was in fact the New Deal which marked the passage from dual federalism to unitary federalism. However, in the construction of Europe we have still not reached the post-American Civil War stage, let alone the New Deal.

The fact is that the imbalance between capital and labour makes a European "new deal" of this kind impracticable. The early implementation of the single market, the pressure for the liberalisation of trade on a world scale, and the crisis in and still predominantly national nature of trade unions are a few more of the obstacles to the rebalancing of forces. The historical compromise behind the European Welfare State was based on a parity of negotiating power between capital and labour.[35] Today, only the political strength of democracy can—and then only partly—make up for the current disproportion. Only through democracy can the single market be "civilised" and the shortcomings of a true European civil society be balanced.

On top of all this, the fragmentation of social structures means that the social question either also appears here in the garb of an inter-state question, or does not appear at all. For now, the only interpreters of the social question that actually have the capacity to take decisions are the Member States. This in turn means that that question cannot entirely be identified as one which is specifically and directly European, nor can it call for the use of either the arbitral or the cohesive function of

[34]Streeck 1994, p. 12.

[35]See Caporaso 1996, p. 47.

a hypothetical European State—functions that are indeed always problematic in such a plural society.[36]

All this is why the social and employment policies that were approved in Amsterdam are still essentially based on the idea of the coordination of national policies and unanimous decision-making. Areas such as wages, the right to strike and lockouts will remain the sole competence of national legislators and unanimity is required for matters such as social security, dismissal, worker representation, employment conditions for third-county nationals, and the funding of employment-promotion policies (Statement for Final Minutes, in respect of Article 5.3).

On the other hand, policies for improving the work environment, working conditions, informing and consulting workers, integrating the excluded, and equal opportunities for men and women in the labour market (Article 118) will be decided by a qualified majority and subject to the co-decision procedure (Article 189B).

The Community's social policy will also certainly retain a predominantly "regulatory" nature,[37] as it will continue to have an extremely limited budget and to lack implementation instruments, which are still in the hands of the national states. It will be able to address flaws in the market, but cannot systematically intervene as a social policy. In any case, it will also have to respect very narrow limits in terms of subsidiarity, which is moreover a concept created by the Catholic doctrine on the social question and was already objectively taken into account on this level before the Maastricht Treaty.[38] I would thus say in conclusion that a centralised social redistribution path would not be consensual and would enjoy neither the conditions it needed in order to be efficient, nor the instruments it needed in order to be operable.

There are still constraints of an economic nature. Firstly, as Alain Liepietz[39] has noted, employment and social policy do not depend exclusively on Europe. Moreover, eighty per cent of the socialised production of most of the people who live in Europe occurs within a twenty-kilometre radius around their homes. Liepietz says that it is possible to create jobs whatever the European policy may be, and that it is the proximity dimension that must be deemed the priority to that end—a conclusion which in fact matches the indications suggested by the principle of subsidiarity.

Equally important are the financial limits on any EU intervention in this field. The 1.27% of GDP ceiling which Agenda 2000 says will be the EU's budgetary limit during the five-year period beginning in 2000 says it all. Even in the long-term, the inflation-free model of growth on which the single currency is based

---

[36]On the issue of social cohesion in the pluralistic societies that the various national societies themselves now are, see Berger 1997.

[37]See Majone 1996, pp. 124 *et seq.*

[38]See Lucas Pires 1991.

[39]*Apud* Moscovici 1997, p. 65.

will not leave room for whims. Taken as a whole, the entire Community perspective on development for the near future seems very reductionist because of that.

The Community budget is unlikely to represent more than three to four per cent of the average of the national budgets of the Fifteen, which in any case are themselves experiencing growing difficulties in accommodating any social policy. For these and other reasons, policies such as those for the trans-European networks that were also vital to the employment policy have fallen by the wayside; and going forwards, the European Community budget will still have to divert considerable sums in order to fund the enlargement or the reform of the CAP.

There is also an aggravating circumstance that is not making anything any easier: little credit is attached to the Community's redistribution policies. The CAP, for instance, is infamous for the fact that even after its worst imbalances were corrected by the last reform, over fifty per cent of its resources benefit less than twenty per cent of farmers—precisely the ones that are already the richest or least in need of assistance. The European Social Fund itself has failed to acquire the best of reputations in countries like ours, and although positive in overall terms, still corresponds to an idea of a social policy that serves as an instrument for the market or limits itself to supporting the creation of occupational qualifications needed to access that market.

The shortcomings in an ideological and intergovernmental consensus are an ultimate block to any further progress. The most liberalist commentators, for instance, invoke the counterproductive nature of more surcharges on the economy and enterprises at a time when globalisation is pointing in the opposite direction—towards deregulation, which is precisely the first criterion in the classification of countries by the international rating agencies.

The thing is that Europe is likely to attribute about 27.5% of its production to social protection, in contrast to the United States' fifteen per cent;[40] and this when we still do not have the diplomatic, political, military and even monetary means that would enable us to discuss the defence of our interests at the global level on an equal footing and to help reflect the famous European "model" through the various world institutions.

At the same time as they are warning of the dangers of more burdens on the economy, the Union's richest countries are advocating a broader legal harmonisation of national social systems in order to protect themselves against the social dumping caused by the fact that labour and the measures to protect it cost less in the poorer countries. The latter, on the contrary, naturally oppose that wish, because the price of the labour factor is often their primary or only competitive advantage—an argument which has often set the goalposts for the Portuguese positions in the debate[41] and ultimately led to the proposal to replace the concept of

[40]D'Intigenano, Paris, 1997.

[41]The cost of labour varies enormously between Member States: in industry, it is twenty-five euros/hour in Germany and five in Portugal (Annual Report on Employment in the EU, *apud* European Report No. 2245 of 27 September 1997, p. 4).

"unemployment" with that of "employability", with a view to mitigating the effects of the first of those coefficients on future cuts in the structural funds.

Protection clauses must remain in line with economic capacity. A sudden increase in levels of pay and in the other social policy demands would lead to the export of unemployment from the richest countries to the poorest ones, and that would be disastrous,[42] not only for the latter but also for solidarity and integration projects.

Different or even opposing strategies subsist beyond the precise wording of the Commission's texts and positions. On the eve of the Extraordinary Council on Employment, the Executive Committee proposed a plan based on four axes—entrepreneurship, adaptability, employability, and equal opportunities—apart from anything else because it knew that it is easier to negotiate difficult dossiers in the Community when one uses "packages" and polyhedral perspectives in which everyone can see themselves reflected or have a share.

On the one hand, the question is more one of common orientation proposals than concrete actions. On the other, while they maintain an enormous degree of openness, in practice those kinds of indicative suggestions tend to end up being reduced to three goals or conclusions: favour terms and conditions of employment by enterprises and make them more flexible; support the preparation of workers for the labour market[43] by means of education and vocational training; and provide bureaucratic and fiscal relief for SMEs, which do the really hard work when it comes to the offer of jobs.[44]

Ideas like reducing the fiscal burden on work are being taken up again, but the creation of fixed goals is being abandoned. Initial objectives include the creation of twelve million jobs over five years and the reduction to seven per cent of the average unemployment rate, which currently still stands at 10.8%—a type of illusory quantification that had already been heavily criticised by the European Parliament.[45] However, all this is entrusted to concertation between the Member States—a process that continues to present the usual difficulties.

Moreover, a war in which no one listens to anyone else persists behind this more proactive attitude. While the prospect of programming common concrete actions does exist, the call for trans-European networks is probably more focused on the East, while that for research and development would almost automatically favour the largest enterprises and the richest countries. The old rich consider themselves to be the new poor and the old poor prefer to become the new rich, but without the problems faced by old wealth. Be that as it may, it is still the states and large

[42]See Donges et al. 1996, p. 55.

[43]Only ten per cent of unemployed persons pursue vocational training and a twenty-five per cent coverage is now being asked for (see the Velzen Report on an Active Anti-Unemployment Strategy, submitted to the European Parliament on 22/10/97).

[44]According to figures published in the newspapers at the time of the Extraordinary Employment Summit (20 November 1997), SMEs have created an average of two hundred and fifty thousand jobs for every two hundred thousand destroyed by large enterprises.

[45]See Minutes of the plenary session of 22 October 1997, in Strasbourg.

organisations that will determine these choices, rather than the struggle between the main interested parties.

On a more general level, that struggle is in turn primarily between three positions: those who would like the fight against unemployment to be one aspect of the fight for economic and social cohesion, including by increasing the funds available to the latter (Portugal is among this group); those who would like it to be a horizontal priority, driving the Communities' sectoral options and perhaps diverting even structural funds to support countries and regions with more employment problems (the case of France); and those who think that this problem should continue to be first and foremost a national one, namely from the financial standpoint (a group that includes Germany and the UK).

Finally, we should bear in mind how globalisation modifies labour-market conditions and restricts the possibilities of intervening in relation to that market, even in a dimension that is more suited to facing up to it, such as the European one. In fact, the logic underlying the new world framework is asking for more "economy for the economy" and less "economy for well-being". It is more about seeking productivity than employment. It absolutely prioritises the consumer over the producer, worker or entrepreneur. It differentiates between the ways of valuing work, which increasingly involve the new technologies and teleworking. It includes new problems that are shaking up the whole social fabric, such as the growing incorporation of women and emigrants.

Topicality and the Need for a Response

There is little room for manoeuvre in this scenario: it does not seem easy to either move ahead with a tailor-made social policy, even if it is a complementary one, or define a kind of common third way in relation to such a policy and in the light of the global economy. Despite this, people have been acknowledging the growing reasons for the constitutionalisation of the social and employment policies at the European level.[46]

There have even been upsets such as the dismissal of three thousand workers at the Renault factory in Vilvoorde, Belgium, in which the process of public accountability has already reached the European institutions—unlike that which happened on a similar occasion in the past, albeit on a smaller scale, in a country that is a net beneficiary of intra-European delocalisations, which is to say in the Setúbal region of Portugal.

France's position with regard to this European constitutionalisation of the social policy is particularly symptomatic. This is one of the topics on which there is a consensus between a right-wing President of the Republic and a left-wing Prime-Minister, despite the country's "Gaullist" tradition in Europe and the

[46]See Lucas Pires 1995, pp. 142–148.

growing reticence in relation to any federalising evolution of the European integration process. At the end of the day, both the Amsterdam rules on employment and the social policy and the convening of the Extraordinary Summit on the 20th of November were also a result of that vigorous consensus between France's left and right wings which, albeit without much of a subsequent echo, reached the point of dramatizing the said events.

The more economies converge, the more social problems and their solutions will tend to be identical. Besides, the industrial policy which, from Maastricht onwards, gained a legal albeit not very operational basis, will always be inseparable from a more dynamic social policy.[47] Especially now, when States have lost devaluation as an instrument with which to defend their competitiveness, the sole alternative lies in the creation and permanent upgrading of a qualified labour force—although this is merely the more "preventive" and less "therapeutic" path taken by the social policy.

One should also be aware that a single market that is virtually complete and on its way to the finishing touch in the shape of the tying of the final knot of the single currency will, apart from anything else, certainly favour a partial harmonisation of social systems, as the Treaty itself admits (see the last paragraph of Article 117). And while on the one hand it is true that the international competition to which labour markets are subject will be intensified by the single currency,[48] on the other the more perfect unity of the single market made viable by the euro will also mean that the respective labour market cannot be seen as a mere combination of various national markets.

Both the man/economy relationship itself and the concept of work will tend to be reconstructed on the basis of this simultaneously vaster and more advanced position. To the point that it will only be possible to retie the knots that have come undone in a new social contract on that level. Even politically, the new possibilities in terms of "increased cooperation" (flexibility) also require other parallel possibilities in terms of "strengthened solidarity" (Vítor Martins). The political densification of the Union also entails its social densification at a moment when more dangers of disintegration are lurking around the corner. Only thus will it be possible to sustain and mobilise the albeit modest progresses that have been made in terms of the Political Union.

Indeed, there is starting to be a sort of "cross-contamination" of new solutions in the social area between different European countries. After all, it was the Italian adherence to the thirty-five-hour week—in the wake of France, albeit under internal pressure from the "Communist Refounders"—that saved the support of the left-wing bloc for Romano Prodi's budget and government in October 1997.[49]

---

[47]See Moussis 1997, pp. 10–11.

[48]See Donges et al. 1996, p. 54.

[49]However, another argument is that alongside eighteen million unemployed, there are nine million "overburdened" workers in Europe (Van Velzen Report, *op.cit.*).

Most important of all may, however, be the fact that the construction of Europe offers the *great opportunity for the post-modern reconstruction of "the social". Apart from anything else, because at the end of the day the social in Europe will be that of the "information society" and not the "industrial society". It is only as part of that new European plan that it is simultaneously possible to emancipate the social from the bureaucratic rigidity to which it would be doomed as a prisoner of the former framework of the Welfare State, and reconcile it with the economic shapes which the single market and the single currency have now assumed and which the national state can no longer attain.* It is on this terrain and with this leverage that Europeans could change their social culture without having to renounce the essence of their own model.

Possibilities: Up Until Amsterdam

The Treaty of Rome remained very distant from this perspective, however. Its approach to the social policy issue (Articles 117 to 128) was fairly poor and partly involved rules directed towards free movement (Articles 47 and 51, 117 and 118). After that, the first constitutional, legislative and jurisprudential advances mainly concerned emigrant workers (Articles 47 and 51 and Article 121)—the first European citizens, in a sense.

Until the Single European Act (SEA, 1987), the possible legal bases for the development of the social policy were either indirect or exceptional in nature (Articles 100 and 235), and required such legislation to be tied to the implementation of the single market—something that only allowed social objectives to be addressed (and then in an oblique way) as the result of a spill-over or incidental effect.

Two significant progresses are occurring with the SEA. The first is indirect and results from the introduction of a qualified majority for decisions on many of the questions linked to the completion of the single market. The second is derived from a new competence (Article 128) to decide on health and safety conditions in the workplace and on the latter's specific environment in the broad sense.

The support for vocational training, the establishment of minimum daily and weekly rest requirements and the protection of pregnant women's rights have seen substantial progresses since then. Although the European legislation was already quite complete in many of these areas, in general terms the social legislation was still one-off, fragmentary and residual in nature.

Despite its limitations, the Community Charter of the Fundamental Social Rights of Workers that was finally approved at the Strasbourg Summit in December 1989 was to represent a remarkable milestone. It abused two of the long-standing formal notions of International Public Law—"Charter" and "Declaration"—but did not possess binding force under either that Law or Community Law. However, it did link back to certain provisions of the Treaty and was able to serve as "guide" to the interpretation of its subject matter.[50]

From a substantive standpoint, the Charter enlarged the array of concerns but was still centred on improving living and working conditions. In addition, many of the rights it proclaimed already fell within the scope of the Community's legislative competence with regard to matters such as the freedom of movement (Articles 7 and 48 to 51), promoting social dialogue (Article 118-B), the right to association and collective bargaining (Article 118), and paid holidays (Article 120). However, the Charter was dependent on the success of the legislative programme which the Commission set in motion in the Charter's shadow and whose final outcome was to prove quite limited.

The TEU would come to add a Protocol and a Pact on Social Policy that were annexed to the Treaty, but the decisions adopted under or pursuant to those texts were not to be binding all twelve Member States—the UK would remain outside their purview. In addition, the newly amended Article 2 was to charge the Community with the mission of attaining both "a high level of employment" and "social protection", and higher levels of quality of life and "social and economic cohesion".

Indeed, all this showed how the first signs of recession were stimulating the attention paid to social questions. More symptomatic still of some systematic interpretations of Articles 1, 2, and 3, the social policy was already becoming an essential way in which to lend more body to the "increasingly closer union" of European peoples that was then decided on.[51]

At the same time, the TEU also created a new status for individuals—that of European citizenship, which in its own right enriched all the remaining rights, including the social ones, that were recognised through the primary law and derived from the Community. In addition, the protection of the freedom of movement and the right of residence as citizenship rights also served to expand the range of Community social rights, eventually emancipating them from their necessary connection with a labour activity[52] and in any case setting the seal on the first necessary step towards the recognition of a common "social citizenship".

Meanwhile, the Commission consolidated its goals for 1995–1999 with regard to cooperation and coordination between Member States in its White Paper on Social Policy. In order to promote these objectives, it used not only interministerial meetings, but also an annual conference, an observatory and a European employment service.

Even though it remained far from its own "road to Damascus", a European path to a certain reinvention of the social dimension began to be outlined in the place that was actually its natural starting point: *the reinvention of the notions of labour and the labour relationship*. One example is the broader formulation of the first of

[50]Hepple 1990, pp. 643–654.

[51]O'Leary 1995, p. 171.

[52]Ibid.

the two, which is no longer restricted to employment. It was not by chance that the Charter of the Social Rights of *Workers* was initially going to be called the Charter of the Social Rights of *Citizens*, and in fact its purposes and the way it attributes rights refer not only to employed workers, but also to people young and old who engage in social, community or charity services and volunteering.

The case law of the Court of Justice of the European Communities (see cases C-159/91 and C-160/91, in respect of Articles 85-86 TEC) seems to be pointing in the same direction. Albeit with different objectives, the Atypical Workers Directive and the Working Time Directive go in a parallel direction in which both seek to adapt the rules on the nature and rate of work to the worker, in such a way as to recover his/her autonomy as a subject and reconcile his/her occupation with family life and the social context.

The solutions that have been put forward with a view to achieving greater participation by and more information and consultation of workers, which now enjoy a constitutional basis in the Treaties (Article 118), can also be seen as seeking a working relationship that is less authoritarian and less based on subordination, contrary to the traditional approach. The European Social Fund's efforts to ensure something close to lifelong vocational training would, in turn, point towards the concrete implementation of a fundamental right to continuous training, and thus an embryonic social citizenship.

Possibilities: After Amsterdam

With the Amsterdam Treaty, however, a new point of departure and a wider basis for future development have been created. To begin with, the simple fact that it talks about social and employment rights—i.e. that it accepts an active, guarantee-based mandate on these levels—implies a counterattack against a radical type of market-driven globalisation.

There is now a set of principles, objectives, rights and institutional action instruments that not only rank higher in the regulatory hierarchy, but are also organised in a more systematic and functional way. We have moved on from the social "dimension" and "space" to the "constitutionalisation" of rights and the social policy, thereby at a single stroke making social rights—hitherto reliant on simple derived law, or even solely on the case law of the ECJ—less unstable and precarious. This represents above all a contribution to the emancipation of these rights from their fundamental link to the market.

It is likely that we have already begun to move from a phase in which the Treaty of Rome defined the *status negativus* of mere economic freedoms to one in which the Amsterdam Treaty has created a *status activus* (TUE citizenship) and a *status positivus* (social rights).[53] A particularly significant example of this mutation could be said to be the transformation of the question of non-discrimination between men and women. In the previous Article 119, this only covered a function linked to pay and the market, but has now been turned into a more general principle of and a fundamental right to equal treatment and opportunities for both sexes (see Articles 2, 3, 6-A, 118, and 119, TEC).

The same can be said about both the fact that the fight against exclusion has now been enshrined as one of the objectives of the Community social policy (Articles 117-A and 118), and the horizontal nature of the promotion of a "high level of employment" (Article 3§2), or the creation of institutional instruments such as the Employment Committee or the social dialogue process with legally recognised contractual effects. This has actually reached a point at which some people, overly lulled by the acquisitions of the past, are already asking for the implementation of social convergence criteria and for the convergence process to be phased in exactly the same way as the monetary union process.[54]

The referrals to the European Social Charter and the Charter of the Fundamental Social Rights of Workers—to begin with in the new Article 1 of the TEU, and then in Article 117 of the TEC—and the integration of the Protocol whereby the United Kingdom has now adopted the CFSRW already constitute a significant framework for a European social citizenship, notwithstanding the fact that it is not possible for citizens to directly invoke them in the courts.

The many reasons I have already set out clearly mean that expectations cannot be excessive. Even so, Amsterdam is the first draft of a social citizenship and policy without which the new European civil society would not be able to see itself as anything other than a market, much less as possessing power and freedom within that market, in a situation that nevertheless challenges its identity to an extent that even goes beyond its so-called "social model".

Many even see the "social" and closeness-to-the-citizen elements as the priority direction taken in this new Treaty,[55] as if they constituted an attempt to "civilise" the single market and in parallel make a European civil society and democracy viable. Be that as it may, the employment and social policies in their entirety now form part of the Community mainstream.

Indeed, none of this prevents the new Treaty from continuing to safeguard the priority and precedence of the Member States in social matters and from primarily taking a perspective that gives preference to complementarity, coordination,

[53]Reich 1997, pp. 131–164 suggests that this cycle had already begun, pointing to the social, environmental and consumer rights that have been created by a combination of primary law and derived Community law and in many cases have been put into practice with direct effect.

[54]See the Van Velzen Report, *op. cit.*

[55]See e.g. Wessels 1997, p. 121.

cooperation, incentives and information, both in relation to the Member States and with regard to the social partners and social dialogue.

Even regarding matters that have been moved from the "cooperation" to the "co-decision" process, such as the Maastricht Social Protocol [Article 118(3)], the requirement for unanimous votes in the Council remains, despite the fact that the rule in European Parliament-Council co-decision cases is one of a qualified majority. In addition, the last paragraph of Article 109-R actually precludes the idea of harmonisation by expressly saying that coordination actions regarding employment and provided for therein "shall not include the harmonisation of the laws and regulations of the Member States".

In this regard, the decisions taken in Amsterdam are designed on the one hand to enable the Member States to continue to control the social policy, and on the other to indicate that it is a priority goal to ensure the "development of human resources" (Article 117) in order to obtain a qualified labour force (see Article 109-N) that is trained for and adapted to a labour market which is both competitive and capable of creating jobs.

The Treaties already included various references to the question of employment (Articles 2, 102-A, 103, 105, 118, 119, 122, 123, and 127), over and above those contained in the Social Protocol (Articles 1, 2, and 4). However, those references were flawed by their scattered nature, the disconnect between them and both the mechanisms for coordinating economic activity and the goals in that field (Article 103), and the fact that they did not enjoy enough resources to become effective (Article 118) and either required unanimity or were not applicable to all the Member States (the UK, in the case of the Social Protocol). It is in this context that the creation of a special chapter for employment in Amsterdam inevitably possesses an important systematic significance in terms of the coherence and overall efficiency of this policy.

What this new "file" in the overall dossier of the Treaties means is that people didn't trust, and were unable to trust, in the pure social spill-over effect of the single market—which was actually leading to a mere economism instead. Nor was there just a mere declaration of new social rights—although some have just been taken from elsewhere, this time from the Charter of the Fundamental Social Rights—seen from a perspective of social citizenship which, together with the mandatory definition of minimum standards, had probably thus far been the most important, if not almost the only, point of view.

A number of institutional information mechanisms were created. Examples include the annual joint report by the Council and the Commission (Article 109-K), mechanisms for making recommendations to the Member States, for coordination between them (the Employment Committee is one example here), and now, with the help of the Extraordinary Summit, also for "multilateral supervision", like the one implemented at the level of the Monetary Union.

In addition, specific legal bases were defined not only for drawing up policies to counter exclusion—which is the social problem of the 20th century, as opposed to that of "exploitation" in the 19th century[56]—but also for organising the social dialogue, consulting the social partners (Articles 117, and 118-A and B), or granting incentives in relation to innovative pilot projects, which will certainly serve as catalysts for more homogeneity and social security; and the same can be said about the progress in improving the situation of women in working life and the equality of male and female workers.

An apparent formal symmetry between the Employment Committee and the Monetary Committee now suggests a greater fellowship between or reconciliation of the social and economic dimensions, even though the social policy is still expressly confined to the boundaries of its nature as a policy that must be "consentaneous" with the economic policy [see e.g. Articles 109-O(1), and 109-K(2)]. The social dimension has not only risen many places in the overall ranking of priorities on the Community agenda, but is also approaching a degree of parity with the economic dimension, albeit within a dominantly liberal internal and external framework.

From now on there will be fewer obstacles along the way for the progresses that have already begun to be outlined in matters such as the creation of workers' committees or councils within European enterprises, the right to parental leave for both men and women, and equality between part-time and full-time workers.

However, the limits I describe above once again show that we should not harbour too many illusions. Although the climate is what one might call "neo-voluntarist", to use Streek's[57] expression, it was not with empty pockets that the Extraordinary Employment Summit[58] could have done much more than reaffirm the priority of fighting unemployment in all the various EU policies.

In general, it was mostly about continuing the task of improving the definition of and implementing generalist initiatives, ideas and proposals, which in many cases had already been rehearsed by Delors and Santer and essentially aimed at improving the capacity to achieve insertion into the labour market, developing entrepreneurial spirit, encouraging the capacity of enterprises and their workers to adapt, and strengthening equal opportunities policies.

Trans-European networks, support for SMEs, reducing the fiscal burden on labour, ecotaxes, social VAT, incentives for competitiveness, pilot initiatives against exclusion, the transition from salaried to independent workers, making the labour market more flexible and continuous vocational training will all continue to be on the menu of desirable solutions, either taking small steps forwards or waiting for better opportunities. At one point it was suggested that the Treaty should include a minimum income principle, albeit one that would not have a set value, would vary

[56]Ricouer, in the *Figaro* newspaper of 25 March 1998.

[57]Ibid.

[58]Despite it all, the Summit's conclusions show that the European Investment Bank was ready to mobilize ten billion euros for SMEs that are actively present in the new technologies field, while the EU was also able to make four hundred and fifty million available for a three-year period.

from one Member State to another, and would thus be funded entirely from national resources. However, in the end the idea was not actually adopted due to a lack of consensus.

In the meantime, some of the proposals that have been deferred or actually frozen will inevitably give rise to practical obstruction by many countries that have either solved the employment problem better than most, or consider that these days only creating new businesses can open the way to job creation or that the only way to make it possible to create new jobs is to also make it possible to dismiss staff.

Even so, subsidiarity and the need to "preserve the competitive capacity of the Community economy" (Article 3-B) will continue to exist as unavoidable parameters. In addition, the flexibilisation of labour markets will also go on expanding, albeit with an increase in both the process of preparing people for that change[59] and the direct "social" responsibility of enterprises, namely in the training field, in relation to which there are already voices calling for "corporate citizenship".

However, those directions must in turn be compatible with the principle of solidarity (Article A§3, TEU), which goes beyond the primarily passive forms of solidarity which still prevail at the moment and which, albeit more generalised and generous than the American ones, mainly provide security for large organised social groups.[60] An active solidarity with the capacity to create a better distribution of opportunities at the European level… that kind of solidarity will at least require a bigger vision and a systematic link between European and domestic policies.

The Community's Social Constitution is thus subjected to a tension between cohesion and competitiveness, solidarity and subsidiarity. Neither of the poles in this dialectic can be interpreted separately. In a way, the second would in fact seek to avoid a situation in which the first remained without someone to take adequate responsibility for it. Solidarity would at least tell us how to apply the concept of subsidiarity, apart from anything else by horizontally and vertically distributing roles.[61]

The answer to this question is neither easy nor obvious, nor will it be able to do without a continuous fight on the ground for the pre-eminence of one or other of the two principles. After all, they reflect the conflict between the liberal ideology of the single market and the superimposition of a "European civil society" on the latter. *The only way in which this tension will not pose difficulties will be when the concrete implementation of the social rights also contributes to the "efficiency" or at least the "pacification" of the market.*

Where "social citizenship" is concerned, the expectations of the latter's densification cannot be very great, but at least they are now pointing towards what João Carlos Espada calls a "common ground" or access and "non-exclusion" by the

---

[59]The proportion of people working part-time in the European Union increased from 4 to 5.5% from 1990 to 1996, while in 1996 itself, 31.5% of all women workers worked part-time (Annual Report on Employment in the EU (*op. cit.* p. 4).

[60]Ponzini 1996, p. 12.

[61]See Bercusson et al. 1997, p. 193.

market.[62] In other words, going beyond Hayekian and neoliberal radicalism and falling short of its symmetrical socialist alternative, it is now possible for a citizenship that is simultaneously based on the domain of the "material conditions which enable individuals to use their freedom" and the equal right that everyone has to access that value[63] to start "constructing itself" on the level of the single market and on the basis of Amsterdam.

The difficulties with the ideal, normative, institutional and practical Europeanisation of these perspectives are great, but a framework of constitutional norms has already been created and will allow at least three types of evolution that are all communitising and to that extent will possess the virtue of civilising the market: the creation of standard norms with an exemplary meaning and the ability to be reproduced at the level of the Member States; the improved coordination of national social policies, both with each other and with the Community's economic policies; and the development through social dialogue of forms of "assisted" self-regulation at a macro-European level. In many of these fields the normative result will mostly be soft law, but on the other hand, achieving the consensus needed to obtain it will also be easier.

From now on, the "social" will in any case cease to be a "clandestine" or merely "supplementary" Community policy, gaining a dignity that is virtually identical to that of the economic and monetary policy, in addition to a priority with a degree of urgency[64] that was moreover underlined at the Extraordinary Summit of 20 November 1997.

The then President of the Council (Jean-Claude Juncker) spoke of a "starting point", and the European Parliament's report on the Summit says that "the seed has been sown".[65] The harvest will primarily depend on the vitality and autonomy of European society, and a social policy that is increasingly inherent in that society is likely to develop side-by-side with it. On that level it is crucial that "social dialogue"—another form of anti-exclusion—be institutionalised. That way, workers will automatically see their negotiating capacity strengthened in the "big space", while unions may even find it offers a way to renew trade unionism.

Paradoxical though it may seem, it is liberal Europe itself that will be dependent on an effective "citizenship" and "social dialogue" becoming viable at the European level. While it is true that a liberal construction of Europe cannot impose identical social concepts on every Member Country, failing which it runs the risk of becoming as fundamentalist as any other "religion of the social", nor can it dispense with rules of conviviality that are legitimated by agreement between the continent's various organised groups and conceptions.

The richness and strength of the liberal conception lie simultaneously in the coexistence of different approaches to its dialectic tension with equality, and in the

---

[62]See Direitos Sociais de Cidadania, Lisbon, 1998, pp. 263–265.

[63]Ibid.

[64]See Chirac 1997, p. 157.

[65]Report by Mèndez De Vigo 1997, p. 31.

assumption that they are on the same level and can come to an understanding with each other. From this standpoint, democratisation, politics and citizenship, and social dialogism will actually be simple tempos in the same musical score.

Epilogue

Social Policy as an Institutional Question and One of Political Authority

Ranging from the technological revolution to the denationalisation of the economy and the globalisation of the labour markets, the conditions that exist today are forcing an in-depth reformulation of the so called "European social state", in relation to which the European dimension must play a growing, albeit subsidiary role. Having said this, minimal though that dimension's role may be, its action in this respect is the only means of placing the keystone in the dome of the possible coherence between politics and the economy on the one hand and the social dimension on the other. This is the path that Amsterdam, albeit timidly and within a framework of very tight limits, is already essaying.

What has grown more than anything is the evidence that, as Habermas[66] says, on this plane it is necessary to "construct bodies that are capable of functioning on the supranational level", given that only intergovernmental structures of the European-Community type are still in a position to condition the global system from a perspective of "internal policy taken to the world level (*weltinnenpolitik*)".

The problem is an even more general one. *On the one side (European Union), we have a market with weak institutions; on the other (national state), we have strong institutions without a market. The remedy for this reciprocal inadequacy is both essential to and must come before the resolution of the social question, so that it is possible to face up to both the external competitive pressure and the possible internal conflicts.* This means that besides the supranational dome, the reconstruction of the social needs to be institutionally underpinned with sufficient capacity at that level.

The social question—which was the last to be resolved on the constitutional level of the national state—cannot in fact be seriously reopened except by an institutionally and politically more consistent Europe. This is not just an issue of its internal democratic structuring, in that the European social model will only be "competitive" if it possesses proportional means of control, influence and refraction in relation to the global economy.

One might even say that it is perhaps on this plane that Europe is still far from enjoying the conditions needed to make its future social identity viable. It was also in this domain that Amsterdam fell furthest short of expectations. What I hope is

[66]Zagrebelsky et al. 1996, p. 371.

that reality rapidly imposes the perception that the Europe of the single currency—especially that Europe—will only acquire its full meaning and operationality as a political Europe.

At the end of the day the new European "social" contract will be as "political" as the one that gave birth to the modern national democracies. To put it another way: on this plane too, the political "contract" required by the notion of a European "constitution" will concurrently require a true "social contract". This does not mean that the framework and meaning of a European post-liberal democracy—even when seen as a "democracy of democracies"—must coincide with the shapes taken by the foundation of the modern constitutional state. What they will have to do is breathe with the spirit of a new renaissance which, like the previous ones, would still be the best way to face up to and anticipate the new "globalisation" from the European side.

References

Ackerman B (1993) La Justicia Social en el Estado Liberal (transl. Rosenkrenz C). Barcelona

Albert A (1997) Reconstruire d'Urgence. Sociétal, No. 12, October

Archibugi F (1996) Beyond the Welfare State: Planning for a Welfare Society. In: Greve B (ed) Comparative Welfare Systems. London and New York

Bercusson B et al (1997) A Manifesto for Social Europe. European Law Journal, Vol. 3, No. 2, June

Berger PL (ed) (1997) Limits of Social Cohesion

Caporaso J (1996) The European Union and Forms of State: Westphalian Regulatory or Post-Modern? Journal of Common Market Studies, Vol. 34, No. 1, March

Chalmin P (1997) De Charles Quint à la Sécurité Sociale. Sociétal, No. 12, October, p. 10

Chirac J (1997) Memorandum on the European Social Model. Employment: A European Strategy, ep/ppe, July

Cohen E (1996) Europe between Market and Power: Industrial Policies. In: Mény Y et al (eds) Adjusting to Europe. London

D'Intigenano B (1997) La Protection Sociale. Paris

Donges J B et al (1996) (Kronberger Kreis) A Social Union for Europe? Bad Homburg

George V (1997) The Future of the Welfare State. In: George V and Taylor-Gooby P (eds) European Welfare Policy: Squaring the Circle, pp. 22–27

Greve B (1996) Post-Fordism and the State. In: Greve B (ed) Comparative Welfare Systems. London and New York

Hayek F (1967) Studies in Philosophy, Politics and Economics. London

Hepple B (1990) The Implementation of The Community Charter of Fundamental Social Rights. The Modern Law Review, 53, September, pp. 643–654

Jordan B (1997) Globalization and the European Social Model. In: What Global Role for the EU? Brussels, the Philip Morris Institute for Public Policy Research, September

L'Épée R (1993) L'Identité Européenne. In: Edifie LLN (ed) Des Valeurs pour L'Europe. Brussels

Lucas Pires F (1991) A Política Social Comunitária como exemplo do Princípio de Subsidiariedade. Separata da Revista de Direito e Estudos Sociais, Year XXXIII, V, 2nd Series, Nos. 3–4

Lucas Pires F (1995) Constituição Social: Superar o Oito Sem Cair no Oitenta. In: Portugal e o Futuro Da União Europeia, pp. 142–148

Lucena D Globalização, Tecnologia E Desigualdades. Revista V, No. 0

Majone G (1996) Which Social Policy for Europe? In: Mény Y et al (eds) Adjusting to Europe. London, pp. 124 et seq
Mèndez de Vigo I (1997) Textos Sobre El Tratado De Amsterdam (Doc-Po/Rr/339/3391644 of 5 November
Miegel M and Wahl S (1994) Das Ende des Individualisms. Die Kultur des Westens zerstört sich selbst. Bonn
Moscovici P (1997) Emploi et Objectifs Sociaux. In: Moscovici P (ed) Réinventer L'Europe
Moussis N (1997) Manuel De L'Europe Social
Murray R (1999) Fordism and Post-Fordism. In: Hall S and Jacques M (eds) New Times, the Changing Face of Politics in the 1990s. Lawrence and Wishart, pp. 38–47
Nadal E (1997) Brotéria, Vol. 145.
O'Leary S (1995) The Social Dimension off Community Citizenship. In: Rosas A and Antola E (eds) A Citizen's Europe. London
Ponzini G (1996) La Dimensione Sociale De L'Unione Europea. In: Barbieri A et al (eds) Lo Stato Sociale in Italia. Donzelli, Rome
Reich N (1997) A European Constitution for Citizens. European Law Journal, Vol. 3. No. 2, June, pp. 131–164
Rhodes M (1996) Globalisation and West European Welfare States: A Critical Review of Recent Debates. Journal of European Social Policy, 6 (4)-1996
Smith M P (1997) The End of German Social Partnership? CEPS Review, No. 2, Summer
Sorz F (1996) Políticas De Empleo En Europa. Meridiano Ceri, August, No. 10
Streeck W (1994) From Market-Making to State Building? Reflections on the Political Economy of European Social Policy. Florence
Toulemon R (1996) L'Europe et l'emploi. Revue Du Marché Commun et de l'Union Européenne, No. 400, July-August, pp. 485 et seq
Wessels W (1997) Der Amsterdam Vertrang – Durch Stückswerksreformen Zu Einer Efizienteren, Erweiterten Und Föderalen Union? Integration, 3/97
Whiteford E A (1995) W(h)ither Social Policy? In: Show J and More G (eds) New Legal Dynamics of European Union. Oxford
Zagrebelsky G et al (1996) Una Costituzione per l'Europa? Osservazioni Sui Dieter Grimm. In: Zagrebelsky G et al (eds) Il Futuro Della Costituzione. Turin

Chapter 4
Asylum Law and Policy in the European Union Before and Beyond Amsterdam

For a Greater Juridification of the Community Law on Asylum

Francisco Lucas Pires

In memory of Aristides de Sousa Mendes, the Portuguese man who made historical rehabilitation possible.

The way in which the asylum problem[1] is handled is especially symptomatic of the relationship between Europeans and non-Europeans, and thus helps reveal what is one of the "border issues" facing the new Europe. The path which the process of European construction is taking in this domain is conditioned to a large extent by the domestic and international aspects of the question, and up until Amsterdam the different views and decisions in relation to it were entirely the province of intergovernmental procedures within the scope of the third pillar. In order to be able to evaluate this process, we need to go further back and look beyond the Community tradition, to the end of Second World War.

There were more than six million displaced people in Europe at that time—a fact that was to make a major contribution to the creation of the Office of the United Nations High Commissioner for Refugees in 1950, and to inspire the approval of the Refugee Convention in Geneva in 1951. The Hungarian exodus (two hundred thousand people) following the Soviet invasion in 1956, and the return to the various

[1]The bibliography on this topic is extensive. Limiting myself to a few of the most current works, I would suggest the following authors and titles: Christiansen and Kjaerum 1990; Martin 1994; ECRE 1993; Goodwin-Gill 1983; Meijers 1990; D'Oliveira 1994; Handoll 1995; Joly 1996; Joly and Cohen 1989; Joly with Nettleton and Poulton 1992; Weiler 1992; Hailbronner 1990 and 1995, pp. 182–206; Araújo Torres 1995; Gorjão-Henriques 1996; Garrone 1993; Minority Rights Group No. 5, Refugees in Europe: The Hostile New Agenda, 1996; Hoogenboom 1992; Den Boer 1997.

This chapter was originally published in Portuguese by PRINCIPIA, Cascais, Portugal in the book *Amsterdão: do Mercado á Sociedade Europeia?* (ISBN 972-8500-04-1) in 1998, which was translated from the Portuguese by Luís Tirapicos Nunes and Richard Rodgers. For more information, contact the editors of the present book via the following e-mail address: martinholucaspires@fd.lisboa.ucp.pt.

F. Lucas Pires (Deceased) (✉)
Lisbon, Portugal
e-mail: martinholucaspires@fd.lisboa.ucp.pt

M. Lucas Pires and F. Pereira Coutinho (eds.), *What Market, What Society, What Union?* https://doi.org/10.1007/978-94-6265-371-9_4

home countries following decolonisation in the 1960s and '70s, were to cause massive forms of displacement of people or pressure on certain borders and populations. Especially in the first of these cases, the concept of "individual refugee" that provided the basis for the Geneva Convention definition would in fact be jeopardised, and in the end it was accepted that the nationality of the applicants sufficed.

Despite all these convulsions and changes of perspective, both the Treaty of Rome and actual Community practice were silent on this subject and remained immune to the problem, as they were to the issues of asylum and emigration, at a time when the European growth rate and model seemed happy to absorb the cheap labour coming from elsewhere. The European panorama of the day was one of a contradictory range of emigration and asylum policies, namely with strong North/South and West/East contrasts. However, with the first great recession caused by the oil price shock, this tendency would begin to be reversed in the mid-1970s.

Between the Single Act and Maastricht

The History of Schengen and Dublin

Nevertheless, only a decade later, in October 1986, the Ministers of Internal Affairs of the Member States of the European Union decided to create an "ad hoc immigration group", in what was a first attempt to coordinate the asylum and immigration policy. This step forward was then supplemented by the need to prepare the adoption of the Single European Act, pursuant to which all internal borders were to be eliminated and freedom of movement assured by 1993 and in accordance with Article 7a of the TEC.

Two years later in Rhodes, the Council created the position of "coordinators" in order to strengthen intergovernmental cooperation and force concrete results in the freedom of movement field. One outcome of the mission entrusted to the coordinators was to be the "Palma document", which was presented in Madrid in 1989 and provided a list of the measures that were necessary or desirable in order to put the free movement of persons in motion.

On 15 June 1990, the Dublin Convention, which was subsequently signed by all the members of the then EEC, stipulated that the first Member State to authorise the entry of an asylum seeker into its territory should also be responsible for examining his/her request for asylum, regardless of his/her country of origin. Its Preamble expressly says that one of the Convention's objectives is to avoid the movement of asylum seekers from one state to another without any country taking responsibility for examining their requests. The second goal was to guarantee applicants that those requests would indeed be examined by one of the Member States; while the third was to avoid too long a wait for an answer as to whether asylum would be granted.[2]

[2]This description of the Dublin Convention's objectives is taken from Pereira 1993, p. 37.

On practically the same date—19 June—and in the place that would eventually give its name to the document, the Governments of the Benelux, the Federal Republic of Germany and the French Republic signed the Convention implementing the Schengen Agreement, which the same countries had already agreed on 15 June 1985. Spain and Portugal adhered to the Agreement on 25 and 26 June 1991, shortly after Italy and before Greece. Schengen was scheduled to enter into force on 1 September 1993, for application as of March 1996.

Objectives, Principles and General Rules

Where the asylum policy was concerned, Schengen's objective was to coordinate all the above-mentioned policies by defining criteria for the responsibility of the Member States to examine asylum requests and exchange relevant information (Articles 28 to 38). However, while the Dublin Convention is a first step on the path to harmonisation in asylum-related matters, Schengen develops a whole range of cooperation and follow-up measures that are not limited to asylum and more generally concern the elimination of internal borders and other questions that fall within the scope of the states which signed it, whose collective territory some people have since called "Schengenland".

Dublin and Schengen thus partly overlap, but at the same time constitute a sort of experimental shipyard for freedom of movement. In order to prevent the possibility of conflict between the two, on 26 April 1997 Schengen's Executive Committee approved a protocol whereby the Schengen Agreement's provisions on asylum would cease to apply when the Dublin Convention entered into force. That entry was in fact postponed in the meantime due to the paradoxical delay in ratification by the country whose capital gave the Convention its name, but then occurred on 1 September 1997.

On asylum, the core question in both Conventions is the determination of the country that is responsible for granting it. The concern behind the centrality of this problem lies in the need for the responsibility to examine an asylum request to fall on a single country—the principle of exclusivity or sole opportunity. The intention was thus to avoid both the submission of multiple requests as a result of asylum-shopping—i.e. a sort of auction of simultaneous requests—and the possibility of having refugees "in orbit", which is to say a kind of "merry-go-round" of candidates going round and round countries that are not interested in examining the request in question. Additionally, the system has the desired effect of making the designated state responsible for the applicant's departure from Union territory in the event that his/her request is not granted.[3]

---

[3]On this point, see Hailbronner and Thiery 1997, pp. 964 *et seq.*

This principle nonetheless safeguards the possibility of exceptions, first of all insofar as it is not mandatory for third-party states to recognise the exclusivity of the first state's responsibility to examine the request, namely in cases in which the applicable process has ended with a negative outcome. In addition to being one more manifestation of the idea of sovereignty in the sensitive area of asylum, this exception can be especially relevant in the countries in which this right of asylum is directly founded on the wording of the Constitution.[4]

This stance on the Convention's part also elucidates another important aspect of the issue. Its only addressees are likely to be states. It is thus probably not about legally establishing true subjective rights pertaining to the subjects in question, and namely a right of asylum. It has more to do with solving procedural and almost technical questions, avoiding the additional conflicts between states which a borderless space might foster in that respect. More than "fundamental", the rights that are at stake here could be seen as "functional", in a sense that could be said to be equivalent to that of the four freedoms on which the single market was built.

Nor does this prevent applicants for asylum from being recognised to possess a certain number of rights—namely of a procedural nature—not only in Schengen and Dublin, but also in other related conventions and resolutions. This is the case of rights such as those to a prior hearing and an appeal, to temporary leave to remain, to the protection of the applicant's personal data, to access to translation and legal assistance, to the guaranteed provision of means of subsistence by the state that is examining the request until such time as the final decision is taken, and to family reunification.

It is also in the light of the primary function referred to above that the criteria for determining the responsible state can be said to be not only objective, but also clearly ranked. In principle, it is the state with the largest share of responsibility for the asylum seeker's presence in Schengen territory that will be under the obligation to examine the relevant request. To put it more clearly, "the more a state manifests its agreement to the entry or continued presence of an asylum seeker, the more that state becomes responsible".[5] Other criteria follow, such as consanguinity with a refugee to whom another Member State has already granted refugee status, the issuance of a residence permit, the grant of a visa, the grant of permission to enter without a visa, or current residence. The principle of family reunification is also solidly established, albeit limited to the spouse, unmarried offspring under the age of eighteen, and the father or mother of an unmarried minor offspring when the latter has already been guaranteed asylum status (Article 35 Schengen, and Article 4 Dublin).

[4]Ibid., p. 965.

[5]European Commission, *Avant-Projet de Proposition de Directive de Conseil au Rapprochement des Règles Concernant le Droit d'Asile et le Statut de Réfugiés*, June 1998, p. 31.

Critical Assessment

Despite the fact that they established a set of principles and rules of the type described above, which are in fact often relatively indeterminate or exceptional, Schengen and Dublin did not give rise to a substantive or even formal harmonisation of solutions. Both immigration and asylum remained outside the Community framework and within the area of competence reserved to the Member States, sometimes individually, and sometimes in the form of the need for unanimous decisions within the scope of intergovernmental cooperation. In fact, this was the only possible interpretation of the precepts contained in the Conventions, which were thus to a large extent more dependent on inter-state consensus than on their own literal texts.

These Conventions did not even seem to jeopardise the advances that had already been secured in terms of guarantees on this front, either internationally or domestically. The solutions for an embryonic harmonisation which they have rendered viable not only represent a relatively low minimum common denominator, but also rationalise and ideally even expand the possibilities for free movement within the European space by asylum applicants who have obtained a positive answer to their request from the Member State that is concretely deemed competent to that end. In addition, while the grant of asylum substantively depends on the Member States as such, at the same time their decision is still bound by the Geneva Convention and the European Convention on Human Rights, to which all the Member States are parties—a fact that constitutes a basis which is reliable and sufficient enough to serve as a guarantee.

Over and above this effort at rationalisation and at producing a normative guarantee, the European Community was also demonstrating its commitment to finding an overall response to the problem on the prelegal level—i.e. in the political, economic and social field. For instance, it became the biggest international contributor to the budget of the Office of the United Nations High Commissioner for Refugees. In November 1992 its participation reached the significant sum of 215,065,978 USD. At the same time, the Commission was funding around forty-five per cent of the humanitarian resources employed in the former Yugoslavia.[6]

The Commission was also proving itself very diligent as an observer within the scope of the negotiations at both the Community level and between the States Party to the Schengen Convention. In 1991 it even submitted two documents to the Member States on the right of asylum and emigration policy, describing the measures to be adopted with a view to harmonising those areas and serving as the pillars of future policy.[7] Those documents were not only the basis for a number of future developments, but also retain a great deal of their currency today.

Later, in its 1994 Communication to the European Parliament and the Council, the same Commission made a clear distinction between the immigration policy, as

---

[6]See Drüke 1993, p. 20.

[7]Ibid., p. 21.

part of which it would be necessary to act in a restrictive and preventive manner, and the policy with regard to refugees, in relation to which the Commission essentially pointed out that it was impossible to reduce the number of refugees the Member States have to receive.

Notwithstanding all these efforts and good intentions, just recently (October 1997), Günter Grass—speaking about the regulations on asylum in Germany at the ceremony to award a Peace Prize to a Kurdish writer in Frankfurt—protested against what he called the reintroduction of "barbarism" within the very same citadel of the rule of law. In turn, at a more general level within the European Community, the criticisms of the effects of Dublin and Schengen have been as numerous as they have been virulent.[8] The objects of those criticisms can be summarised as follows:

(a) Their regulatory and bureaucratic complexity and opacity, which make the mere attempt to provide a systematic description extremely valuable from a scientific standpoint. These characteristics favour ignorance and the manipulation of interested parties, and they also increase the number of controls, to the point at which one can now say that they can be carried out anywhere and anytime, except when one crosses the old borders.
(b) The lack of parliamentary and judicial review of the ways in which they function—a shortfall which, in the parliamentary case, is equally true of the various national parliaments and the European Parliament—thereby creating a real "hole" in the process of legitimation and political/legal accountability.
(c) The absence of any reference in either document to the European Convention on Human Rights, and the clear distancing from the Council of Europe's first (1976) and second (1981) Recommendations on the Harmonisation of National Legislations on Refugee Status and Asylum, which sought to establish a number of undisputable international reference standards, such as the principle that a "fair and objective trial" is indispensable.
(d) Doubts as to whether some of the measures in these Conventions are in legal conformity with either Community law itself or the principle of a "community of law" that underlies it, with an even more notorious deviation in employment-related matters.
(e) The fact that the solutions contained in Schengen and Dublin are miserly compared to the standards set in the Geneva Convention, with the latter's significance in danger of becoming increasingly residual, namely as a result of the operation of the so-called "objective doctrine", which is tending to interpret Geneva's Article 1 on the notion of a "well-founded fear of persecution" in such a way as to require that the author of the persecution be "politically motivated".
(f) Doubts as to a possible abuse and obscure use of the personal data that circulate in the Schengen Information System (SIS), whose protection rules are broader and more precise compared to those in other international conventions with a

[8]See e.g. Ward 1997, pp. 79–95; Meijers 1990.

more generic application, but can only be invoked by European citizens and not by those of third countries—i.e. asylum seekers.

(g) The lack of democratic review, transparency and political accountability of Schengen's Executive Committee—a shortcoming which, like the previous allegation, suggests that we are in an area where the idea of secrecy prevails and "reasons of state" may have discovered their new oasis…

(h) The existence of discrepancies between certain requirements imposed in Schengen and those contained in other conventions or resolutions. One example is in relation to the provisions of the Convention on Controls on Persons Crossing External Frontiers with regard to the movement of refugees and asylum seekers within the limits of the overall territory of the Community. The Schengen Convention allows both categories of persons to transit from one Member State to another, subject to possession of a valid travel document and to the requirement that travellers declare their entry into the country of destination within three days of arriving there. The Convention on the Crossing of External Frontiers deals with refugees and asylum seekers in different ways, with the former able to stay in another EU country without the need for any visa, whereas the latter must register with the police within seventy-two hours following their arrival.

Schengen and Dublin came about as a compensation for doing away with the Union's internal borders. They were thus primarily intended to be control and regulation mechanisms. At the same time, the spectre of a new invasion of the Union caused by the dismantling of the communist regimes in the East or the demographic discrepancies in the South, the confusion between economic, humanitarian and political reasons or between emigration and asylum in the preparation and procedural details of requests, and the considerable rise in the number of refugees due namely to the war in the former Yugoslavia, have all combined to exponentially increase applications for asylum and reinforce the fears felt by both states and populations within the Union.

The sharp increase in unemployment in the Community countries and the budgetary restraint caused by the single currency has contributed to a climate of isolation and restriction which often took on xenophobic or racist hues. In a borderless Europe, some might even want states to use this path as a way to seek to reaffirm their control over their territorial boundaries and peoples, both of which are being eroded as much by globalisation as by Europeanisation, but also by localist and corporativist trends.

All the above factors may also have stimulated the restrictive effect of the Conventions, with regard to which the statistics seem undeniably conclusive. Whereas the requests of sixty-five per cent of asylum seekers were still successful in 1980, that figure is thought to have fallen to well below twenty per cent by 1990. Probably for the same reasons, the flow of asylum seekers, which grew exponentially over the course of a decade—from 73,700 casefiles in 1983 to 692,685 at the end of 1992—has gradually fallen ever since. In 1995 there were only 283,416 requests, and this number is likely to have decreased by thirty thousand in the first three quarters of 1996, compared to the same period of the previous year.

Albeit intended to provide guarantees, the new regulations end up containing factors that tend to dissuade asylum seekers, especially considering the context of absolute deprivation in which most of the people who apply for this type of protection find themselves. Particular examples of those factors include: the new and more complex requisites and procedures for granting visas; the fact that international transport companies are now held jointly liable and subject to heavy fines;[9] long periods of detention in refugee camps, with prisonlike conditions; the fear of deportation to the country of origin—a factor in relation to which the aforementioned Günther Grass criticised Germany with regard to the Kurdish issue; the very limited means of subsistence granted to applicants; the progressive reduction in the extent of and opportunities for family reunification; the difficulties in finding a job after being granted asylum; the obstacles that exist before actually reaching the country of asylum;[10] the ever greater strengthening of border controls; the creation of buffer zones; the prohibition of multiple or so-called "orbiting" requests; the almost total reliance on the "first host country" criterion; the threat of being sent back to the first host country outside the EU; the *in limine* refusal of requests on the grounds of their "manifestly unjustified" nature; and so on…

Between Maastricht and Amsterdam

The Treaty on European Union, which was signed in February 1992 but only entered into force in 1993, was not to alter this situation at all. It would practically restrict itself to providing a single framework for all the previous agreements on the asylum and immigration policy—namely the Dublin and Schengen Conventions—much of which were thereby made into law that was derived from or subsidiary to the Treaties. The policies in question were in turn to be subject to Article K, TEU, on cooperation in the fields of justice and home affairs—i.e. the so-called "third pillar".

Article K.1 now considers asylum policy to be "a matter of common interest", while Article K.3, which refers to K.1, promotes information, consultation and coordination of their action in this field between the Member States. At the same time, both these provisions are invoked in a very short Declaration on Asylum annexed to the TEU, which reiterates the intention to achieve greater cooperation on the matter. The only aspects of the immigration policy that are seen as reliant on the TEU's "first pillar" and therefore subject to the current Community procedure can be summed up as the drawing up of a list of countries whose citizens must hold a visa when crossing the EU's external borders, the requirement that those documents

[9]See Cruz 1996.

[10]On this and other difficulties referred to below, see, e.g., O'Keeffe 1994, pp. 24–26.

possess a uniform format, and the possibility of making them provisionally mandatory with regard to countries that find themselves in an emergency situation (Article 100-C of the EC Treaty, as inserted by Article G.23, TEU).

As I said earlier, the Schengen and Dublin Conventions are more about determining the country that is responsible for examining the request to exercise the right than any substantive criterion for recognising the right itself. The state that is considered responsible will then base its decision on its own criteria, which must in principle be in line with the Geneva Convention, to which the TEU in turn pays homage (Article K.2). An applicant's transfer to a third state, for instance, depends on the terms of the Geneva Convention.

In parallel, national governments are pursuing a path of harmonisation in the light of a number of resolutions, recommendations and conventions on "manifestly unjustified" requests, "first host countries", "crossing of external borders", "safe countries of origin". "family reunification", "practices regarding the deportation of persons who remain in a territory illegally", "minimum guarantees with regard to asylum procedures", "controls and deportation of third-country nationals residing or working without authorisation", and "sharing responsibility for the admission and resettlement of displaced persons"…

In accordance with this logic, the TEU continues to include the regulation of asylum-related matters in the intergovernmental sphere (third pillar), although it is one of the areas that could be transferred to the Community sphere (first pillar) under the terms of Article K.9—a move that has not taken place. The ultimate criterion of each state's sovereignty has thus been fully preserved in practice. Right up until the negotiations of the Amsterdam Treaty were concluded, the Member States failed to display any willingness to give way to the European Parliament's proposals that such a transfer should take place. The Parliament would like to intervene in this field within the scope of the first pillar, apart from anything else in order to make its wishes—namely that an international court should have the final say on the interpretation of the rules governing the right of asylum laid down by both the Member States and international conventions—viable.

These positions on the part of the Union's democratic/parliamentary body may serve to show the way in which it is the sometimes "national" and sometimes "intergovernmental", but basically non-Community, nature of the right of asylum that may also be responsible for the propensity to interpret that right in a way that lessens its content. Along these lines, one can imagine that the criterion adopted by the most restrictive state will end up becoming the common one. After all, it would be natural if the sum of the separate fears of fifteen small and medium states, whose combined area is no larger than that of the Amazon, were to be greater than those that would scare a broader and more consistent political unit.

One can therefore conclude that notwithstanding a few progresses, the situation continued to cause apprehension. This is in fact what emerges from what could be considered some of the most constant trends in the way things evolved on the road to Amsterdam.

1. While there was no common policy on asylum and emigration until 1980, in the mid-nineties Schengen and Dublin were to simultaneously initiate a convergence process in the domain of those European policies and an amplification of the common defensive attitude. From the initial position of controlling access, the path then gradually led to a European versus Non-European dialectic and a tendency to move on towards a… "general refusal of access".
2. Against the Commission's advice that asylum and emigration should be treated separately and differently, in practice the former increasingly reflected and suffered from the fears about the latter, to the point of generalising the suspicion that asylum seekers would primarily be "dissimulated emigrants" and that the policy towards them would merely be a part of the policy on emigration.
3. The tendency to reduce the scope of asylum was also evident in the preference for alternative and diminished asylum statuses—above all that of "temporary protection", but also "humanitarian status", both of which were fashionable in the aftermath of the Yugoslavian conflict.
4. The fight against the causes of population displacement in the areas of origin and the attempt to contain it in the regions concerned became generalised, like a kind of preventive action designed to handle the phenomenon.[11]
5. In contrast to the trend towards "turbo-procedures", a minimum set of procedural rights in favour of asylum seekers was defined. However, this was counterbalanced by increased threats to the "centrality" and "pre-emptive nature" of the non-refoulement principle (Article 33§1 of the Geneva Convention and Article 3 of the UN Convention against Torture), as were the other international-law principles[12] on the matter.
6. The individual establishment of the requisites for asylum has been partly replaced or completed by group decisions that are sometimes negative (safe country of origin) and sometimes positive (vulnerable groups coming from armed-conflict zones).[13]
7. The phenomena of emigration and mass displacement of refugees have put the traditional asylum model under stress and are increasingly moving it towards a redefinition.[14]

It is thus no wonder that the situation was to prove increasingly unsatisfactory, even from the Community and national standpoints themselves. The European institutions and most of the Member States now began to say that they favoured an expansion of the Community's powers with regard to the policy on asylum and its transfer to the first pillar. In general, they also proposed to immediately make use of the transitional provision contained in Article K.9 of the TEU in order to deal with the problems linked to these policies. Only the United Kingdom appeared to continue to prefer intergovernmental cooperation in these fields.

[11]See Minority Rights Group No. 5, Refugees in Europe: The Hostile New Agenda, 1996.

[12]See Mortimer 1997, pp. 201–202.

[13]Ibid., footnote 11, *op. cit.*

[14]On these, see Goodwin-Gill 1983.

Amsterdam and Afterwards

Amsterdam brings a few benefits and may help improve not only the existing legal guarantees, but also the political willingness itself in relation to this question. This is due firstly to the new context of how the question of the fundamental rights and the third pillar are handled in the Treaty. In relation to the former, not only does the text clearly affirm a principle of the rule of law, breach of which will be subject to review by the Court of Justice, but it also provides for very harsh sanctions for states that violate the fundamental rights and/or that principle (Article F.1). Also helpful to some extent is the enlargement of the principle of non-discrimination by Article 6A to include motives such as gender, race, ethnic origin or religion.

Where the third pillar is concerned, the Treaty creates an "area of freedom, security and justice" and partially communitises the pillar—indeed, it does so precisely in relation to the questions of asylum, the crossing of external borders and immigration (Article K.1). At a time when so much is being said about the limitations of a neo-functionalist explanation, at the end of the day this is another demonstration of how the single market is gradually generating a proportional need for integration within the internal security area, thereby continuing the path towards the juridification of the borderless market.[15]

One could even say that the Treaty of Amsterdam implies the communitisation in this domain of matters as important as determining which state is responsible for examining an asylum request, and defining minimum rules on the reception of asylum seekers, the grant of refugee status to third-country nationals, and the procedures which Member States must follow in order to grant or withdraw that status.[16]

At the same time, the conditions needed to ensure the efficacy and review of the right in question have been reinforced by these advances. Incipient though it may have been, communitisation was in fact a precondition for the ability to overcome the inefficiencies, ambiguities, overlaps, imbalances and even contradictions that continue to exist between the asylum policies of the Fifteen, which are having the effect of relativising the operability of Schengen and Dublin. At the same time, the possibility of a review by the Court of Justice—albeit one that is also limited—opens the way towards more effective conditions for accountability and control.

In general, although it is also still very small, the progressive involvement of more EU institutions (the ECJ, the European Parliament, and the Commission) ensures a greater prevalence of the common principles and objectives over the reservation of power to purely national bodies, which was serving as a barrier to

[15]Müller Graff 1997, pp. 273 and 282.

[16]Perez-Prat Durbán 1997, pp. 22–25. According to some reports, along with Sweden, Denmark, the UK and France, Portugal was probably one of the countries that were most recalcitrant in relation to the communitisation of the third pillar (see Arbeitskreis Europäische Integration, Der Amsterdamer Vertrag—Eine vorläufige Bewertung. Integration, 4/97, p. 307). This fact is probably explained by concerns about citizens from Brazil and the Portuguese-speaking countries in Africa, whose position, however, we can go on intermediating and protecting within the new framework.

action in this field. At the same time, it is likely that within a framework of greater transparency and institutional co-accountability, the values of freedom, democracy and the rule of law can achieve a better balance with security-related concerns.

With regard to the Treaty of Amsterdam norms that are relevant to this end, we should begin by mentioning Article 73i of the new Title III-A of Part III (numbering of the consolidated text of the Treaties). It provides for the progressive implementation of an "area of freedom, security and justice" (AFSJ), which in turn implies the adoption within five years by the Council of the measures designed to ensure the free movement of persons, as well as follow-up measures regarding the control of external borders, asylum, immigration, and the prevention of and fight against criminality. It also says that the Council must also adopt measures in the areas of asylum, immigration, the protection of the rights of citizens of third countries and so on.

Secondly, Article 73j says that within the same five-year time limit, measures must be adopted to ensure the total elimination of controls in relation to persons crossing internal borders, irrespective of whether they are citizens of the Union or of third countries and thus including people who have been recognised to possess a right to asylum.

In addition, although the new Treaty excepts certain aspects of the action undertaken in this regard, in Article 73k it also provides for a five-year deadline for the adoption of measures in relation to asylum, refugees, displaced persons and the immigration policy. Following an express reference to the Geneva Convention, para 1 and its subparagraphs now contain the essence of the policy of "minimum rules" in matters concerning asylum and the reception of refugees, which henceforth possess the normative force of a constitutional type of grounds for legitimation.

However, Article 73l includes an old caveat, which serves to protect "the exercise of the responsibilities incumbent upon Member States with regard to the maintenance of law and order and the safeguarding of internal security". It also allows the Council, acting by qualified majority on a proposal from the Commission, to adopt provisional measures with a duration of no more than six months for the benefit of a Member State in an emergency situation due to a large inflow of nationals of third countries.

With regard to the procedural aspect of this question, Article 73o provides for the existence during the same transitional period (five years) of a dual power of initiative pertaining to both the Commission and the Member States, with action subject to consultation of the European Parliament and unanimity in the Council (para 1). After that, the Commission will possess the sole right to make proposals to the Council, which must again consult the European Parliament and decide unanimously whether to enlarge the co-decision mechanism to all the areas covered by this new Title, or only some of them.

Setting aside the initial five-year period, the Commission's proposals on the list of third countries whose citizens will require a visa to cross internal borders and of those that are exempt from this obligation will be adopted by qualified majority, once again following consultation of the European Parliament. The same is true of the uniform model for visas. The same regime will apply to the procedures and conditions for the issue of visas and the rules governing the uniform visa, but this time—and once more—following a five-year period after the Treaty's entry into force.

A "Protocol on Asylum for Nationals of Member States of the European Union", was also inserted into the Amsterdam Treaty, and apart from anything else was to influence in advance the revision of the Portuguese constitutional provision on extradition. This Protocol establishes a presumption that asylum requests made to one Member State by citizens of any of the others are without grounds. Indeed, such citizens were never covered by the Schengen/Dublin mechanisms, which only concern citizens of third countries—i.e. from outside the EU.

As of the entry into force of Amsterdam, any asylum request by a European citizen will thus be considered in principle to be "manifestly unfounded", on the basis of the idea that all the "Member States shall be regarded as constituting safe countries of origin". The exceptions are clearly specified. The most important one concerns the hypothesis that the applicant's state of origin has engaged in "a serious and persistent breach" of the Treaty, as duly recognised by the Council—this in fact corresponds in principle to the conditions for the application of the sanctions provided for in Article F.1.

The progresses made in the Treaty that was signed on 2 October 1997 are significant, but no less cautious. To begin with, the decision to maintain the requirements for unanimity in the Council is regrettable, although the idea that there will be a progressive movement from unanimity and dual initiative to a qualified majority and the Commission's monopoly on the initiative to make proposals seems to impose itself in the background.[17]

The Community institutions (EP and ECJ) are the biggest winners of this Amsterdam round.[18] Where the European Parliament's role is concerned, there has been criticism of the fact that it has not been given a co-decision power with regard to legislative acts, but rather a simple consultative part in the process. What is more, the already excessive deadline (five years) for the possible transition from consultation to co-decision is not automatic and is dependent on a criterion that must be established and unanimously decided by the Council.[19]

When it comes to the Court of Justice, there are two clear examples of communitisation: the competence to issue a preliminary ruling at the request of the highest instance of a national jurisdiction; and the capacity to interpret the various types of Community rules at the request of the Council, the Commission and the Member States. However, Article 73p does limit the submission of these questions of freedom of movement to the preliminary ruling regime to cases in which a domestic court considers the intervention of the Court of Justice to be necessary.

---

[17]The author's more general point of view on these solutions generically matches that of the majority within both the European Parliament and the latter's task force that accompanied the IGC.

[18]See Rupprecht 1997, p. 269.

[19]This assessment is identical to that contained in the Report of the European Parliament's Institutional Committee, which was drafted by MEPs Iñigo Méndez De Vigo and Dimitros Tatsos (see the Exposition of Motives, Doc. PO/RR/339/339164 of 5 November 1997, p. 26).

We should also note the exclusion of any competence on the part of the ECJ to rule on measures regarding the crossing of borders which have been adopted by a Member State on the grounds that it needs to maintain public order or safeguard domestic security. Finally, while on the one hand the new Treaty makes it possible to ask the Court of Justice to rule on a question of the interpretation of the norms contained in Title IIIa, or of acts adopted or undertaken on the basis of the latter, on the other the resulting judgment is nonetheless not deemed applicable to decisions which courts or tribunals of the Member States have already taken on exactly the same matter.

There is thus is no doubt that even though the enlargement of the ECJ's competences in this area is "encouraging",[20] the Court's ability to intervene is excessively small compared to that given to it by the Community pillar (Article 177, TEC). The emerging risk of this solution is that it will cause a breach of the principle of uniform interpretation, which is so dear to the Community legal system. This consequence would only be avoidable if, as the European Parliament had called for and would have preferred, a full jurisdictional review had been implemented.

Finally, it was necessary to safeguard the UK, Irish and Danish positions by means of their optings-out and optings-in, paying the price of a relative communitisation of these policies. In what is yet another blatant demonstration of not just complexity, but also complication, Article 73q says that the new Title is to be applied subject to the provisions of Protocols Y and Z and without prejudice to protocol X… The concern revealed in this "delimitation" of the three countries in question may, however, be a further confirmation of the expectations that a significant amendment of the asylum situation can be expected in the post-Amsterdam period.

Conclusion

The old third pillar was thus dismembered into three parts by the new Treaty: a new Title on free personal movement, asylum and immigration, which combines all the provisions regarding the free movement of persons within the Community; the integration of Schengen, constituting a second layer and governed by a "specific regime" set out in a protocol which, in the event of a deadlock, provides for a form of "functioning by thirteen members"; and lastly, a series of measures designed to strengthen what is left of the third pillar—i.e. in the domain of the cooperation between police forces and judicial authorities in criminal matters.

Overall, this represents important, albeit not radical, progress. It may in fact be the most important conquest made by this Treaty. Moreover, it also pays homage to the idea of a European civil society, apart from anything else in that it seeks to

---

[20]Report of the European Parliament's Institutional Committee on the Treaty of Amsterdam, *op. cit.* p. 26.

provide for, protect and prioritise what every opinion barometer says is the "Europeans' primary concern as Europeans"—the freedom to move safely around a "borderless Europe".

Despite that, it falls far short of the expectations that were created before and even during the IGC. In fact, the sought-after communitisation of the third pillar has lost in élan and substance due to the excessively long deadline (five years) for the adoption of the measures in question, the absence of an automatic transition from unanimity to qualified majority during the period after that, and the non-generalisation of the co-decision process.

At the end of the day, the Council retains an excessive pre-eminence (requirement for unanimity) in the process, reaffirming the continued prevalence of the intergovernmental method to the utmost extent. According to the forecast made in Agenda 2000, the asylum policy will therefore not be communitised before the middle of the coming decade (in 2004) at best—i.e. at the time of the first accessions of Central and Eastern European countries. Until then, we will continue to witness the confirmation that national states are more willing to surrender sovereignty to the market than to the aspirations concerning European citizenship, democracy and security.

One of the no less substantial flaws in the situation also continues to be the excessive amalgam of law and politics at the Community level with regard to the matter of asylum. This would only change if the Court of Justice or an independent international judicial entity were able to more clearly remedy that perverse pairing, and the right of asylum were able to constitute a true fundamental right in the Community's constitutional order.

This evolution is linked to a broader one. The freedom of movement was not born as one of the component parts of European citizenship, and it will only be possible for it to be perceived as such little by little. Nevertheless, once again that evolution is dependent on both a "democratisation", and as I mentioned earlier, a "jurisdictionalisation" of the Union. The former would serve as the fundamental dynamic and interactive factor within the new framework, countering the more static or disruptive ones. Amsterdam precisely opens up the path to a number of progresses in terms of the jurisdictionalisation and democratisation of the right of asylum, while the international and economic situations in the EU also seem to be helping a bit more than the social situation.

Most of all, it is necessary to impose the awareness that the right of asylum is the best cornerstone or litmus test of the reality of Europe's desire to be seen by the world as an exemplary defender of fundamental rights. Moreover, no one has a greater interest than Europe in reviewing and being mindful of the painful lessons of its own history in this matter, which show us that whenever and wherever the rights of others were not taken into account, our own also collapsed.

References

Araújo Torres M (1995) Introdução. Direito dos Estrangeiros, Lisbon.

Christiansen A P and Kjaerum M (1990) Refugees and Our Role in the European House. IJRL (special issue).

Cruz A (1996) Nouveaux Contrôleurs d'Immigration: Transporteurs Menacés de Sanctions. Paris.

D'Oliveira J (1994) Expanding External and Shrinking Internal Borders: Europe's Defense Mechanisms in the Area of Free Movement, Immigration and Asylum. In: O'Keeffe and Twomey (eds) Legal Issues of the Maastricht Treaty. London.

Den Boer M (ed) (1997) Schengen, Judicial Cooperation and Policy Coordination.

Drüke L (1993) Einleitung. In: Dücke L and Weigelt K (eds) Fluchtziel Europa. Munich/ Landsberg, p. 20.

ECRE (1993) Asylum in Europe: An Introduction. Vol. 1. ECRE, London.

Garrone P (1993) La Libre Circulation des Personnes. Zurich.

Goodwin-Gill G S (1983) The Refugee in International Law. Clarendon Press, Oxford.

Gorjão-Henriques M (1996) Aspectos Gerais dos Acordos de Schengen na Perspectiva da Livre Circulação de Pessoas na União Europeia. Vol. 1, No. 2, Coimbra—Rio de Janeiro.

Hailbronner K (1990) The Right to Asylum and the Future of Asylum Procedures in the European Community. International Journal of Refugee Law, Vol. 2, No. 3.

Hailbronner K (1995) Aüslanderrecht, Kommentar, loose leaf edn., Heidelberg.

Hailbronner K and Thiery C (1997) Schengen II and Dublin: Responsibility for Asylum Applications in Europe. Common Market Law Review, 34, pp. 964 et seq.

Handoll J (1995) Free Movement of persons in the EU. Chichester.

Hoogenboom T (1992) Integration into Society and Free Movement of Non-EC Nationals. EJIL, Vol. 3, No. 1.

Joly D (1996) Heaven or Hell? Asylum Policies and Refugees in Europe. Macmillan, Basingstoke.

Joly D and Cohen R (eds) (1989) Reluctant Hosts: Europe and its Refugees. Gower Press, Aldershot.

Joly D, Nettleton C and Poulton H (1992) Refugees: Asylum in Europe. MRG, London.

Martin D (1994) La Libre Circulation de Personnes dans L'Union Européenne. Brussels.

Meijers H (1990) Refugees in Western Europe: "Schengen" affects the entire Refugee Law. IJRL, 428.

Mortimer E (1997) The Treatment of Refugees and Asylum-Seekers. Journal of Refugee Studies, Vol. 10, No. 2, pp. 201–202.

Müller Graff P C (1997) Justiz und Inneres nach Amsterdam – Die Neuerungen in erster und dritter Säule. Integration 4/97.

O'Keeffe D (1994) Reflections on a European Immigration Policy. In: O'Keeffe and Twomey (eds) Legal Issues of the Maastricht Treaty. London, pp. 24–26.

Pereira P (1993) The Draft Convention on External Borders and Asylum Policy on the Level of the Twelve Member States. In: Korella G D and Tworney P M (eds) Towards a European Immigration Policy.

Perez-Prat Durbán L (1997) La Unión Europea, ¿Tierra de Asilo? Meridiano CERI, August, pp. 22–25.

Rupprecht R (1997) Justiz und Inneres nach dem Amsterdam Vertrag. Integration 4/97.

Ward J (1997) Law and Other Europeans. Journal of Common Market Studies, Vol. 31, March, pp. 79–95.

Weiler J H H (1992) Thou Shall Not Oppress a Stranger: On the Judicial Protection of the Human Rights of Non-EC Nationals—A Critique. European Journal of International Law, Vol.3, No. 1.

Chapter 5
Postface

The New Order of the Euro

Francisco Lucas Pires

This year we have become contemporary witnesses of the victorious apogee of what is both the initial throw of the dice and the biggest milestone in the construction of Europe—economic and monetary union. It also entails the consummation in our countries of something that can be seen as the emancipation of European civil society, while a currency that is now controlled by an independent central bank seeks to be much more of an expression of that society than of any new political power. Let us say that although Europeans may still be like the *gentilhomme sans epée*,[1] they are no longer like the *bourgeois sans argent*,[2] and in that regard an effort is being made to take the opportunity to provide European citizenship with a concrete content.

The path that has already been travelled enables us to cherish such hopes. There is in fact a triple dimension to the success of this ephemeris. Firstly, it means that the Rubicon of irreversibility has now been now crossed and a formidable driving force for political union has been created. Secondly, because this was a question of the triumph, not of the wealthy European minority, but of the majority (eleven) of the Member States, including the more peripheral ones in the South, some of which—like us—reached integration thirty years late. Thirdly, because it coincides with a period of stable and inflation-free economic renaissance such as we have not

[1]Gentleman without a sword.

[2]Penniless bourgeois.

This chapter was originally published in Portuguese by PRINCIPIA, Cascais, Portugal in the book *Amsterdão: do Mercado á Sociedade Europeia?* (ISBN 972-8500-04-1) in 1998, which was translated from the Portuguese by Luís Tirapicos Nunes and Richard Rodgers. For more information, contact the editors of the present book via the following e-mail address: martinholucaspires@fd.lisboa.ucp.pt.

F. Lucas Pires (Deceased) (✉)
Lisbon, Portugal
e-mail: martinholucaspires@fd.lisboa.ucp.pt

M. Lucas Pires and F. Pereira Coutinho (eds.), *What Market, What Society, What Union?* https://doi.org/10.1007/978-94-6265-371-9_5

seen in Europe since the 1960s and which, thanks above all to the fall in interest rates, has turned into a sort of virtuous circle that is only overshadowed by high unemployment rates, which in any case are now falling back.

A no less important sign of this triumph—and this is another reason why it is "revolutionary"—is the conversion of the sceptical, whether they were won over by force or by argument, with the additional advantage that the consensus is thus now less permissive and more enlightened and motivated. After all, even for the pessimists, the problem is no longer Europeanisation; on the contrary, Europe is once again the solution. Instead of change, it means protection against the fears of a rapid transformation and a sudden immersion in the "problem"—the real one—of globalisation, which, together with digitalisation, increasingly hangs like a Sword of Damocles over middle-class jobs, which are the traditional vehicle for the facts of liberal modernity and stability. This is why people are thinking of using Europe as a means of giving a boost to what is now being referred to, namely in electoral terms, as the "new centre".

It is after reaching this point, this consensual platitude, that some people are even asking whether it is still worth holding a referendum on Europe, notwithstanding the fact that it is the first time in Portugal's history that this form of consultation is being called for and that those calls are being made with the vehemence of a political crusade. However, it is upon attaining this starry-skied plateau that we are becoming aware of a new crossroads ahead of us: on the one hand, as Europeans, squeezed between the centripetal force of the euro and the centrifugal force of the enlargement; on the other, as Portuguese, between a nominal convergence that makes us equal with the frontrunners and a competitive capacity which makes us unequal even among those who are second from last.

What this means is that while the next referendum may not count as much in terms of a choice between "yes" and "no" with regard to the present and to Amsterdam, it is nevertheless increasingly counting as a debate on the options regarding the new Europe, which is now in the process of gestating out of the difficult marriage between the single currency and the enlargement. If the former and the latter simultaneously act as a convergence of a "second" Europe in the west with "another one" in the east, that which lies ahead of us is in any case is a "new" Europe, with regard to which the least we can do is to awaken a spirit of a new beginning and a new game. For instance, the fact that not only the PP,[3] but also the PC,[4] recognise that Europe is no longer a choice but a need, is one more reason why pro-Europeans in particular can now go from criticising the insufficiency and impotence of present-day Europe to asking that which is logically the next question: Yes, but what Europe?

Indeed, it was by winning the major "stage in the race" which has now been concluded that we left the red carpet at the finishing line behind us. In this respect, the combination of receiving the victor's laurels and the inertia which victories

---

[3]Portuguese Popular Party.

[4]Portuguese Communist Party.

generate could only blind us. The change is more structural and swifter than any previous one and is incompatible with the complacent attitude taken by those who inherit something. The arrival of the single currency is in fact the "first anchor" of a "new order" in Europe, which is self-generating a chain of transformations that go far beyond the economy. This is not just about change in the relationships between sovereignty and supra-nationality, but concerns the institutional suitability of the state and the transformation of the very culture and structure of the various national societies, in relation to which it will operate, like a revolution, with "immediate effect" and in the "first degree".

This is why the questions we have not answered during this new, historic launch of the construction of Europe must become clearly intelligible for everyone—something which the occasion of a referendum renders possible. A first question, which looks inwards and depends entirely on us, is about what has to be done in order to succeed in a much more exposed and competitive situation like the one that will follow the introduction of the single currency. Are we ready? A second, which looks outwards and possesses the nature of a negotiating proposal, is about which European model will enable us to best defend our interests and reflect our identity after the enlargement. Do we have an idea, or are we just going to pick one of proposals made by the others?

We hope the referendum debate will make the first of these two questions clearer and establish the decisive nature of the fact that achieving the single currency cannot continue to be an excuse for the absence of the necessary structural reforms—on the contrary, it should be the wasp-sting that makes people act, now that the conditions for growth are favourable. With regard to the second, we should better understand the Portuguese interest in a less intergovernmental and sectoral and more democratic and political Europe, without which not only could the process of "social and economic cohesion" break down, but the single currency and the ECB themselves would become scapegoats for every crisis, with the inevitable consequences in terms of instability in the economic and monetary field itself.

In short, this year the celebration of the construction of Europe is the closure of one era and the beginning of a new one. The fact that it is of a new type does not prevent it from being a revolution; and in our case it would be useful for the forthcoming referendum to be the opportunity to discover this new horizon, redefine objectives and assume collective aims in terms of reform and action to be undertaken along the hard path ahead of us, both here in Portugal and "out there", in this "second" and other, post-single currency and post-enlargement "Europe". The longer we wait the more we lose, and it is precisely in times of prosperity that one must act. Otherwise, we will be like a patient who puts off his surgery and thereby worsens his condition. All this on the assumption that a stronger Europe in the competition at world level will also be a tougher Europe when it comes to intra-European competition.

ECB: Independent but Not Deaf

The appointment of the President of the ECB and the launch of the euro have already been ratified by the markets and recognised by the United States and the dollar. One could say that it would be hard to achieve a greater democratic legitimacy than that… And while there were problems with the presidency of the ECB, they resulted from both an "excess" of intergovernmental democracy and a shortfall in parliamentary democracy—the requirement for unanimity in the Council. With a qualified majority and the parallel requirement for the "assent" of the European Parliament, we would not need a split term of office for Duisenberg and Trichet.

Another thing is certain though. The rotation which the Council has decided in relation to the presidency will not be automatic. When Mr Duisenberg steps down—if he steps down—in the middle of his term, the process will have to begin anew, once again with the requirement for hearings at and assent by the European Parliament, not to mention the unanimous vote in the Council. At the end of the day, the masterpiece of ambiguity that has been painted is dissipating the scruples of those who used to talk about monetary authoritarianism, while at the same time failing to become the tragedy which the guardians of orthodoxy were afraid of and ending up being just a minor drama.

Meanwhile, both the vote by the European Parliament on 2 May regarding the choice by the Council of the eleven founding members of the euro, and the hearings on 7 and 8 May for the parliamentary scrutiny of the nominees for the ECB, are symptomatic manifestations of the intensity of the democratic control that the representatives of the European people want to exercise over the single European currency.

These indicators probably allow us to draw two immediate conclusions: first, that given the concrete, albeit very hypothetical, possibility that from now on, the parliamentary scrutiny of the persons who are nominated to be members of the Executive Committee may end in their voluntarily standing aside, that review may go beyond what is provided for in the Treaties; and second, that the requirements which have already been formulated seem to favour a more Anglo-Saxon model of absolute transparency of the ECB's decisions, rather than a model in which the ECB's position is less public or is even capable of surprising the markets.

What may thus emerge from the experiment is a kind of range of implicit review and control powers, which may or may not then turn into explicit competences at a later date. However, there are also forms of review and control that are defined in both the Treaties and the ECB's own Statute. Suffice it to say that the European Parliament's report on this matter lists no less than thirty-one cases in which the Parliament possesses an explicit competence in this regard, although a large proportion of them refer to a single article—Article 109—of the Treaties.

In general terms, on the one hand the Parliament's role encompasses taking part in the drawing up of rules and the appointment of officers, and on the other ensures information, transparency and public discussion in relation to the ECB's action. One of the things it guarantees is the existence of what could be called a procedure for dialogue between the ECB and the European Parliament about the policy that is to be pursued, particularly with regard to its effects on both economic activity as a whole and the social situation within the scope of the Community.

It would even be natural if an interinstitutional-type agreement between the ECB and the European Parliament were to come to institutionalise the formats taken by this dialogue, which people will probably try to conduct discreetly in order not to alarm the markets. What is excluded is the ability to issue any guidelines for the ECB's monetary policy, whose absolute priority will be to ensure price stability and which will enjoy the highest degree of autonomy in pursuit of that end, namely with regard to the definition and scope of that notion of "stability" itself. In short: the ECB will be independent, but not deaf.

One could thus say that where the ECB is concerned, the European Parliament will exercise more of a right to engage in dialogue than any power to interfere. The ECB's extreme degree of independence is, however, offset by the requirement for a proportionate degree of transparency, which not only includes the submission of annual and quarterly reports to the Parliament, but also the publication of its decisions and an explanation of the grounds on which they were taken, albeit who voted for or against those decisions will not be made public.

For now, the Parliament's main demand concerns the democratic control of the way in which the EU Council of Ministers coordinates the economic policies—a demand that will inevitably be intensified once the single currency is in place. For now, this is the point in relation to which there continues to be a democratic deficit that is clamouring for attention. If the euro functions like an enormous spotlight on the entire life of the market, it will be one more reason why the Council's policy in that area should also be subject to review—a review on which the policy's credibility and the confidence in it rely.

In the end, the emergence of the ECB confirms that the more power neutral administrative institutions like it possess, the greater the need to intensify the democratic control over them—in this case, in the shape of the role of the European Parliament.

If the euro is the first common language shared by the three hundred million citizens of the new eleven-nation Europe, or a kind of password that only they know or understand, and thus the driving force behind a first glimpse of a European public opinion in the economic/monetary sphere, it is natural for the only institutional form of representation and active voice of this incipient public opinion—the European Parliament—to become more prominent in this respect.

The single currency is the "enzyme" for not only an internal and external multiplication of European power, but also multiple social transformations, in the generic sense of greater flexibility. The minimum outcome must therefore be a proportionate democratisation of the Community's decision-making structures. What is more, the euro is the most fiduciary currency in the world, or at least the one that needs more consensus-generating conditions, and this is why the role which the peoples' representatives play with regard to it must be proportionately enhanced.

Part II
What Market, What Society, What Union?

Chapter 6
Constitutionalism, Federalism and Constitutional Reforms in Francisco Lucas Pires' Thought

Giuseppe Martinico

Abstract In this chapter I shall make three points. The first point is a terminological point and insists on the notions of constitution and constitutionalisation employed in Lucas Pires' essays, at least in those that have been translated into English on this occasion and in two other books available in Portuguese. The second point regards the importance of these reforms for the creation of a kind of "federal type Europe" (to quote Stein). The last point concerns the substance of these reforms and the importance of the "social question" at the supranational level.

Keywords Federalism · Constitutionalism · Social Question · Constitutionalisation

Introduction: The Relevance of Francisco Lucas Pires' Thought

There are two reasons why Francisco Lucas Pires' thought is still important today: the first one is of course the newness of many of the intuitions present in his essays. In this sense, it is really difficult to believe that pages like these were written almost 20 years ago. In order to understand the brightness of Francisco Lucas Pires' mind it is sufficient to read the considerations made about the flaws in the European asylum system, those concerning the need for a supranational "financial constitution"[1] and those aimed at overcoming the ambiguity of the European Monetary Union.

[1]Lucas Pires 2020, Chap. 1 in the present book.

This chapter is part of the Project Jean Monnet Module "Eur.Publ.IUS" (European Public Law-IUS). giuseppe.martinico@santannapisa.it.

G. Martinico (✉)
Scuola Superiore Sant'Anna, Pisa, Italy
e-mail: giuseppe.martinico@santannapisa.it

M. Lucas Pires and F. Pereira Coutinho (eds.), *What Market, What Society, What Union?* https://doi.org/10.1007/978-94-6265-371-9_6

The second reason why his work is interesting to me is the following: while EU law scholars normally tend to emphasise the importance of the Maastricht Treaty in the history of European integration, Francisco Lucas Pires was able to grasp the motives which made the Amsterdam Treaty an important step in the progressive federalisation of Europe.

Indeed, starting from 1992, the Maastricht Treaty has been described as a turning point in the narrative of European integration:

> However political and legal, especially judicial, developments surrounding the adoption of the Treaty of Maastricht (ToM), caused a significant blow to the vision of integration espoused by the classical constitutional narrative. In 1993 the Treaty of Maastricht introduced the (in)famous three-pillared temple structure of the European Union, consisting of the pre-existing Community pillar and of two, so called, intergovernmental pillars of the EU, namely the Common Foreign and Security Policy (CFSP) and the Justice and Home Affairs (JHA). Moreover, it introduced a set of protocols and declarations that granted some Member States exemption from the *acquis communautaire* of the Community pillar.[2]

Such a set of protocols and declarations was defined by Curtin[3] as an attempt to "hijack" the *acquis communautaire* and, in this jungle acts, the *Danish Second Home*, the *Grogan* and the *Barber* protocols deserved special attention in this respect. The choices made in Maastricht still condition the uncertain economic integration at supranational level as Diane Fromage stresses in Chap. 9. Although Amsterdam did not have the impact reached by the Maastricht Treaty over the integration process, it did represent a crucial point as Francisco Lucas Pires pointed out in this research:

> The result seems thus sufficient. In the beginning it was promised at least a Maastricht 2. Maybe it is merely a Maastricht 1,5. If the glass is still half empty, whomever is thirsty only needs to immediately drink it to fill it up again. It is also for that reason that Amsterdam is worth a ratification and the sooner the better.[4]

These are the words of a politician and a scholar who was aware of the difficulties in the negotiation and ratification process and who did not want to miss the opportunity to achieve an important goal. Indeed, Indeed, the Amsterdam Treaty introduced important novelties: it increased the powers at the supranational level, reinforced the role of the European Parliament, introduced important institutional reforms for the future enlargements and the germs of what today we call enhanced cooperation. It also provided for the incorporation of the Agreement on Social policy and the extension of the Community method to some important areas. After all, it is not a detail that commenting upon the provisions of the Amsterdam Treaty Ingolf Pernice presented his famous theory of the multilevel constitutionalism.[5]

---

[2]Avbelj 2008, 8.

[3]Curtin 1993, 21.

[4]Lucas Pires 2020, Chap. 2 in the present book.

[5]Pernice 1999.

Francisco Lucas Pires defined the Amsterdam Treaty as the "First Social Constitution of Liberal Europe"[6] with an oxymoronic formula which reveals the weaknesses of a still incomplete constitutionalisation. To confirm this, in another passage the same Author stressed that "The Community's Social Constitution is thus subjected to a tension between cohesion and competitiveness, solidarity and subsidiarity".[7]

For the purpose of this short chapter I shall limit myself to three points: while all these points revolve around the idea of constitutional reform, they differ in nature. The first is a terminological point and insists on the notions of constitution and constitutionalisation employed in his essays, at least in those that have been translated into English on this occasion and in two other books available in Portuguese (*infra*). The second point regards the importance of these reforms for the creation of a kind of "federal type Europe" (to quote Eric Stein[8]). The last point concerns the substance of these reforms and the importance of the "social question" at supranational level.

Constitution and Constitutionalisation in Francisco Lucas Pires' Works

In his *Introdução ao Direito Constitucional Europeu*[9] Francisco Lucas Pires reflected a lot on the nature and notion of a European Constitution. It is clear from his works that his notion of European Constitution is not limited to the wording of the Treaties, since "in any case, Treaties are not the only source of constitutional evolution of the Communities".[10]

Another element that one can identify is the acknowledgement of the role of the Court of Justice in the progressive constitutionalisation of the European Treaties.

Before analysing these aspects and for the purpose of this section it is also convenient to clarify what constitutionalisation means in the EU. It is possible to identify at least two different meanings in European Studies. By that formula scholars[11] mean the progressive shift of EU law from the perspective of an international organisation to that of a federal entity. This is the understanding of

[6]Lucas Pires 2020, Chap. 3 in the present book.

[7]Lucas Pires 2020, Chap. 3 in the present book.

[8]Stein 1981.

[9]Lucas Pires 1997, 14.

[10]Lucas Pires 2020, Chap. 2 in the present book.

[11]For example, Cartabia and Weiler 2000, 73. About the ambiguity of the notion of constitutionalisation in EC/EU Law see: Snyder 2003.

constitutionalisation in Stein's works, for instance.[12] In a different meaning "constitutionalisation" can be understood as progressive "humanisation" of the law of the common market, i.e., the affirmation of the human rights issue at the supranational level.[13]

In its second meaning, it refers to the progressive "constitutionalisation" of the EU, a process through which the EU over the years has partly overcome its purely economic nature, becomes something more, a union based on fundamental rights as acknowledged in the national constitutions. According to the traditional narrative,[14] this provision should be read as the confirmation of a long process which started after *Solange I*, a direct product of the dialectic existing between the national Constitutional Courts and the European Court of Justice (ECJ). The rapprochement between the national and the supranational legal orders has been extensively studied, and I am not going to recall such a well-known story.[15]

By European Constitutional Law one can thus mean both the *corpus of fundamental principles*[16] devised by the Court of Justice of the EU in attempting to transform Europe[17] (this set of principles can also be understood as the European Constitution) and a field of studies that emerged after the ideal turning point represented by the Charter of fundamental rights of the EU, in other words European constitutional law refers to an autonomous discipline.

For Francisco Lucas Pires, European Constitutional Law and a sort of European Constitution already exist, as he pointed out in his *Introdução ao Direito Constitucional Europeu.*[18] In the collection of essays translated into English on this occasion, Francisco Lucas Pires refers to these concepts many times by depicting the process of Europeanisation as an example of "transnational constitutionalisation"[19] or as a phenomenon of "gradualist constitutional development".[20]

[12]His essays about Europe and America in a comparative perspective have been collected in a book (Stein 2000). The first part of this work contains a very famous article with its very famous incipit: "Tucked away in the fairyland Duchy of Luxembourg and blessed, until recently, with the benign neglect by the powers that be and the mass media, the Court of Justice of the European Communities has fashioned a constitutional framework for a federal-type structure in Europe" (Stein 1981, 1). However, that was not the first piece in which he used the constitutional jargon to describe the effort of the ECJ. As Boerger (Boerger 2014) recalls, in 1960 he wrote that "the techniques and the procedures of the Community resemble in many respects those of the public law of a state—predominantly of administrative law, but also those of constitutional law—rather than those of international organizations and international law" (Stein 1960, 19).

[13]On this process, see Lenaerts 2000.

[14]Slaughter et al. 1998.

[15]On this process, see Gordillo 2012, 66. The Author describes a process, consisting of two stages: "the establishment of the red lines" and "the rapprochement of positions".

[16]On constitutionalisation as a creation, development and impact of general principles of the EU law legal order, see Groussot 2006, 3.

[17]See Weiler 1999.

[18]Lucas Pires 1997, 14.

[19]Lucas Pires 2020, Chap. 1 in the present book.

[20]Lucas Pires 2020, Chap. 1 in the present book.

Here one can notice the use of terms such as "gradual" and "evolution", which suggest that in Francisco Lucas Pires' mind the European Constitution responds to a form of evolutionary constitutionalism.

More recently Leonard Besselink regained the famous distinction between evolutionary and revolutionary constitutionalism to define the European partly unwritten Constitution as an example of evolutionary constitutionalism.[21]

There are other leading scholars who have supported a similar thesis[22] while other colleagues have questioned this reconstruction. In any case, in this gradual constitutionalisation a very important role has been played by the European Court of Justice.[23]

Federalism and Constitutionalisation

There are many other passages in his works where Francisco Lucas Pires shows a certain preference for a federal Europe without however renouncing political realism, advocating a realistic interpretation of Amsterdam, "even if melancholically realist".[24] States are still necessary[25] and Europe is not yet ready for a European federal State.[26] That realism led him to disagree with the those who labelled themselves federalists about the concrete choices to make at that time:

> The people in a hurry who are asking for a 'revision of the revision, now' are primarily looking for a reweighting of votes in the Council. I ask some of my colleagues at the EP who claim themselves as federalists solely because they confuse federalism with speed.[27]

In his view, in fact, Europe was (and to a certain extent is) not America which had experienced a Civil War and a New Deal before achieving the federal form we know:

> In the constitutional history of the United States, it was in fact the New Deal which marked the passage from dual federalism to unitary federalism. However, in the construction of Europe we still have not reached the post American Civil War stage.[28]

---

[21]"These revolutionary constitutions tend to have a blueprint character, wishing to invent the design for a future which is different from the past … Old fashioned historic constitutions are, to the contrary, evolutionary in character", Besselink 2007.

[22]Anne Peters once wrote the "the European Constitution was not 'given' in a specific constitutional moment by a single authority. There was no single event which created a European Constitution, but only an accumulation of steps of diverse legal character", Peters 2006, 51–52.

[23]Lucas Pires 1997, 25.

[24]Lucas Pires 2020, Chap. 2 in the present book.

[25]Lucas Pires 1997, 14.

[26]"It is more urgent to consider the idea of European society and its democratic organization instead of the idea European (federal) State" (p. 38).

[27]Lucas Pires 2020, Chap. 2 in the present book.

[28]Lucas Pires 2020, Chap. 3 in the present book.

However, Francisco Lucas Pires was a kind of proto-federalist and devoted important page to the idea of federalism in the European integration process.[29] In another book, Francisco Lucas Pires also added that the federal solution was possible for Europe even in the absence of a formalised European Constitution.[30]

Throughout the essays now translated into English, federalism is frequently opposed to intergovernmentalism[31] and in other passages it is clear that federalism, in his mind, does not necessarily correspond to the theory of a federal (European) State, as it has a broader concept. This reminds me of the understanding of federalism employed by other eminent scholars in European Studies. This is the case with Peter Hay, for instance. In 1968 Hay wrote about certain "federalizing features"[32] of the common market Treaty system, thus participating in the spreading of a "comparative language" and above all applying the concept of federalism to "supranational organizations".[33] In his fundamental book *Federalism and Supranational Organizations* he wrote that: "One of the important reasons for the success of European integration is the organizational form which it adopted for the three 'European Communities'. Described as 'supranational' … these organizations possess both independence from and power over their constituent states to a degree suggesting the emergence of a federal hierarchy".[34]

Even earlier, in 1963, in an article published on the most important comparative law review (the *American Journal of Comparative Law*), Hay also wrote of an "imperfect" federalism which "derives from the limited economic federalism of the organization" need not change the characterization, especially since the developing case law may correct imperfection.[35] According to Hay, supranationalism is connected to the idea of federalism because both concepts are based on a transfer of power from the State to a higher entity. He started from a dynamic notion of federalism without regard to the institutional form and he distinguished "the federal elements from the international elements":

> 'Federal' is therefore used in an adjectival sense: it attaches to a particular function exercised by the organization and is used to denote, as to that function, a hierarchical relationship between the Communities and their members.[36]

Hay used the notion of "functional federalism" in order to describe the jurisdiction/activity of the ECJ and the relationship between national and supranational law. Such a formula might sound as oxymoronic for a European scholar who is used to the contraposition federalism/functionalism, nevertheless Hay

[29] Lucas Pires 1997, 85.

[30] Lucas Pires 1992, 737.

[31] Lucas Pires 2020, Chap. 2 in the present book.

[32] Hay 1968.

[33] Hay 1966.

[34] Hay 1966, 4.

[35] Hay 1963, 24.

[36] Hay 1966, 90.

explained what he meant by this formula when he clarified that his notion of federalism does not consider the institutional form of the organization.

Here Hay stressed the possible gap between the federal functions of an organization and its possible definition as a federation. In other words, his approach to federalism is a dynamic one and resembles that adopted by Carl J. Friedrich.[37]

The Substance of the Institutional Reforms

Francisco Lucas Pires suggested concrete reforms were required in order to make the EU more democratic and to reduce the "distance" existing between itself and its citizens.

Indeed, as he wrote in the essays on the Amsterdam Treaty collected in this volume: "it is thus no wonder that the Amsterdam Treaty has incorporated the social topic into the Union's constitutional programme".[38] Francisco Lucas Pires listed some possible reforms that—after the entry of the Amsterdam Treaty—were necessary to adopt:

> What is at stake here is the decision method in its entirety, from the Commission's initiative, **whose autonomy and transparency need strengthening**, to the implementation, which needs to be distanced from the Council, which must increasingly become a body that serves to establish political and regulatory directions.
>
> **Reducing comitology and extending the European Parliament's co-decision powers to cover one hundred per cent of legislative matters are parallel movements that need to be undertaken and foundations that are inseparable from and preeminent elements of the construction of a democratic Europe**. Identifying responsibilities is no less crucial, namely **in terms of attaching greater value to the role and democratic nature of the President of the Commission**, apart from anything else in order to compensate for the increase in the number of commissioners – and even to stop Kissinger from continuing to ask: 'Who do I call if I want to speak to Europe?'.
>
> […] The simultaneous **revalorisation of the Council** and of politics should lead to the reformulation of both its membership (appointment of the first vice-presidents?) – and its competences, which should possess a more general nature.
>
> It is necessary to reinforce the political decision and the **democratic accountability inherent in its legitimation**. Without such an increase in political authority, instead of becoming the undisputed and glorious arbitrator, the **European Central Bank** would on the contrary end up being turned into the go-to scapegoat. **At the same time, it is important to strengthen the control/review, transparency and subsidiarity mechanisms**, by awarding true powers of inquiry to the European Parliament and **possibly creating a Constitutional Court** alongside the Court of Justice. In other words, the tasks at hand are more about democratisation than a reweighting of the Member States' powers within the Council.[39]

[37]Friedrich 1968.

[38]Lucas Pires 2020, Chap. 3 in the present book.

[39]Lucas Pires 2020, Chap. 2 in the present book.

This is an ambitious agenda that has been partially implemented in the subsequent rounds of Treaty revisions. If it is true that the role of the Parliament has been strengthened (especially after the entry into force of the Lisbon Treaty), at the same time, it is evident that many of these proposals are still burning issues, starting with the improvement of the mechanism of transparency and control. Something similar can be said with regard to the role of the European Central Bank. Another very original proposal is the possible creation of a supranational Constitutional Court. This set of proposals were in Pires' thought the next thing to be done after the compromise of Amsterdam which had postponed "questions like institutional reform, which had previously seemed to need solving first and more urgently".[40] Without going into details (leaving the analysis of their concrete details to the other authors of this collection) I would like to emphasise two methodological guidelines —so to say—that characterise his approach to the changes to be introduced in the Treaties. The first guideline is the necessity to think of Europe in a global context and this implies two main things: the need to adapt Europe to the globalised scenario but also the necessity to rely on Europe to tame some negative consequences of globalisation. In this sense the overcoming of the silence of the European Treaties about the "social question" was already seen as a good starting point by Francisco Lucas Pires. At the same time, Francisco Lucas Pires stressed the need for more solidarity and cohesion in the EU and these words sound incredibly topical nowadays, especially after the climax of the financial crisis and its impact over the European integration.[41] The key word in his view was "democratisation" as he repeated throughout this collection of essays ("Institutional reform: The tasks at hand are more about democratisation than a reweighting of the Member States' powers within the Council"[42]). The polemic spirit of these words echoes the necessity to go beyond the national interests and the short—term logic in order to achieve a higher goal which could give the supranational project added value and bring Europe closer to its citizens.

Europe and the Social Question

An important achievement of the Amsterdam Treaty was the incorporation of the Agreement on Social policy which put to an end the "social frigidity" of the European Treaties to quote Federico Mancini.[43] Indeed an important element of Francisco Lucas Pires' thought is the centrality of the social question which has

[40]Lucas Pires 2020, Chap. 3 in the present book.

[41]The debate is huge, I tried to sum up the transnational literature on that in this piece: Martinico 2014. See also Ioannidis 2016; Beukers 2015.

[42]Lucas Pires 2020, Chap. 2 in the present book.

[43]Mancini 1988, 26.

been crucial in the history of constitutionalism. It is sufficient here to recall the considerations made by Hannah Arendt in *On Revolution.*[44]

That was an important piece of a puzzle which is far from being completed. It is no coincidence that the "European Social Model" is one of the most ambiguous formulae existing in EU studies, as it refers to a very diversified set of sources and acts (EU Treaties, secondary EU legislation, *soft law*):

> One of the fastest growing European catchwords at the present time - the 'European Social Model' (ESM) - is used to describe the European experience of simultaneously promoting sustainable economic growth and social cohesion. The use of the concept of European Social Model in academic and political debate is characterized by two main and interconnected features: on the one hand, the usually taken-for-granted assumption of the reality of the concept (the reality called 'Europe' becomes a naturally occurring phenomenon); on the other hand, the highly ambiguous and polysemic nature of this concept.[45]

One of the main reasons for scepticism towards the European Social Model is the high diversity in terms of welfare policies present at national level, almost never questioned by the EU. This is a point also raised by Francisco Lucas Pires who wrote that:

> In this regard, the decisions taken in Amsterdam are designed on the one hand to enable the Member States to continue to control the social policy, and on the other to indicate that it is a priority goal to ensure the "development of human resources" (Article 117) in order to obtain a qualified labour force (see Article 109-N) that is trained for and adapted to a labour market which is both competitive and capable of creating jobs.[46]

This can be understood in light of the coexistence of the many "worlds if welfare" present in Europe.[47]

This is one of the reasons for the difficulty of harmonisation in the field of social policies, and partly explains why more recently the EU has resorted to soft law instruments and to the Open Method of Coordination (with questionable results in some cases).[48]

This variety induced Francisco Lucas Pires to conclude that: "the fragmentation of social structures means that the social question either also appears here in the garb of an inter-state question, or does not appear at all."[49] The necessity to stress the link between the principle of solidarity and the European Social Model has been pointed out, among others, by Ottmann:

> The reference to solidarity in these European legal texts underlines a continuous process of addressing social policy issues in the European Union throughout the past decades: Whereas the emphasis of the European Social Model lies, above all, in the creation of common labour law standards which are ultimately designed to enhance the European

---

[44]Arendt 1973, 60.

[45]Jepsen and Serrano Pascual 2005, 231.

[46]Lucas Pires 2020, Chap. 3 in the present book.

[47]Esping-Andersen 1990.

[48]Hatzopoulos 2007.

[49]Lucas Pires 2020, Chap. 3 in the present book.

> common market, solidarity is also considered one of the common values and objectives of the Union. In this respect, solidarity relates to the cohesion between Member States and their people(s) in a way that transcends the notion of a mere common market. This concept of solidarity is intended to create and enhance cohesion in a community – a European community. However, it has to be born in mind that the concept of community at the level of the European Union has to be distinguished from the concept of community at national level. The European Union is, above all, a community of law. Therefore, the discussion of solidarity in the European Union cannot simply revert to theoretical foundations in national solidarity; the discussion has to revisit periodically the universal philosophical foundations of social solidarity.[50]

After many years the EU still suffers from the disease described in these words. Indeed, when looking at the recent developments it is possible to notice a sort of terminological paradox present in the latest developments in European law (*largo sensu* understood): when describing the amendment to Article 136 TFEU[51] in response to the EU economic crisis, in an excellent article Borger[52] argued that this provision "embodies both the change in normative solidarity and the transition from negative to positive solidarity". The paradox is that neither Article 136 nor the Treaty on Stability, Coordination and Governance in the Economic and Monetary. Union (TSCG) use the word solidarity in their texts. A partial exception to this trend is represented by the Preamble of the ESM Treaty.[53]

The current situation, in my view, confirms the intuitions by Francisco Lucas Pires who already stressed the need for a transnational solidarity a long time ago:

---

[50]Ottmann 2008.

[51]

1. In order to ensure the proper functioning of economic and monetary union, and in accordance with the relevant provisions of the Treaties, the Council shall, in accordance with the relevant procedure from among those referred to in Articles 121 and 126, with the exception of the procedure set out in Article 126(14), adopt measures specific to those Member States whose currency is the euro:

    (a) to strengthen the coordination and surveillance of their budgetary discipline;
    (b) to set out economic policy guidelines for them, while ensuring that they are compatible with those adopted for the whole of the Union and are kept under surveillance.

2. For those measures set out in para 1, only members of the Council representing Member States whose currency is the euro shall take part in the vote.
   A qualified majority of the said members shall be defined in accordance with Article 238(3)(a).
3. The Member States whose currency is the euro may establish a stability mechanism to be activated if indispensable to safeguard the stability of the euro area as a whole. The granting of any required financial assistance under the mechanism will be made subject to strict conditionality.

[52]Boerger 2013.

[53]"This Treaty and the TSCG are complementary in fostering fiscal responsibility and solidarity within the economic and monetary union."

> The social question – which was the last to be resolved on the constitutional level of the national state – cannot in fact be seriously reopened except by an institutionally and politically more consistent Europe.[54]

After more than 20 years these considerations still inspire generations of scholars and contribute to the never-ending debate regarding the finality and nature of the European integration, confirming, this way, the bright legal and political mind of Francisco Lucas Pires.

References

Arendt H (1973) On Revolution. Pelican Books, New York.

Avbelj M (2008) Questioning EU Constitutionalism. German Law Journal, Vol. 9, Issue 1.

Besselink L (2007) The notion and nature of the European Constitution after the Reform Treaty, http://papers.ssrn.com/sol3/papers.cfm?abstract_id=1086189.

Beukers T (2015) Legal Writing(s) on the Eurozone Crisis. EUI Working Papers LAW 2015/11, http://cadmus.eui.eu/handle/1814/35418.

Boerger V (2013) How the Debt Crisis Exposes the Development of Solidarity in the Euro Area. European Constitutional Law Review, Vol. 9, Number 1.

Boerger A (2014) At the Cradle of Legal Scholarship on the European Union: The Life and early Work of Eric Stein. American Journal of Comparative Law, Vol. 62, Number 4.

Cartabia M and Weiler JHH (2000) L'Italia in Europa. Il Mulino, Bologna.

Curtin D (1993) The Constitutional Structure of the Union – A Europe of Bits and Pieces. Common Market Law Review, Vol. 30, Issue 1.

Esping Andersen G (1990) The Three Worlds of Welfare Capitalism. Princeton University Press, New Jersey.

Friedrich CJ (1968) Trends of federalism in theory and practice. Pall Mall, London.

Gordillo LI (2012) Interlocking Constitutions Towards an Interordinal Theory of National, European and UN Law. Hart, Oxford.

Groussot X (2006) General Principles of Community Law. Europa Law Publishing, Groningen.

Hatzopoulos V (2007) Why the Open Method of Coordination is Bad for You: A Letter to the EU. European Law Journal, Vol. 13, Number 3.

Hay P (1963) Federal Jurisdiction of the Common Market Court. American Journal of Comparative Law, Volume 12, Number 1.

Hay P (1966) Federalism and Supranational Organizations. Patterns for New Legal Structures. University of Illinois Press, Urbana.

Hay P (1968) Supremacy of Community Law in National Courts. A Progress Report on Referrals Under the EEC Treaty. American Journal of Comparative. Law, Vol. 16, Issue 4.

Ioannidis M (2016) Europe's new transformations: How the EU economic constitution changed during the Eurozone crisis. Common Market Law Review, Vol. 53, Issue 5.

Jepsen M and Serrano Pascual A (2005) The European Social Model: An Exercise in Deconstruction. Journal of European Social Policy, Vol. 15, Number 3.

Lenaerts K (2000) Fundamental rights in the European Union. European Law Review, Vol. 25, Number 6.

Lucas Pires F (1992) O que è a Europa. Difusão Cultural, Lisbon.

Lucas Pires F (1997) Introdução ao Direito Constitucional Europeu. Edições Almedina, Coimbra.

[54] Lucas Pires 2020, Chap. 3 in the present book.

Mancini F (1988) Principi fondamentali di diritto del lavoro nell'ordinamento delle Comunità europee. In: Il lavoro nel diritto comunitario e l'ordinamento italiano. Cedam, Padova.
Martinico G (2014) EU Crisis and Constitutional Mutations: A Review Article. Revista de Estudios Politicos, Number 165.
Ottmann J (2008) The Concept of Solidarity in National and European Law: The Welfare State and the European Social Model. Vienna Online Journal on International Constitutional Law, Vol. 2, Issue 1.
Pernice I (1999) Multilevel Constitutionalism and the Treaty of Amsterdam: European Constitution-Making Revisited. Common Market Law Review, Vol. 36, Number 4.
Peters A (2006) The Constitutionalisation of the European Union – Without the Constitutional Treaty. In: Riekmann S and Wessels W (eds) The Making of a European Constitution Dynamics and Limits of the Convention Experience. Dynamics and Limits of the Convention Experience. VS Verlag für Sozialwissenschaften/ GWV Fachverlage GmbH, Wiesbaden.
Slaughter AM, Stone Sweet A and Weiler JHH (eds) (1998) The European Court and National Courts: Doctrine and Jurisprudence. Legal Change in Its Social Context. Hart, Oxford.
Snyder F (2003) The unfinished constitution of the European Union. In: Weiler JHH and Wind M (eds) European constitutionalism beyond the state. Cambridge University Press, Cambridge.
Stein E (1960) In: Stein E and Nicholson TL (eds) American Enterprise in the European Common Market: A Legal Profile. University of Michigan Law School, Ann Arbor.
Stein E (1981) Lawyers, Judges, and the Making of a Transnational Constitution. American Journal of International Law, Vol. 75, Number 1.
Stein E (2000) Thoughts from a Bridge: A Retrospective of Writings on New Europe and American Federalism. University of Michigan Press, Ann Arbor.
Weiler JHH (1999) The transformation of Europe. Yale Law Journal, Vol. 100, Number 8.

Chapter 7
The EU Democratic Governance in Francisco Lucas Pires' Thought and Its Enduring Topicality

Cristina Fasone

Abstract This chapter reflects on the idea of democratic governance proposed by Francisco Lucas Pires along three dimensions that look especially significant in his vision of Europe: democratic governance in terms of representative democracy and traditional institutional tools; democratic governance as participatory democracy which complements and supports the role performed by representative institutions; democratic governance as a civilising force on the market with more socially oriented policies. These different though complementary understandings of democratic governance are briefly analysed here in the current EU framework, 20 years after the first publication of this seminal book by Francisco Lucas Pires.

Keywords Democratic Governance · EU Representative Democracy · EU Civil Society · Social Europe · Francisco Lucas Pires

Introduction: Setting the Scene

Francisco Lucas Pires' book provides a critical and thought-provoking endorsement of the Treaty of Amsterdam's innovations on EU democratic governance. The volume is shaped by the idea of creating a truly European civil society as a precondition to develop the process of European integration. It should go beyond the "simple Habermasian 'public sphere'" in order to make the single market and

This chapter is part of the Jean Monnet Module on "Parliamentary accountability and technical expertise: budgetary powers, information and communication technologies and elections (PATEU)". cfasone@luiss.it.

C. Fasone (✉)
Department of Political Science, LUISS Guido Carli, Rome, Italy
Faculty of Law, Nicolaus Copernicus University, Toruń, Poland
e-mail: cfasone@luiss.it

M. Lucas Pires and F. Pereira Coutinho (eds.), *What Market, What Society, What Union?* https://doi.org/10.1007/978-94-6265-371-9_7

currency (still under construction at that time) operate properly.[1] Indeed, "civil society" is possibly one of the most cited concepts in this work.

The author considered that, aiming to foster the sharing and the support for common values, "Amsterdam put the questions of society and democracy before that of European power",[2] i.e. of institutional reforms and of the organization of those powers, for example through a "European (federal) State".[3] Indeed, every subsequent Treaty revision after Amsterdam has endorsed this vision to strengthen European democracy, even though the results often have not fulfilled the expectations, for a number of reasons.

Many of the brilliant insights he proposed in this book have eventually materialised in the EU governance. Being at the same time a bright scholar and smart politician, Francisco Lucas Pires was also able to predict, in a completely different context compared to where we live now,[4] some key threats for the advancement of the process of EU integration: from the flow of Euroscepticism all over Europe,[5] to the dismantlement of Welfare States and the attacks on the principles of the rule of law, to the role of the EU as a global actor, in prospect, in the field of common commercial policy.[6]

Following the Maastricht Treaty, as rightly observed by the author, the Treaty of Amsterdam intended to promote a more "civilised internal market" and "achieve a more democratic and less economics-based culture of European construction—taking advantage of Lincoln's definition of democracy, one could say a culture that seeks a "government" that is more for the people (social and employment policies), more of the people (substantial strengthening of the European Parliament's powers of co-decision and assent), and more by the people (new rights in relation to non-discrimination, substantive equality and participation)".[7] He was, however, perfectly aware of the shortcomings of the Amsterdam Treaty, in this regard, for example the lack of a truly "financial" (maybe fiscal) Constitution with a tiny EU budget and the multiannual packages regime that can hardly allow to pursue an

[1]Lucas Pires 2020, Chap. 1 in the present book.

[2]Lucas Pires 2020, Chap. 2 in the present book.

[3]Lucas Pires 2020, Chap. 2 in the present book.

[4]In fact, in Chap. 1, Francisco Lucas Pires refers to a time "that the issue of European disunion is solved", which of course appears at odds with the current Brexit process and the many internal tensions the EU is currently facing, but that was the reality at the end of the last century.

[5]For example, where he warns not to ignore the dissatisfaction of pro-Europeans: Lucas Pires 2020, Chap. 2 in the present book.

[6]He regrets, for instance, that in respect of external commerce Amsterdam had hesitated (Lucas Pires 2020, Chap. 3 in the present book) and after the Treaty of Lisbon we can witness the fast growth of trade agreements concluded by the EU in every region of the world.

[7]Lucas Pires 2020, Chap. 1 in the present book.

ambitious social agenda for Europe. He was in fact quite disappointed by the minimalist approach of Agenda 2000, which had just been launched,[8] towards the "European civil society project".

In subsequent years, the White Paper on Governance (2001),[9] fuelled by the corruption scandals surrounding the Santer Commission, and the turbulent process of "constitutionalisation" of the European Treaties, with the shocking results of the French and Dutch referendums of 2005, contributed towards putting democracy and civil society at the top of the Union agenda. Indeed, it is precisely in this context that the polysemic notion of EU governance came to the fore.[10]

The type of governance that the author advocated for the Union was intended to increase the openness and the transparency of the European institutions and to provide more opportunities of participation and consultation of European citizens within the Union decision-making procedures, in addition to the strengthening of the role of parliamentary institutions and to streamline the chain of democratic accountability. Thus, using categories that have been developed more recently, we can infer that Francisco Lucas Pires possibly endorsed the so-called "hybridity thesis"[11] on the EU governance whereby traditional legal and institutional mechanisms of production of binding norms, based on the powers conferred upon EU institutions, co-exists and interacts with new governance tools structured around mechanisms of participatory and deliberative democracy with the bottom up participation of societal actors. Indeed, they are deemed to be mutually inter-dependent and complement the strengths and weaknesses of each other.

In the following pages, short reflections will be developed around the idea of democratic governance proposed by the author in this book along three dimensions that look especially significant in his vision of Europe: (i) democratic governance in terms of representative democracy and traditional institutional tools; (ii) democratic governance as participatory democracy which complements and supports the role performed by representative institutions; (iii) democratic governance as a civilising force on the market with more socially oriented policies. These different though complementary understandings of democratic governance will also be briefly analysed in the current EU framework, 20 years after the publication of this seminal book that Francisco Lucas Pires' family, with the support of the European People's Party, has kindly made available to a foreign readership.

---

[8]See European Commission 1997.

[9]See European Commission 2001.

[10]Governance is traditionally referred to as "a range of processes and practices that have a normative dimension but do not operate primarily or at all through the formal mechanism of traditional command-and-control-type legal institutions": De Búrca and Scott 2006, 3. The White Paper on European Governance (European Commission 2001, 10–11), defined a set of guiding principles for the decision-making within the EU governance systems: openness, participation, transparency, accountability, effectiveness, coherence, proportionality and subsidiarity. See also Scharpf 2001.

[11]De Búrca and Scott 2006, 5.

The Advancements and Pitfalls of EU Representative Democracy

In 1997, like today, the discussion on the institutional methods of EU governance still revolves around the dichotomy of inter-governmentalism (old, neo and new) and supranationalism (or federalism as Francisco Lucas Pires calls it) or perhaps a combination of both, denominated the "Union method".[12] Because the inter-institutional balance is significantly policy-dependent, there is no ultimate and final say on the predominant method of governance that also tends to change over time. For example, what was once a traditionally intergovernmental area, justice and home affairs, has been turned into the Treaty of Lisbon's area of freedom security and justice mainly subject to the supranational-community method. Within this framework, some argue that intergovernmental institutions have been strengthened; others consider that there has been a shift over time in favour of supranational institutions, like the Commission and the European Central Bank and, finally, a small group of scholars support the existence of a re-parliamentarisation of the EU, meaning that both national parliaments and the European Parliament have been reinforced.

The latter is also the direction of development envisaged by Francisco Lucas Pires, following the Amsterdam Treaty, the steady growth of legal bases subject to co-decision and the role assigned to the Conference of parliamentary committees on EU affairs (COSAC), of which the authors had been members on behalf of the European Parliament (p. 32). In particular, through COSAC national parliaments were given a direct acknowledgment of their democratic role in the EU through Protocol no. 1 annexed to the Treaty of Amsterdam.[13] It marked a first attempt to rehabilitate the losers of and latecomers to the EU integration, as national legislatures have been described.[14] When represented inside the Parliamentary Assembly of the European Community, national parliaments did not count for much, due to the primarily consultative role of the Assembly and besides the fact that their real participation in this institution had been discontinuous in some cases (like Italy). Moreover, in the light of the conferral of powers to the EU, national parliaments had "lost" part of their legislative authority over an increasing number of subject matters.

The trend detected by Francisco Lucas Pires was further strengthened at the next Treaty revisions, including the experience of the two Conventions, where MPs occupied most seats though probably lacked the greatest influence on decision-making. The Treaty of Lisbon, described by some emphatically and probably overstating its novelties, as the "Treaty of Parliaments" has formally reinforced both the European Parliament as co-legislator and as veto-player, for

[12]See also Merkel 2010.

[13]Francisco Lucas Pires in his book (Lucas Pires 2020, Chap. 2 in the present book) talks of them as the winners of Amsterdam.

[14]Maurer and Wessels 2001.

example on international agreements concluded by the EU, and has given to national parliaments a series of prerogatives, like in the revision of the Treaties, in the control of compliance with the subsidiarity principle and in the political control of Europol, to mention just a few (Article 12). They are expected to contribute to the good functioning of the Union, according to Article 12 TEU. However, the appraisal of the effects of the "Treaty of Parliaments" on the parliaments themselves is uncertain. While the strengthening of their formal powers is unanimously recognised, many consider that their influence over policy-making has steadily declined in the case of the European Parliament[15] and has never been effective for national parliaments.[16]

Whatever the assessment on the strengthening of parliaments in the EU, as pointed out by Francisco Lucas Pires, this is not enough for the sake of democratic legitimacy, in many regards.[17] First of all, because there are governments next to parliaments as representative institutions (Article 10 TEU) and governments are expected to be democratically accountable to their own parliament or directly to the citizens, depending on the system of government. However, when, from the national level of government we move to the European one, intergovernmental decision-making at least in part disrupts the work of the chain of accountability as there is a shift from the individual executive's position to the formation of a collective will. The European Parliament, already discredited for its representative capacity,[18] is not equipped with effective tools to scrutinise the Council—also because, if we follow the many that today consider the European Parliament and the Council as the two chambers of the EU legislative body,[19] we would be in the strange situation of a Lower Chamber that is called to control the Upper House—and even less so the European Council.[20]

Also, on the side of the democratic accountability of supranational institutions, like the Commission and the European Central Bank, both part of the EU "fragmented executive", Francisco Lucas Pires recommended an increase in the power of scrutiny and oversight of the European Parliament.[21] While on the European Central Bank he advised proceeding with a caution, given its statutory

[15]As reported by Schmidt 2018, 1545, and in particular on budgetary powers, see Fasone and Lupo 2018, 843–846.

[16]De Wilde 2012.

[17]Lucas Pires 2020, Chap. 2 in the present book.

[18]Lacking a uniform electoral procedure for the European Parliament (see recently the Council Decision (EU, Euratom) 2018/994 of 13 July 2018) and a transnational electoral constituency, as well known, the seats are still assigned to Member States according to the very much criticised principle of degressive proportionality, which has come under the attack of the German Constitutional Court on many occasions: see, for example, the judgment on the Treaty of Lisbon, BVerfG, 2 BvE 2/08, 30 June 2009, paras 284–285.

[19]Schütze 2015, 223–262 and Fabbrini 2017.

[20]Wessels and Rozenberg 2013, 14–60.

[21]Lucas Pires 2020, Chap. 2 in the present book.

independence,[22] Francisco Lucas Pires suggested transforming the Commission "into a sort of Government legitimised by the European Parliament and constituted within it"[23] as well as enhancing "the role and democratic nature of the President of the Commission, apart from anything else in order to compensate for the increase in the number of commissioners".[24] Despite the idea having many detractors,[25] EU primary law has codified the proposal of a "parliamentary endorsement" (if not election, according to Article 17.7 TEU) of the European Commission and, hence, of a sort of "parliamentarisation" of the EU form of government. In addition to the Treaty provisions designing the President of the Commission as something more than a *primus inter pares*, the suggestion of reinforcing the position of the Commission's President has been followed by practice through the experiment of the *Spitzenkandidaten*, despite its uncertain enforcement after the 2019 European elections.[26]

Nonetheless with a multilevel system of governance that has become increasingly complex, it appears that these remedies are only palliative rather than the therapy to the democratic malaise of the Union. Indeed, with (the raise of) decision-making procedures that are carried out partly at national level and partly at European level, of which the best example is possibly the European Semester, political responsibilities and the democratic accountability become dispersed and difficult to trace. This nourishes the phenomenon that has been described as "EU executive dominance",[27] whereby executive bodies (including the Commission), individually and collectively, can play their multilevel game blaming other institutions or other levels of government (typically the EU) for the decision taken without bearing the burden of the responsibility of their choice. Parliaments, both at EU and national level, with their big administrative machineries and long times of reaction, are rather displaced in this "game" and even when informed by their executive, are hardly able to direct the government's action.

The politicisation of the Commission and of EU policies at domestic level contributes to creating greater confusion.[28] If, on the one hand, the fact that at least certain EU policies have become politically salient and occupy a central stage in national political conflicts should be seen as a positive sign of citizens' mobilisation towards the EU, on the other hand, given the way EU institutions and

[22]See also Fromage 2020, Chap. 9 in the present book.

[23]Lucas Pires 2020, Chap. 2 in the present book.

[24]Lucas Pires 2020, Chap. 2 in the present book.

[25]Fabbrini 2015 and Kreppel 2012.

[26]Goldoni 2016. For a critical assessment of the politicization of the Commission, see Lupo 2018 and Dawson 2018.

[27]Curtin 2014.

[28]Schmidt 2018, 3.

decision-making are depicted by national media and many political leaders, the sense of attachment and loyalty to the EU, if ever in place, is undermined.

Therefore, as clearly understood by Francisco Lucas Pires, the democratic improvement of the EU governance cannot just come from changes in the institutional design and in the composition and tasks of representative institutions.[29] The democratic enhancement of the EU integration process also derives from a bottom up movement, through civil society participation and the boost of common values, which could reconnect citizens and institutions.

The Construction of a Truly European Civil Society

Although it is never clearly mentioned by the author, Francisco Lucas Pires' book seems to be written with the awareness that the end of the permissive consensus towards the European integration project,[30] coupled with the concrete prospect of a Union that was about to double its size, risked endangering the very foundations of the integration process and facing a society that could become increasingly diverse and fragmented, while being reunited under the common perception of an irreversible disconnection between EU citizens and institutions.[31]

Moreover, with the crises that have occurred in the last decade, many years after the completion of the book, in particular the Eurozone crisis and the migration-refugee crisis, the traditional legitimacy of the Union, grounded in its capacity to deliver based on the objectives enshrined in the treaties, the output legitimacy,[32] has been irremediably undermined.[33] At the same time, the Union input legitimacy has always been considered weak and, for the reasons described above (The Advancements and Pitfalls of EU Representative Democracy) can hardly be rehabilitated without Treaty reforms. As rightly observed, "it is precisely the distance from the world of parties, parliaments, and referenda that contributes to suspicion about the legitimacy of the EU which also protects some of its core institutions from political turbulence".[34] The Union, after all, is structurally unable to inject democratic credentials into national decision-making: it was designed as a technocratic and elite-driven process aimed at the rationalisation of national

[29]As contended, amongst many, also by De Búrca 2018, 357, "Despite parliamentary elections, a powerful European Parliament, democratically elected representatives in the Council of Ministers, a legally enshrined principle of transparency, a strong EU court, and various layers of legal and constitutional rights protection, the European Union still lacks real responsiveness to the preferences of its citizens".

[30]Hooghe and Marks 2009.

[31]Lindseth 2010, 234.

[32]Scharpf 1999.

[33]Weiler 2012.

[34]Sabel and Zietlin 2008, 272.

democracies after World War II.[35] And until the crises the EU performed this role quite well.

This is why it has been suggested by some authors that throughput legitimacy can be a solution to enhance the Union's legitimacy.[36] Throughput legitimacy resorts to a procedural view of democracy and puts the emphasis on deliberation and discursive interaction, in other words on the inclusiveness, dialogic and the participatory nature of the procedure leading to a decision as the standard against which the quality of that decision is assessed.[37] Although the elaboration on throughput legitimacy is far more recent than the EU Governance Agenda, it seems useful to understand certain shortcomings that the EU governance has shown and that Francisco Lucas Pires has clearly identified in this book, though in prospect.

For example, back at the time of the Commission's White Paper on Governance, with an approach that survives consistently today,[38] the Commission proposed building up this governance around a few major projects of great appeal rather than trying to shape forms of collective identity. This cautious and short-term view, harshly criticised by scholars,[39] does not help to create a sense of European identity that can boost the legitimacy of the integration process. What Francisco Lucas Pires highlights, alongside many authors after him,[40] is the need to create a community of values. And, indeed, there are values that were at that time, and still are, shared by Member States, like the refusal of death penalty, a certain way to see inter-state relationships, based first on dialogue rather than on the use of force, or the need to combine market economy with social dignity and social policies. It is not just a matter of procedure, but also of substance.

At the same time, in this book Francisco Lucas Pires did not engage with the problem of the lack of a single European people and of the co-existence of multiple demos within the EU "demoi-cracy" as has been described lately.[41] It appears that for him the terms of the problem are different: rather than promoting the view of an homogeneous and "organic entity which is delimited in time and space",[42] he opts for a vision of the European civil society that mirrors Gidden's notion of society "as a set of procedures and mechanisms for representing and organising social relationships".[43] For example, Francisco Lucas Pires complains about the lack of

[35]Maduro 2010, 3.

[36]See the essays in Fromage and Van der Brink 2018.

[37]Schmidt 2013.

[38]Cf., for instance, European Commission 2017 and the critical appraisal by Avbelj 2017.

[39]Weiler 2001.

[40]Ibid.

[41]Nicolaïdis 2004.

[42]Lucas Pires 2020, Chap. 3 in the present book.

[43]Lucas Pires 2020, Chap. 3 in the present book.

"associative structures"[44] at Union level, both political and social, like truly European political parties[45] and trade unions.

Especially today, with the Euroscepticism matched with populism on the rise, it is even more difficult to find transnational "associative structures" promoting the process of European integration or that, at least, provide a constructive critique to the EU policies and policy-making. Rather, as pointed out recently, Euroscepticism has become the main aggregating factor linking together parties and associations originally supporting very different values and programs.[46] Mainstream parties were mainly pro-European, so extremist parties, particularly from the right, used the pro-European stance against mainstream parties to gain electoral consensus.

Moreover, compared to the period when the Treaty of Amsterdam was adopted, the democratic malaise has spread from Union to national level, where the crisis of liberal constitutionalism has become evident (not only in Eastern Europe) and it entails what Peter Mair, with a visionary intuition, had in 2006 described as a general sentiment of "polity-scepticism",[47] hinting at the lack of political engagement by citizens, distrust in representative institutions, and decline in voter turnout.

To counter the political weaknesses of the integration process from the perspective of the democratic legitimacy, the EU has also tried to respond with a strategy that strengthens and refines participatory democratic tools,[48] thus aiming to improve the quality and the throughput legitimacy of its decision-making processes. This, however, has further favoured a technocratic-managerial path of decision-making and has little to do with politics if not in the sense of a call for more civic engagement, which has not materialised in practice or, when shown, has been disappointed in the end.[49] Thus far the poor performance of participatory tools for the sake of EU democratic legitimacy has been confirmed by the assessment of the reality of the consultation processes that the European Commission launches: mainly economic interest groups, trade associations or firms are participating and, to redress the strength of these economic and business interests, the Commission started to co-finance certain associations thereby creating further problems, in particular of independence.[50]

Likewise, the experience of the European Citizens' Initiative, recently reformed, has proved to be of little help in creating a European civil society, in particular from

---

[44]Lucas Pires 2020, Chap. 3 in the present book.

[45]Even though European political parties have been recognized in EU primary law since the Treaty of Maastricht and are regulated in detail today, they are still evanescent and devoid of a shared identity based on common values, as the internal divisions inside the European People's Party and the case of the Hungarian ruling party Fidesz prove.

[46]Hooghe and Marks 2018, 119–20, affirm that Euroscepticism has become a "new and distinct social cleavage that has not easily been internalized or prioritized by traditional political parties whose core programs did not adapt to reflect its salience".

[47]Mair 2007, 16.

[48]See, extensively, Kohler-Koch and Quittkat 2010.

[49]Klüver 2013, 59.

[50]Saurugger 2008, 1284.

the side of its impact on the decision-making. Even when successfully registered, at present no European Citizens' Initiative has entailed a follow up by the Commission through the adoption of legally binding measures.[51]

The support for more openness and transparency in the EU, clearly stated in this book,[52] has indeed led to many steps forward, for example in the rules of procedure of the EU institutions, including the Council,[53] in EU legislation through Regulation 1049/2001, and in the Court of Justice case law, though primarily within the legislative procedures.[54] However, many have warned against the blurred divide between rule-making by institutional actors and by networks of interested parties as a consequence of the EU strive for more openness and inclusion.[55] Indeed, next to de-regulation the EU governance has also favoured co-regulation by EU institutions and private parties,[56] like social dialogue that Francisco Lucas Pires also repeatedly evokes.[57] It has been observed that this practice risks further undermining responsiveness and accountability towards citizens.[58]

The idea to involve stakeholders and private parties in public rule-making, however, is consistent with one of the pillars of the EU multi-level governance though being often contested, the principle of subsidiarity. Not easy to manage from a purely legal perspective,[59] subsidiarity has been described as expressing the political philosophy of self-government,[60] although it has been used by the EU primarily to expand the reach of its policies in matters of non-exclusive competence. Also, because of this move from the EU side, in the current time of rising Euroscepticism in power, the principle is invoked instrumentally as a justification for taking powers back and regaining control at State level of certain key issues.

---

[51]Dougan 2011 and Cuesta-López 2012, 257.

[52]Lucas Pires 2020, Chap. 2 in the present book.

[53]See Council of Ministers of the EU 2016.

[54]See the Judgment of the General Court (Seventh Chamber, Extended Composition) of 22 March 2018, *Emilio De Capitani v European Parliament*, T-540/15 and the Judgment of the Court of Justice, Grand Chamber of 4 September 2018, *Client Earth*, C-57/16P, compared to the Judgment of the General Court (Second Chamber), 19 March 2013, *Sophie in 't Veld v European Commission*, T-301/10, on international agreements, in particular ACTA.

[55]See Schiek 2007, 443.

[56]See the Inter-institutional Agreement on Better Law-Making of 2003 (OJ C321/01), while the Inter-institutional Agreement on Better Law-Making of 13 April 2016, OJ L231/16 does not refer to co-regulation.

[57]Lucas Pires 2020, Chap. 3 in the present book.

[58]Joerges 2008.

[59]This explains the attempt to involve national parliaments in the Treaty of Lisbon: see Bartl 2015.

[60]See Føllesdal 1998, 190, and Barber 2005, 308 and 323.

The Idea of a Social Europe

Subsidiarity and the idea of subsidiary policies between the national and supranational level are often evoked in Francisco Lucas Pires' book, particularly in connection with the construction of a Social Europe. Following the Treaty of Amsterdam's prioritisation of the social question,[61] the author calls for a shared responsibility on social policy between the European and local level.[62] Aware of the impossibility to merely rely on the social spillover effects of the internal market, the "Union's responsibility lies above all in ensuring that which is no longer possible on a state-by-state basis: the re-adaptation of the essentials of a specific social model".[63]

Although, the EU, as a macro-regional platform, could work "like a necessary regulatory counterweight […] to the way in which the markets are overflowing across and above borders"[64] triggered by globalisation and directly affecting social protection, this has not happened in practice or the EU has not been perceived as a counterweight to this process in the common discourse. Despite the fact that European policies also included policies aimed at correcting the negative external effects that markets and productive activity determine, for example on the environment and human health,[65] the EU has been accused of pursuing exclusively economic liberalisation and de-regulation and, in the aftermath of the Eurozone crisis, to second ordoliberal policies[66] in contrast with the EU social "constitutional identity" based on a constant "tension between cohesion and competitiveness, solidarity and subsidiarity".[67] Solidarity, in particular, which also gives the name to Title IV of the Charter of fundamental rights and that requires the active engagement of the European civil society besides the States, is seriously in trouble nowadays. The bailout programmes, the strict conditionality and the flawed management of the refugee crisis have further split Europe and its society rather than fostering solidarity. Despite the commitment of the Juncker Commission towards a Social Europe—from the Juncker Plan to the 2018 State of the Union Speech, solemnly titled "The Hour of European Sovereignty"—there are clear signals that speak of a social "impasse" in Europe, for example when looking at the European

[61]Lucas Pires 2020, Chap. 3 in the present book.

[62]Lucas Pires 2020, Chap. 3 in the present book.

[63]Lucas Pires 2020, Chap. 3 in the present book.

[64]Lucas Pires 2020, Chap. 1 in the present book.

[65]Héritier and Lehmkuhl 2008.

[66]Joerges 2012 and Menéndez 2017.

[67]Lucas Pires 2020, Chap. 3 in the present book.

Pillars of Social Rights[68] or the weak coordination of social policies and of social reforms among Member States, which Francisco Lucas Pires considered as a target.[69]

Concluding Remarks

Twenty years after the publication of the book, many of the crucial claims that Francisco Lucas Pires put forward have not been addressed by the EU and still represent the most significant weaknesses in the governance system of the Union: the (lack of) European civil society, democratic accountability, solidarity, to mention just a few.

Compared to the period when the Treaty of Amsterdam was signed, the EU has become a different "beast". In 1997, Lucas Pires wrote that on the side of the European Union "we have a market with weak institutions"; on the national side, "strong institutions without a market".[70] In 2018 we witness a situation in which all EU institutions, both supranational and intergovernmental, have become stronger in many policy areas, though the inter-institutional balance is different and highly dependent on the subject matter. However, undeniably the institutionalisation of the Union has proceeded, even outside the EU legal framework, strictly speaking.

By contrast, national institutions are in crisis, of power and legitimacy. Using Vivien Schmidt's words:

> the characterization of the EU level as consisting of 'policy without politics', based on the tendency to apolitical and/or technocratic decision-making, no longer fully describes EU governance, which has increasingly become 'policy with politics' in the more contentious areas. At the same time, what Schmidt (2006) identified as national level 'politics without policy' has only worsened, so much so that it arguably no longer fully describes the current situation, which has increasingly become 'politics against policy' or even 'politics against polity'.

While it is clear on both levels of government that representative institutions have seen their legitimacy and their capacity of intermediation weakened, it is also true that citizens are eager to be more involved in decision-making,[71] so there is hope for the fostering of a European civil society. Some opportunities have been missed at EU level, with regards to the adoption of a truly European electoral procedure and for the creation of transnational electoral lists or of a transnational constituency, even this year, at the time of the redistribution of the UK seats in the

---

[68]See, in particular, COM (2017) 250, 251, 252, 253, 254, final and the critical comments by Giubboni 2017.

[69]Lucas Pires 2020, Chap. 3 in the present book.

[70]Lucas Pires 2020, Chap. 3 in the present book.

[71]Though under the form of "counter-democracy", in a deconstructive manner, rather than in constructive terms. See Rosanvallon 2010, 173–190.

European Parliament. Indeed, the 2019 European elections could have been a key moment in this regard, marked by a general increase of the voters' turnout.

In a multilevel system of relationships and accountability, where it is difficult to see a clear correspondence between power and responsibility and where the political directions come from, the invitation of Francisco Lucas Pires to draw particular attention to the coordination, connection and interdependence between levels of government, institutions and citizens should be taken into account, for example under the form of revised and refined mechanisms of interplay between representative institutions and of participatory democracy, the latter having being merely a fig leaf for participation, without any detectable institutional implications for citizens.

Finally, Francisco Lucas Pires' book shows a model of a politician (and scholar) that is not easy to find in today's Europe and of which, therefore, there is an urgent need: able to provide a clear and constructive vision of where Europe should go, how and with which objectives, and to set ambitious standards for the institutions to reach; very sensitive to the social reality behind institutional engineering but, at the same time, having lived the institutions from within, perfectly aware of the limits of the inter-institutional and inter-State dynamics.

References

Avbelj M (2017) What Future for the European Union? Discussion Paper SP IV 2017–802, Center for Global Constitutionalism, WBZ—Berlin Social Science Center.

Barber N (2005) The Limited Modesty of Subsidiarity. European Law Journal, Vol. 11, 308–325.

Bartl M (2015) The Way We Do Europe: Subsidiarity and the Substantive Democratic Deficit. European Law Journal, Vol. 21, 23–43.

Council of Ministers of the EU (2016) Council's Rules of Procedure and comments on Council's Rules of Procedure, http://www.consilium.europa.eu/en/documents-publications/publications/council-rules-procedure-comments/ Accessed January 2019.

Cuesta-López V (2012) A Comparative Approach to the Regulation on the European Citizens' Initiative. Perspectives on European Politics and Society, Vol. 13, 257–69.

Curtin D (2014) Challenging Executive Dominance in European Democracy. Modern Law Review, Vol. 77, 1–32.

Dawson M (2018) Evaluating Juncker's Political Commission: The Right Idea in the Wrong Hands? VerfBlog, 2018/9/10, https://verfassungsblog.de/evaluating-junckers-political-commission-the-right-idea-in-the-wrong-hands/ Accessed January 2019.

De Búrca G (2018) Is EU Supranational Governance a Challenge to Liberal Constitutionalism? The University of Chicago Law Review, Vol. 85, 337–67.

De Búrca G, Scott, J (2006) Introduction. New Governance, Law and Constitutionalism. In: De Búrca G, Scott J (eds) Law and New Governance in the EU and the US. Hart Publishing, Oxford.

De Wilde P (2012) Why the Early Warning Mechanism does not alleviate the democratic deficit. OPAL Online Paper, No. 6, University of Maastricht, Maastricht.

Dougan M (2011) What are we to make of the citizens' initiative? Common Market Law Review, Vol. 48, 1807–1848.

European Commission (1997) Agenda 2000. For a Stronger and Wider Union. COM (97) 2000, 15 July 1997.

European Commission (2001) European Governance: A White Paper. COM (2001) 428, 25 July 2001.
European Commission (2017) White Paper on the future of Europe. COM(2017)2025, 1 March 2017.
Fabbrini S (2015) The European Union and the Puzzle of Parliamentary Government. Journal of European Integration, Vol. 37, 571–86.
Fabbrini S (2017) Which Democracy for a Union of States? A Comparative Perspective of the European Union. Global Policy, Vol. 8, 14–22.
Fasone C, Lupo N (2018) The Union Budget and the Budgetary Procedure. In: Schütze R, Tridimas T (eds) Oxford Principles of European Union Law. Oxford University Press, Oxford, 809–46.
Føllesdal A (1998) Subsidiarity. Journal of Political Philosophy, Vol. 6, 190–218.
Fromage D, Van der Brink T (eds) (2018) National parliaments, the European Parliament and the democratic legitimation of the European Union economic governance – Special Issue. Journal of European Integration, Vol. 40.
Giubboni S (2017) Appunti e disappunti sul pilastro europeo dei diritti sociali. Quaderni costituzionali, Vol. 4, p. 953–86.
Goldoni M (2016) Politicising EU lawmaking? The Spitzenkandidaten Experiment as a cautionary tale. European Law Journal, Vol. 22, 279–95.
Héritier A, Lehmkuhl D (2008) Introduction: The Shadow of Hierarchy and New Modes of Governance. Journal of Public Policy, Vol. 28, 1–17.
Hooghe L, Marks G (2009) A Postfunctionalist Theory of European Integration: From Permissive Consensus to Constraining Dissensus. British Journal of Political Science, Vol. 39, 1–23.
Hooghe L, Marks G (2018) Cleavage Theory Meets Europe's Crises: Lipset, Rokkan, and the Transnational Cleavage. Journal of European Public Policy, Vol. 25, 109–135.
Joerges C (2008) Integration through de-legalisation? European Law Review, Vol. 33, 213–237.
Joerges C (2012) The European Economic Constitution in Crisis: Between 'State of Exception' and 'Constitutional Moment'. In: Maduro M et al. (eds) The Democratic Governance of the Euro. RSCAS Policy Papers, RSCAS PP 2012/08, EUI, Florence.
Klüver H (2013) Lobbying as a Collective Enterprise: Winners and Losers of Policy Formulation in the European Union. Journal of European Public Policy, Vol. 20, 59–76.
Kohler-Koch B, Quittkat C (2010) De-Mystification of Participatory Democracy: EU Governance and Civil Society. Oxford University Press, Oxford.
Kreppel A (2012) The normalization of the European Union. Journal of European Public Policy, Vol. 19, 635–45.
Lindseth P (2010) Power and legitimacy. Reconciling Europe and the Nation-State Oxford University Press, Oxford.
Lupo N (2018) The Commission's Power to Withdraw Legislative Proposals and its 'Parliamentarisation'. Between Technical and Political Grounds. European Constitutional Law Review, Vol. 14, 311–31.
Maduro M (2010) Passion and Reason in European Integration, FCE 3/10 Forum Constitutionis Europae. Humboldt University, Walter Hallstein-Institut Für Europäisches Verfassungsrecht, Berlin.
Mair P (2007) Political Opposition and the European Union. Government and Opposition, Vol. 42, 1–17.
Maurer A, Wessels W (eds) (2001) National Parliaments on their Ways to Europe. Losers or Latecomers? Nomos Verlag, Baden-Baden.
Menéndez A (2017) The Crisis of Law and the European Crises: From the Social and Democratic Rechtsstaat to the Consolidating State of (Pseudo)technocratic Governance. Journal of Law and Society, Vol. 44, 56–78.
Merkel A (2010) Speech by Federal Chancellor of Germany at the opening ceremony of the 61st academic year of the College of Europe, Bruges, 2 November.
Nicolaïdis K (2004) The New Constitution as European 'Demoi-cracy'? Critical Review of International Social and Political Philosophy, Vol. 7, 76–93.

Rosanvallon P (2010) Counter-democracy. Politics in the Age of Distrust (transl. Goldhammer A). Cambridge University Press, Cambridge.
Sabel C F, Zietlin J (2008) Learning from Difference: The New Architecture of Experimentalist Governance in the European Union. European Law Journal, Vol. 14, 271–327.
Saurugger S (2008) Interest Groups and Democracy in the European Union. West European Politics, Vol. 31, 1274–91.
Scharpf F W (1999) Governing Europe. Oxford University Press, Oxford.
Scharpf F W (2001) European Governance: Common Concerns vs. The Challenge of Diversity. In: Joerges C et al. (eds) Mountain or Molehill: Critical Appraisal of the Commission White Paper on Governance. Jean Monnet Working Paper 6/01 NYU, New York.
Schiek D (2007) Private Rule-making and the European Governance: Issues of Legitimacy. European Law Review, Vol. 32, 443–466.
Schmidt V A (2006) Democracy in Europe. Oxford University Press, Oxford.
Schmidt V A (2013) Democracy and Legitimacy in the European Union Revisited: Input, Output and 'Throughput'. Political Studies, Vol. 61, 2–22.
Schmidt V A (2018) Rethinking EU Governance: From 'Old' to 'New' Approaches to Who Steers Integration. Journal of Common Market Studies, Vol. 53, 1544–61.
Schütze R (2015) European Union Law. Cambridge University Press, Cambridge.
Weiler J H H (2001) The Commission as Euro-Skeptic: A Task Oriented Commission for a Project-Based Union: A Comment on the First Version of the White Paper. In: Joerges C et al. (eds) Mountain or Molehill: Critical Appraisal of the Commission White Paper on Governance. Jean Monnet Working Paper 6/01 NYU, New York.
Weiler J H H (2012) Europe In Crisis—On 'Political Messianism', 'Legitimacy' And The 'Rule of Law'. Singapore Journal of Legal Studies, December, 248–68.
Wessels W, Rozenberg O (2013) Democratic Control in the Member States of the European Council and the Eurozone Summits. Study for AFCO. European Parliament, PE 474.392.

Chapter 8
European Civil Society, Rights and Non-Europeans: Thoughts Upon Reading *Amsterdam—From the Market to the European Society* by Francisco Lucas Pires

Samo Bardutzky

Abstract The chapter aims to be a reflection on the state of European citizenship (in a wide sense of the word) and civil society. The reflection takes place, on the one hand, during a time of important dilemmas on the course of European integration, and on the other hand, approximately two decades after the entry into force of the Amsterdam Treaty. Accordingly, it is inspired by one the most important achievements of Amsterdam: the reshaping of European law on immigration and asylum. The chapter takes as its starting point the last book of the Portuguese scholar Francisco Lucas Pires, in which he discussed the move, in the Amsterdam Treaty, from market to civil society. The chapter tries to frame the current conflict in the European civil society between those that advocate for future strengthening of European integration and at the same time agree with Europe's moral and legal responsibilities towards the incoming refugees, and those that oppose them. It tries to provide an answer to these dilemmas by recognizing the role of rights, in part drawing upon the thought of Jürgen Habermas.

Keywords Asylum · European integration · Civil society · Public sphere · Amsterdam Treaty · Human rights · Freedom of speech

---

At the time of writing Research Associate, University of Kent, United Kingdom.

S. Bardutzky (✉)
University of Ljubljana, Ljubljana, Slovenia
e-mail: samo.bardutzky@pf.uni-lj.si

M. Lucas Pires and F. Pereira Coutinho (eds.), *What Market, What Society, What Union?* https://doi.org/10.1007/978-94-6265-371-9_8

Introduction

This text is intended to be a reflection on the state of European citizenship (in a wide sense of the word) and civil society. This reflection is written in the aftermath of the arrival of a large number of Syrian (and other refugees) to Europe, a phenomenon inaccurately described as a refugee "crisis". While the number of people who arrived was extraordinary, it was still relatively modest in comparison to the numbers of refugees poorer and smaller developing countries host. The crisis, if anywhere, is to be found in the incapacity of the Member States of the European Union to co-operate in the spirit of partnership, and even more, in the political reactions to these events, which led to the creation of or strengthening of populist, anti-establishment movements, often Eurosceptic, but often also nativist, xenophobic or even outright racist.

Just as with the financial and sovereign debt crisis, the so-called refugee crisis has exposed the poorly veiled differences between the Member States: the differences in their capacity to cope with an extraordinary event, as well as the differences in political attitudes and preferences of their respective electorates. We find ourselves in a European Union where in fact a number of the constituent states is led by people that are advocating or had once advocated for a significant loosening of the ties that bind the European nations (leaving the Euro, holding referendums on continuous membership etc.)

The reflection that I undertake here is inspired by the last book written by Francisco Lucas Pires, a Portuguese scholar of constitutional and European Union law. The topic of his book was the Amsterdam Treaty, signed in 1997. I am grateful for his insights on the developments introduced in the Amsterdam Treaty, and more broadly, on the state of European integration *circa* 1997, which served as a starting point for me to develop my own insights on the state of European integration at the time of the writing, twenty years after Francisco Lucas Pires's untimely passing.

The Amsterdam Treaty and Non-Europeans

The Amsterdam Treaty, in retrospect approximately two decades later, might strike the observer as one of the more modest steps in the development of the European integration project,[1] referred to even as "constitutional bricolage".[2]

There is, however, an element of the development brought about by Amsterdam that stands out, described by Francisco Lucas Pires himself as perhaps the "most

[1]Craig and De Burca 2015, 15; Haratsch et al. 2009, 11–12.

[2]Schütze 2012, 33.

important conquest" of the new treaty: the reform of the Third Pillar.[3] Third Pillar was reorganized into three parts. Most importantly, a new title of the Treaty on the European Community was created (Title IV).[4] Title IV provided "the umbrella for the communitarisation of the parts of the old Third Pillar most closely linked to the internal market (visas, asylum and immigration)".[5]

First, the changes regarding the law on visas, immigration and especially asylum, that took place in the Amsterdam Treaty, and second, the commentary of a contemporary observer, Francisco Lucas Pires, and some of the other scholars writing on the topic at the time, will be at the centre of our attention in this contribution.

A separate part, in the form of a short independent essay, of Francisco Lucas Pires's book was also devoted to 'Law and Asylum Policy in the European Union Before and After Amsterdam'. However, the discussion in this contribution begins with Francisco Lucas Pires's insight that he expressed in relation to the development of the single market in the European Union, right in the beginning of the book.

The insight that we refer to here is a warning against the construction of a "common market, crowned with a single currency" without sufficient political solidarity and moral backing of the European society. Lucas Pires warned that the necessary authority for the construction of the single market can only stem from the civil society.[6]

Francisco Lucas Pires does not expressly make the claim that the creation of a single market will not be sustainable without the authority stemming from civil society in the context of asylum law and policy which he discusses in a separate short essay. But are there reasons to say that such a claim cannot be made with regard to EU asylum law and policy? No. If single currency is a crown on head of the common market,[7] as Francisco Lucas Pires put it, then a harmonization of immigration and asylum is perhaps a sceptre in its hands. Also, participation in the common asylum system, especially as it has developed since the communitarisation in Amsterdam, takes, from the perspective of a Member State, a toll on its sovereignty that is not equal, but is surely comparable to the one resulting from participation in a common currency.

---

[3]Lucas Pires 2020, Chap. 4 in the present book.

[4]Craig and De Burca 2015, 15.

[5]O'Keeffe 1999, 271. The other two elements of the reform consisted of the changes to the Schengen regime and the rebranding of what was left of the Third Pillar: police and judicial cooperation in criminal matters: Lucas Pires 2020, Chap. 4 in the present book.

[6]Lucas Pires 2020, Chap. 1 in the present book.

[7]Lucas Pires 2020, Chap. 1 in the present book.

Civil Society and the Europe of Francisco Lucas Pires

We should also reiterate Francisco Lucas Pires's remark that the most important reform that the Amsterdam brought about, the restructuring of the Third Pillar, paid "homage to the European civil society" since Europeans, in surveys of public opinions, valued very highly the idea of a borderless Europe.[8] It is, then, safe to posit: the authority for a common asylum system cannot come from above. It needs to originate from the civil society.[9]

Of course, the idea of "civil society" is open to a number of different understandings. Francisco Lucas Pires does not so much put forward a normative claim with regard to the content of this idea as he rejects two established ways of understanding civil society. On the one hand, such a strongly pluralist project as the European Union would be entirely incapable of fitting into Hegel's "concrete universal" definition of civil society presupposing a homogeneous nation.[10] But at the same time, a Habermasian idea of a "public sphere" will not suffice. In Lucas Pires's argument, something more will be needed, a "greater community sentiment", a sharing of a moral and cultural will, as well as equality and rights.[11]

But even if Francisco Lucas Pires called for more than only the Habermasian public sphere, this logically still leads to the conclusion that in any case, he would *also* demand what Habermas demands. In other words, while the existence of a Habermasian public sphere may not suffice by itself, it is relatively safe to claim that it is nevertheless indispensable.

The similarity between the civil society of Jürgen Habermas on the one hand and the civil society of Francisco Lucas Pires on the other strikes me as most convincing in the following two characteristics. First, both accounts of civil society envisage a duality between more formal, institutional politics on the one hand and a more spontaneous and pluralist civil society on the other hand. Second, the two levels also do not simply exist in parallel. in Jürgen Habermas's thought, the formal institutions of decision-making have to be "porous to the input of civil society" if the political system is to function well.[12] Informal public opinion-formation needs to be in a state of interplay with formalized institutions that make law.[13]

---

[8]Lucas Pires 2020, Chap. 4 in the present book.

[9]We should note here that in Habermas's thought, which we see is close to Lucas Pires's understanding of civil society, no simple equation mark could be drawn between expressions/surveys of public opinion and civil society as a much more complex phenomenon.

[10]Lucas Pires 2020, Chap. 1 in the present book.

[11]Lucas Pires 2020, Chap. 1 in the present book.

[12]Finlayson 2005, 108.

[13]Sitton 2003, 95.

Rights

The link to Habermas's concepts enables us to refer to another point that was made in Francisco Lucas Pires's book regarding the asylum law and policy pre- and post-Amsterdam. In *Between Facts and Norms*, Habermas recognized the role of the system of rights as a "minimum set of normative institutional conditions for any legitimate modern political order."[14] When the law protects a system of rights, this system of rights in turn protects the civil society and the discourses that take place within it. The civil society, then, provides the input for the formalised decision-making.[15]

The importance of rights is a central message in Francisco Lucas Pires's book and especially in the essay on asylum law and policy. First, the importance of rights is the central argument in the critique of EU asylum law and policy pre-Amsterdam. Second, the strengthening of rights is cause for optimism in the post-Amsterdam era.

Regarding the former, for example, lamentable is the absence of any reference in the Schengen and Dublin Conventions to not only the European Convention on Human Rights but also Council of Europe soft law on asylum. Conformity with the requirements of the Convention Relating to the Status of Refugees is put in doubt as well.[16] The trends identified in the period between Maastricht and Amsterdam were seen as leading towards the reduction of the scope of asylum, with increasing threats to the principle of non-refoulement.[17]

As for the latter, the optimism regarding the level of the protection of rights in the emerging EU asylum law would seem to stem from the fact of the communitarisation of this area of EU law, as well as the promise of the "progressive implementation of an 'area of freedom, security and justice'".[18] Communitarised, the majority of Title IV would now have to be compliant with the general principles of EU law and thus also compliant with human rights.[19]

Francisco Lucas Pires's essay echoes the criticisms of the contemporary observers such as Ian Ward and David O'Keeffe. There was obvious scepticism in relation to the strong intergovernmental character of Third Pillar, which excluded or heavily limited most conventional forms of control in EU law: judicial control, parliamentary control (via national parliaments as well as via the European Parliament), even via the Court of Auditors.[20]

---

[14]Fabienne 2017, https://plato.stanford.edu/archives/sum2017/entries/legitimacy/. Accessed 18 February 2019.

[15]Finlayson 2005, 113.

[16]Lucas Pires 2020, Chap. 4 in the present book.

[17]Lucas Pires 2020, Chap. 4 in the present book.

[18]Lucas Pires 2020, Chap. 4 in the present book.

[19]O'Keeffe 1999, 285.

[20]Ibid., 273.

"We" v "They"

The contemporaries of Francisco Lucas Pires who at the time expressed their criticisms of the Third Pillar provisions of the Treaty saw the absence of legal guarantees for migrants coming from outside of the European Union in the Amsterdam era as an element of exclusion, marginalization and othering of the non-European migrants.[21] This is an exceptionally appropriate point at which we can expand our account here from recapping the discussion as it happens in the last years of the twentieth century to the situation as it is now, in 2019.

The impression that a reader nowadays obtains from reading the accounts written at the time of the signing of the Amsterdam Treaty is that at that time, the development of Union citizenship, the strengthening of the freedom of movement for the "privileged" Union citizens, combined with the security "backbone", the Schengen system, were seen as contributing to the creation of two categories—"We" (the citizens of the Union) v. "They" (the foreigners, the others).[22] The image that one can immediately picture before one's eyes when reading the late 90s accounts is the image of "Fortress Europe". By that we mean that the territory of the Union provides security for the ones "inside", mainly by keeping the ones who do not belong "outside".[23] It should perhaps be added that it is of course not only "We", the citizens of Europe, that may come in. It is also the foreigners, the non-citizens, who may enter as they are deemed "deserving" immigrants.[24]

Fortress Europe

When we compare the situation at the end of the nineties with the situation nowadays, quite a few developments and differences have to be mentioned. The construction of Fortress Europe is successfully underway. It may not yet be successful in achieving its ultimate objective (the keeping out of those who may not come in) but a number of features have been added to the mechanism deployed to achieve this goal. When the first years of the attempts to use the Dublin system have shown that its functioning depends on the goodwill of the transit countries, the destination countries consequently pushed for Eurodac, a fingerprint collection

[21] Ward 1997, 85.

[22] Ward 1997, 87.

[23] Schlenker 2013.

[24] See Bosworth on the construction of the distinction between deserving and undeserving immigrants. Compare also the classification of "Unwelcome", "Desirable", "Suspicious" and "Poor" Foreigners; Bosworth 2008.

system which enables the Member States to identify the asylum seekers that may have been registered in another country beforehand.[25] The human cost of this particular feature of Fortress Europe, designed to help keep asylum seekers in countries where they do not want to stay, was illustrated to a journalist of the Guardian by the Sudanese refugee in Calais.[26] Specifically, by his instructions on burning off one's fingertips, a two-hour long, excruciatingly painful procedure, that however disarms the costly Eurodac system.[27]

The other striking feature of Fortress Europe that has developed since Amsterdam is the increasingly expanding dimension of externalisation of migration control. It was soon after Amsterdam, at the European Council Summit of Tampere in 1999, when mention was made of participation with the 3rd countries in migration management at the European level.[28] Externalisation of migration control has since taken a number of forms, of which perhaps the most egregious is migration co-operation between EU and Libya.[29]

The Other of the Europe of Today

The question whether there is a causal link between the construction of Fortress Europe and the current image of refugees and other immigrants in the European societies is far beyond the scope of this chapter.[30] We can limit ourselves to establishing that indeed, there is not only a semi-finished Fortress, there are also, on some levels and to some extent, the "We, Europeans" and the "They, Non-Europeans". This observation can be made in a Habermasian sense, as was

---

[25]Aus 2006. http://eiop.or.at/eiop/pdf/2006-006.pdf. Accessed 18 February 2019.

[26]Trilling (2015), https://www.theguardian.com/commentisfree/2015/jul/31/europe-migrant-crisis-political-choice-toxic-waste-sanctuary. Accessed 18 February 2019.

[27]The annual cost of EURODAC's central unit in 2013 was over 340,000 EUR. The costs of the Dublin system at the national level continue to be almost impossible to calculate; Fratzke 2015, 15–16.

[28]Kolman 2019, 8.

[29]Libya is not a signatory to the 1951 Refugee Convention. The Danish Refugee Council has quoted the UN Security Council report establishing that "refugees and migrants intercepted by the Libyan Coast Guard are systematically transferred to detention centres where they are held arbitrarily in inhumane conditions for indefinite periods of time, without registration system, judicial oversight or legal process to claim asylum." See: Danish Refugee Council 2018, 4. http://www.integrazionemigranti.gov.it/Documenti-e-ricerche/DRCPolicyBrief_EU-LibyaMigrationCooperation.pdf. Accessed 18 February 2019.

[30]The fear and occasionally hatred of immigrants in Europe has without a doubt also been fuelled by the inadequate responses of the EU Member States to the arrival of the large number of refugees in 2015–2016. This can be compared to the rise of scepticism towards European integration that is without a doubt partly caused by the attempts to solve the economic crisis that have brought along painful austerity cuts and the erosion of intra-European solidarity.

done by Branko Milanovic. When he observed the students, engaged in public debate on the squares of Madrid, a debate that also touched upon Europe and its future, he could not help but notice African immigrants, standing by the side, hoping to sell the debaters soft drinks or snacks and improve their meagre income. The debate, the informal "will-formation", as Habermas probably would have called it, might have touched upon the lives of the immigrants—theoretically, abstractly. But they were not participants in it, and, for the most part, they were likely completely uninterested in it.[31]

However, the picture is much more complex than that. While it is very likely that the students in the open spaces of Madrid were entirely sympathetic to the immigrants standing at the side (it is just that the immigrants do not belong to their public sphere), the sympathy towards immigrants is eroding in Europe 2019. Political parties with radical anti-immigrant and anti-foreigner stances (often also expressly islamophobic), such as Italy's Lega (under Salvini), France's National Front, Hungary's Fidesz, the Dutch Freedom Party etc., have transformed from fringe formations into sizeable parliamentary fractions. They do not only overlook non-European immigrants, as the benevolent students might have. They actively use the Non-Europeans as the "Other", as the "They": a tool with which European nativist identity is to be forged or strengthened.

These parties combine a strong anti-immigrant stance with scepticism towards European integration. While some advocate for an outright withdrawal from the European Union (Geert Wilders' Freedom Party), others instead call for a reversal of the progressive creation of the "ever closer Union" or the withdrawal from the common currency.[32] It would seem that most of them, as for example Hungarian Prime Minister Orbán, defend the idea of a "Europe of Nations", i.e. a union of sovereign states, as opposed to the alleged federalist project of the "United States of Europe".[33]

The euro-sceptic dimension of the anti-immigration parties in Europe leads to an interesting situation where the process of Othering becomes relatively complex and confusing. The non-EU migrant (a Syrian refugee, a victim of human trafficking from sub-Saharan Africa, an economic migrant from Southeast Asia…) will still be

[31]Milanovic 2018, https://braveneweurope.com/branko-milanovic-habermas-and-pimps-the-world-of-the-day-and-the-world-of-the-night. Accessed 18 February 2019.

[32]See, for example: Leonard 2018, https://www.project-syndicate.org/commentary/merkel-migration-and-the-populist-siege-by-mark-leonard-2018-06. Accessed 18 February 2019.

[33]This message was a point of Orban's victory speech after the 2018 parliamentary election. See: Than and Szakacs 2018, https://www.reuters.com/article/us-hungary-election-orban/hungarys-orban-to-seek-eu-of-strong-nations-after-landslide-re-election-idUSKBN1HH12A. Accessed 18 February 2019.

seen the Other by the Salvini voter, but this particular othering will no longer lead the Salvini voter to distinguish between "Us, the Europeans" and "Them, the Non-Europeans". For politics that opposes the European citizenship and ideas of solidarity, emphasising ethnic or national identity instead, the Romanian immigrant in Italy or the Italian immigrant in the Netherlands is perhaps only microscopically less "They" than the Syrian refugee anywhere in the European Union.[34]

The segment of the electorate does not, at the time of the writing, present the majority of the voters in Europe. There is considerable opposition to this trend that has recently been expressed by a number of public intellectuals.[35] Liberal and centrist parties have been warning against the dangers of populism (described by the liberal ALDE group in the European Parliament as a "cancer").[36] It is perhaps safe to posit that there is, in fact, a *conflict* in European civil society.

Just as the Syrian refugee can serve as the 'Other' to Fidesz or Lega, they have begun to play an unusual role of the 'Other' to those Europeans who support further European integration or at least oppose the dismantling its achievements or reversing its course. Very often, these members of the public agree with or even advocate respect for the rights of refugees. It would seem that it is often the image of the refugee and the non-European that provides the impetus for the vision of Europe of rights. The example would be the Europe-wide response to the publication of the photo of dead three-year old Alan Kurdi.[37] It is my claim that at least in part, the reflex that the image of the suffering non-European triggers in a part of the European civil society is connected to the idea that uniting Europe can prevent atrocities and human rights violations. The idea that post-totalitarian constitutionalism in Europe is built to protect human dignity and life and that European integration, or at least a large dimension thereof, in fact serves this purpose rather than any other.

---

[34]I will argue that an analogous expression of the anti-European/anti-immigrant sentiment can even appear in the Member States of the periphery that have since its accession exported labour force. The example is Orban's Hungary where controversial measures have been taken to demotivate young Hungarians from migrating into richer EU Member States after graduating from a Hungarian university. See for example: Bolton (2015). https://www.independent.co.uk/news/world/europe/hungary-is-paying-its-young-emigrants-to-come-back-home-10358509.html. Accessed 18 February 2019. See also: Manca (2013). http://neweasterneurope.eu/2013/08/01/viktor-orban-the-reforms-and-the-students/. Accessed 18 February 2019.

[35]Lévy et al. (2019), https://www.theguardian.com/commentisfree/2019/jan/25/fight-europe-wreckers-patriots-nationalist. Accessed 18 February 2019.

[36]Alliance of Liberals and Democrats for Europe (2016), https://alde.eu/en/news/690-a-new-and-reformed-europe-is-the-solution-against-uncontrolled-globalisation-and-the-cancer-of-nationalism-and-populism-guy-verhofstadt/. Accessed 18 February 2019.

[37]There is an overview of the facts of the case and of the public response, with a number of further references, in this Wikipedia article: https://en.wikipedia.org/wiki/Death_of_Alan_Kurdi. Accessed 18 February 2019.

The Role of Rights

Rights play an important role in the conflict of the pro-refugee pro-European against the anti-refugee nationalist. The intolerance (and sometimes hatred) directed against the migrants coming to Europe from the other continents is blind to the fact that assistance to asylum seekers and refugees is based on commitments made in international and regional human rights law, as well as national constitutions. This goes as far as insults hurled at the non-governmental organisations who provide legal assistance to foreigners. "Anti-Abschiede-Industrie", "deportation prevention industry", was the choice of words of the Eurosceptic Bundestag Member Alexander Dobrindt, a member of the Bavarian CSU.[38]

On the other hand, the politicians and members of the public belonging to the harsher (if not extreme) parts of the right-wing political pole have increasingly employed the language of rights to support their activity.[39] To be more concrete: when someone takes to the social media to express his opposition to the admission —let alone integration—of refugees into European society, he uses as an argument negative prejudice against Muslims, or Arabs, or non-Christians, and invokes constitutionally guaranteed freedom of speech to justify his intervention. Perhaps the most illustrative example of this trend is the existence of the "alternative" social network called Gab. This network markets itself simply as the "Free Speech Social Network"; it is populated almost exclusively by far-right activists who left Facebook or Twitter after they were found in violation of the community standards.[40]

The Polarised Civil Society and Rights

This leaves us with a very curious problem. We have earlier extrapolated Francisco Lucas Pires's thoughts on the euro and linked them to the common European asylum system, thus establishing the necessity that it is the European civil society that provides a fundament for the political decisions creating and shaping European asylum law. But we find ourselves with the members of the public polarised, and with a growing pool of anti-European as well as anti-immigration sentiment.

This situation presents a considerable threat to the quest for a workable, just, and international human rights law compliant European asylum system. The danger lies

---

[38]Der Tagesspiegel 2018, https://www.tagesspiegel.de/politik/csu-landesgruppenchef-dobrindt-beklagt-eine-anti-abschiebe-industrie/21248990.html. Accessed 18 February 2019.

[39]In the American context, with a comparative caveat, this was discussed by Jennifer Delton; Delton 2017. https://www.washingtonpost.com/news/made-by-history/wp/2017/08/22/when-free-speech-becomes-a-political-weapon/?utm_term=.9921abf60ac8. Accessed 18 February 2019.

[40]Bennett 2018, https://www.vice.com/en_uk/article/ywxb95/gab-is-the-alt-right-social-network-racists-are-moving-to. Accessed on 18 February 2019.

in the possibility that every time human rights are used as an argument in the public sphere as part of the debate on the refugees, the anti-refugee voices will invoke human rights as well, trying to rely on freedom of speech to flood the discussion with xenophobia and fear. And try to undermine the positions of those calling for respect for international human rights law by insulting them, implying ulterior motives etc.

A more segmented understanding of the system of rights is thus necessary to escape this trap. It can be rooted in Habermas's concept of the system of rights in relation to the public sphere. The role of basic civil and political rights is to "create a simultaneously legal and thus legally instituted social space in which non-governmental and non-economic associations can operate free of repression."[41] As Habermas posited, there are three categories of rights that define the status of legal subjects and "regulate the relationships among freely associated citizens *prior* to any organized state."[42] Among them is the right to individual legal protection.[43] To these rights I would add the right to enjoy an equal standing in relationships with other individuals, and to have one's dignity and integrity respected. In the next ("ideal") phase, when legal subjects become the authors of the law that in turn addresses them, the right to participate in the "will-formation" is established.[44] Habermas's requirement for legitimacy of a legal norm is that all members of the legal community can assent to it, and among other things that can happen because the rule-making process was open for input from civil society and because the norm conforms with a legally instituted system of rights.[45]

We can expect Habermas's concepts to help us solve the issues of European civil society, revive respect for the rule of law in the form of international human rights law and national constitutional law dictating respect for human dignity and life. But if our expectations are to be realistic, we will first need to pose ourselves the following question. How do we revisit Habermas's requirements for legitimacy of law, which include possibility of assent by all the members of the legal community, given that EU (refugee and migration) increasingly affects the lives not only of non-citizens, but also of those deemed illegal and undeserving? Habermas himself has on occasions advocated for integration of foreigners into European societies[46] and expressed pride in the inclusion of second- and third-generation immigrants.[47] The problem we face is that the people who have begun to serve as 'the Other' may

[41]Fultner 2014, 188.

[42]Habermas 1996, 122.

[43]Ibid.

[44]Ibid., 123.

[45]Finlayson 2005, 116. See also: Sitton 2003, 91.

[46]Habermas 2006.

[47]Habermas (2018), https://elpais.com/elpais/2018/05/07/inenglish/1525683618_145760.html. Accessed 18 February 2019.

not even find themselves on the European continent.[48] Yet it is their right to life and human dignity that defines what kind of Europe (as the title of this edited volume asks itself) we will create and maintain.

The answer to the question posed in the preceding paragraph is beyond the scope of this short reflection. However, we can formulate a tentative answer to the dilemma that poses itself with regard to the European public sphere *circa* 2018/2019. The dilemma, to reiterate, is: how to resolve the conflict between the ostensible freedom of expression of those advocating for human rights not to apply to non-Europeans on the one hand, and the rights that need to be recognized to the non-Europeans and their lawyers and defenders? It seems that from Habermas's concepts, discussed above, we can derive a simple normative claim. Public debates on the future of asylum in Europe can start as soon as the participants agree to treat everyone (not only their fellow national citizens and Union citizens) as legal subjects with a set of rights, who deserve, without any questions asked, to rely upon the guarantees of international human rights law, who have the right to have their case, whatever it may be, heard by a judge, who will be treated with respect etc. After this abstract moment, freedom of speech can be invoked by the participants exercising their public autonomy. Or with the words of Andreas Voßkühle, the president of the German Federal Constitutional Court, replying to Dobrindt: "*Wer rechtsstaatliche Garantien in Anspruch nimmt, muss sich dafür nicht beschimpfen lassen.*"[49]

References

Aus J P (2006) Eurodac: A Solution Looking for a Problem? European Integration online Papers, Vol. 10, 2006. http://eiop.or.at/eiop/pdf/2006-006.pdf. Accessed 18 February 2019

Bardutzky S, Fahey E (2017) The Subjects and Objects of EU Law: Exploring a Research Platform. In: Bardutzky S, Fahey E (eds) Framing the Subjects and Objects of Contemporary EU Law. Edward Elgar Publishing, Cheltenham, pp. 1–27.

Bosworth M (2008) Border Control and the Limits of the Sovereign State. Social and Legal Studies, Vol. 17, Issue 2, pp. 199–215. https://doi.org/10.1177/0964663908089611.

Craig P, De Burca G (2015) EU Law: Text, Cases, and Materials, 6th edn. Oxford University Press, New York.

Danish Refugee Council (2018) DRC Policy Brief EU-Libya migration cooperation: Shipwrecked values of humanity. http://www.integrazionemigranti.gov.it/Documenti-e-ricerche/DRCPolicyBrief_EU-LibyaMigrationCooperation.pdf. Accessed 18 February 2019.

Fabienne P (2017) Political Legitimacy. In: Zalta E N (ed) The Stanford Encyclopedia of Philosophy (Summer 2017 Edition). https://plato.stanford.edu/archives/sum2017/entries/legitimacy/. Accessed 18 February 2019.

Finlayson G (2005) Habermas: Very Short Introduction. Oxford University Press, Oxford.

[48]This question can also be framed with the vocabulary of "subjects" and "objects" of EU Law. See Bardutzky and Fahey 2017.

[49]"No one has to suffer insults only because he or she relied on the guarantees of rule of law." Zeit online 2018, https://www.zeit.de/politik/deutschland/2018-07/andreas-vosskuhle-praesident-bundesverfassungsgericht-rhetorik-csu-fluechtlinge. Accessed 18 February 2019.

Fratzke S (2015) Not Adding Up: The Fading Promise of Europe's Dublin System. Migration Policy Institute Europe, Brussels. www.mpieurope.org. Accessed 18 February 2019.
Fultner B (2014) Habermas: Key Concepts. Routledge, New York.
Habermas J (1996) Between Facts and Norms. The MIT Press, Cambridge.
Habermas J (2006) Opening up Fortress Europe. Let's talk European, http://www.signandsight.com/features/1048.html. Accessed 23 April 2020.
Haratsch A, Koenig C, Pechstein M (2009) Europarecht, 6. Auflage [European Law, 6th edn.]. Mohr Siebeck, Heidelberg.
Kolman K (2019) Eksternalizacija kontrole migracij v EU [Externalisation of Migration Control in the European Union]. Master's Thesis, Faculty of Law, University of Ljubljana, Ljubljana.
O'Keeffe D (1999) Can the Leopard Change its Spots? Visas, Immigration and Asylum – Following Amsterdam. In: Twomey P, O'Keeffe D (eds) Legal Issues of the Amsterdam Treaty. Hart, Oxford, pp. 271–288.
Schlenker A (2013). Cosmopolitan Europeans or partisans of fortress Europe? Supra-national identity patterns in the EU. Global Society, Vol. 27, Issue 1, pp. 25–51. https://doi.org/10.1080/13600826.2012.734281.
Schütze R (2012) European Constitutional Law 2012. Cambridge University Press, New York.
Sitton J F (2003) Habermas and Contemporary Society. Palgrave Macmillan, New York.
Ward I (1997), Law and the Other European. Journal for Common Market Studies, Vol. 35, No. 1, 1997. https://doi.org/10.1111/1468-5965.00051.

Chapter 9
Francisco Lucas Pires' Views on the Economic and Monetary Union and the Single Currency: An Assessment Twenty Years Later

Diane Fromage

Abstract In his volume on the Treaty of Amsterdam, Francisco Lucas Pires provided a thorough and critical analysis of the then recently approved Treaty. In particular, he examined whether the Treaty of Amsterdam marked the shift from a European integration process focused on the market to a European society, and he showed extraordinary capacities to foresee how the European Union (EU) would develop from then onwards. This chapter first examines Francisco Lucas Pires' views on the Treaty of Amsterdam and the single currency in general and assesses the evolution the EU has witnessed since. The following part of this analysis is devoted specifically to the study of the features of the EU's economic institutional governance contained in the postscript). The final section concludes.

Keywords Economic and Monetary Union · Civil Society · European Central Bank · Economic Governance

Introduction

Twenty years ago, in 1998, the volume on the Treaty of Amsterdam (*Amsterdam—from the Market to the European Society*) by Francisco Lucas Pires was published. In this volume, he provided a thorough and critical analysis of the then recently approved Treaty of Amsterdam. In particular, he examined whether the Treaty of Amsterdam marked the shift from a European integration process focused on the market to a European society, and he showed extraordinary capacities to foresee how the European Union (EU) would develop from then onwards.

D. Fromage (✉)
Faculty of Law, Maastricht University, P.O. Box 616, 6200 MD Maastricht, The Netherlands
e-mail: diane.fromage@maastrichtuniversity.nl

M. Lucas Pires and F. Pereira Coutinho (eds.), *What Market, What Society, What Union?* https://doi.org/10.1007/978-94-6265-371-9_9

The EU was undergoing important changes at the time. The fall of the Berlin Wall had intervened a little less than a decade before, the Communities had taken a more political turn with the approval of the Treaty of Maastricht a few years earlier (1992) and the EU's extraordinary expansion had started with the "EFTA enlargement" in 1995 while a dozen additional states—mostly from Central and Eastern Europe—were negotiating their entry in the EU. Crucially, in 1988, Member States had agreed to work towards the establishment of the Economic and Monetary Union (EMU) by 1999.[1] It therefore comes as no surprise that the then imminent introduction of the single currency received prominent attention in Francisco Lucas Pires' analysis; in fact, he viewed the Treaty of Amsterdam as the first step towards a European civil society "capable of 'civilizing' the market while also maintaining popular consensus in favour of the single currency".[2]

His analysis should also be considered in the context of the Portuguese referendum on the Amsterdam Treaty that was originally scheduled but later cancelled; the Portuguese perspective on the Amsterdam Treaty Francisco Lucas Pires provides is particularly interesting and insightful to a foreign reader and contributes to understand better the dynamics of the post-crisis EU we currently live in.

This chapter first examines Francisco Lucas Pires' views on the Treaty of Amsterdam and the single currency in general and assesses the evolution the EU has witnessed since (Francisco Lucas Pires' View on Amsterdam and the Single Currency). The following part of this analysis is devoted specifically to the study of the features of the EU's economic institutional governance contained in the postscript (Francisco Lucas Pires' Analysis of the Structure of Economic Governance Contained in Amsterdam). The final section concludes (Conclusion).

Francisco Lucas Pires' View on Amsterdam and the Single Currency

Before delving into Francisco Lucas Pires' views on Amsterdam and the single currency, a few preliminary remarks are in order. As is logical in the context in which Francisco Lucas Pires performed his analysis of the Treaty of Amsterdam, the single currency is given particular importance despite the fact that the most important steps towards the introduction of the Euro had already been taken with the Treaty of Maastricht.[3] To a generation that has not actively lived through this change, the

[1]This decision was taken at the European Council meeting held in Hannover on 27–28 June 1988 during which the Heads of State and Government agreed to appoint a committee to study ways to achieve a European economic and monetary union. This Committee, chaired by then Commission President Delors, produced a report on economic and monetary union in the European Community in April 1989. Committee for the study of the Economic and Monetary Union 1989.

[2]Lucas Pires 2020, Chap. 1 in the present book.

[3]Indeed, the Maastricht Treaty included a reference to EMU in its text for the first time; it also foresaw the creation of the European Central Bank.

correlation between single currency and Amsterdam could have gone unperceived; most importantly perhaps, the magnitude of the change resulting from the introduction of the Euro becomes increasingly difficult to grasp for those who have lived all their life with the single currency. After the very existence of the Euro has been threatened by the 2008 economic and financial crisis, the analysis performed by Lucas Pires is not only insightful but also particularly useful to think about the way forward. Five main points of his analysis are subsequently presented and analysed.

The Common Currency Cannot Gain Authority by Legal Means Only; a European Civil Society Is Needed

Francisco Lucas Pires' assessment of the EU's deficiencies appears to have been strikingly lucid ahead of time. Indeed, he underlined already then that a single market with a single currency without a political union or without sufficient moral and legal support of a European civil society would present risks because such a civil society is needed to ensure sufficient authority to the market; he thereby underlined the inability of the political and institutional order alone to supply such type of authority.[4]

If we observe how vivid the debate on the exit of some Member States from the Euro has been since the beginning of the economic crisis, it appears that membership to the single currency is still not taken for granted in many States,[5] even if the return to prosperity may have contributed to restoring the support for the Euro in recent years. A Eurobarometer survey published in December 2017 in fact showed that 74% of the population of Eurozone Member States do support the Euro,[6] but only 51% of the population of the States that are yet to introduce the Euro support such an introduction.[7] The Euro could thus be said to not have yet fully gained the popular authority Lucas Pires was referring to whilst a truly European civil society is still yet to emerge.

[4]Lucas Pires 2020, Chap. 1 in the present book.

[5]For instance: Spiegel online, "Germany Open to Possible Greek Euro Zone Exit", 5.1.2015.

[6]Eurobarometer 2017.

[7]Eurobarometer 2018.

Amsterdam and Especially the Single Currency Could Be Turning Points Towards the Establishment of a European Civil Society

In fact, Amsterdam is depicted as a stepping stone towards the European constitution and as a step towards more democracy in the EU with the establishment of what Lucas Pires calls "a single space for citizens".[8] Francisco Lucas Pires appears to have had high hopes on the potential impact of the introduction of the single currency which he thought could be the essential integrationist link capable of promoting the "ever closer Union between European peoples" anchored by the Treaty of Maastricht.[9] He did recognize the fact that the planned enlargement would introduce new centripetal forces, but he considered the Euro's centrifugal force to be stronger and older.[10]

Even if the Treaty establishing a Constitution for Europe failed, it is undoubtable that the Lisbon Treaty is still very similar to the (or a) Constitutional Treaty. And it has indeed contributed to the inclusion of even more elements of direct and indirect citizens' participation into the Treaties. For instance, in addition to the pre-existing right to petition the European Parliament (EP),[11] European citizens can now launch European Citizens Initiatives.[12] Furthermore, national parliaments and the European Parliament have been granted much importance in the new Treaty—so much that it was even dubbed the "Treaty of parliaments".[13] Building up on the improvements the Amsterdam Treaty had brought about with the inclusion of a protocol dedicated to national parliaments, the Lisbon Treaty went one step further and gave them the responsibility to "contribute actively to the good functioning of the Union" (Article 12 Treaty of the EU (TEU)). On the other hand, the European Parliament has also been significantly reinforced; among other things, it now acts as a co-legislator in almost all areas of legislation.

This somewhat positive assessment might need to be slightly mitigated however. The economic and financial crisis that started to hit Europe in 2008 was to later on show how a European civil society still does not exist fully, and how dearly solidarity is still missing among European peoples. Besides the fact that one quarter of the population of the Eurozone Member States still does not support the Euro as mentioned above, we observe that the gap between Northern and Southern (i.e. creditor and debtor) Member States widened on an economic, but also on a political

[8]Lucas Pires 2020, Chap. 1 in the present book.

[9]Lucas Pires 2020, Chap. 1 in the present book.

[10]Lucas Pires 2020, Chap. 1 in the present book.

[11]Further on the right to petition: Tiburcio 2015.

[12]For an assessment, see: Ingravallo 2017 and Karatzia 2017.

[13]Among many other publications: Fromage 2015, Jancic 2017 and Hefftler et al. 2015.

level. Eurosceptic parties actually received exceptionally high levels of support all over Europe in the 2019 EP elections. Even if the civil society Lucas Pires refers to is not to be understood as a society in Hegelian terms, but rather as a public space as conceived by Habermas,[14] it remains that it can be doubted whether such a civil society has emerged, despite the fact that the Euro has now been in circulation for more than twenty years.

Amsterdam and the Single Currency as Anchors of the Irreversibility of the European Construction and the Political Union

Lucas Pires additionally depicts the Amsterdam Treaty, and the introduction of the single currency attached to it, as anchors of the irreversibility of the European construction[15] and of the political Union.[16] As mentioned previously, this aspect of the analysis deserves to be underlined specifically, and this is for at least two reasons in my view. First, it is striking how true this statement is under the current EU Treaty framework whereby the Euro is the currency of Member States by default,[17] and no procedure has been designed for the exit of the Eurozone only. Second, considering the difficulties which the United Kingdom is facing in trying to disentangle its legal order with the EU legal order, an exit from both the EU and the Eurozone reveals itself as being particularly difficult while an exit from the Eurozone only—if it were allowed—would seem hardly feasible at least for political reasons. Taking into account the disruptions provoked by the temporary suspension of the Schengen rules in some Member States only and their economic consequences, a re-introduction of national currencies seems to be indeed close to unthinkable. In fact, even during the acute Greek crisis, no measures were taken in this sense.

Ratifying Amsterdam Means Ratifying the Single Currency and the Continuity of the Integration Process

Lucas Pires also shows in his analysis how several of the initiatives taken in the 1990s, such as the Treaty of Amsterdam and the Agenda 2000, were implemented

[14]Lucas Pires 2020, Chap. 1 in the present book.

[15]Lucas Pires 2020, Chap. 2 in the present book.

[16]Lucas Pires 2020, Chap. 5 in the present book.

[17]This was clearly reaffirmed by Commission President Juncker in his 2017 State of the Union speech for instance. Juncker 2017.

to prepare the introduction of the single currency.[18] For him, the Euro was the most important European revolution since the Russian Revolution since 1917, and he pointed to the resulting possibility to interpret the convergence criteria with some flexibility to guarantee that a maximum number of States would enter.

Looking back at the twenty years that have passed since Lucas Pires developed his analysis, it is striking how important the decisions that were taken then have been for the future of the EU and its development since. As he underlines, the progress made with the Treaty of Amsterdam was not to everyone's satisfaction, but it allowed States to keep going indeed. And States did prove capable of coming to an agreement at the time, whereas proposals for reforms are currently deemed unlikely because they are perceived as unrealistic. Moreover, Lucas Pires underlines the political judgement involved in the introduction of the Euro. It is noteworthy that this same political judgement continued to play an important role in the management of the single currency, with negative consequences leading to the economic and financial crisis (e.g. absence of applicability of the Stability and Growth Pact to France and Germany in 2003).

The New Order of the Euro

In the same vein, Lucas Pires highlights the existence of a new order of the Euro, which shows again the importance of the Euro for the whole European integration process in his view. He interestingly recalls how, by then, even sceptics were convinced and how Europeanisation had passed to be perceived as a solution and means of protection against globalization.[19] He thus hoped for a "new" Europe where not Europe per se but which Europe would be the question.[20]

Twenty years later, the "new" order of the Euro has arguably become the "normal" order and some strives for change have appeared within the EU. The most visible example of this crisis in citizens' and politicians' trust in the EU is certainly the British vote in favour of the United Kingdom's exit. Nevertheless, the increasing popularity of Eurosceptic parties advocating an exit of the EU or of the Eurozone or the return to intergovernmental structures in the form of international Treaties for instance[21] does (again) pose the question of Europe per se. This tendency is further illustrated by the decrease in the turn out to the EP's elections.[22] As

[18]Lucas Pires 2020, Chap. 2 in the present book.

[19]Lucas Pires 2020, Chap. 5 in the present book.

[20]Lucas Pires 2020, Chap. 5 in the present book.

[21]Suffice it to refer to the Treaty on Stability, Economic Coordination and Governance or the Treaty establishing the European Stability Mechanism.

[22]Only 42.61% of European citizens voted in the 2014 elections; the turnout has been steadily decreasing since the first direct elections in 1979. European Parliament, Results of the 2014 European elections—turnout, http://www.europarl.europa.eu/elections2014-results/en/turnout.html (11.11.2018).

shown above, the Treaty of Lisbon had attempted to introduce some of the necessary reforms to increase democracy within the EU, but it has failed to consolidate the "new" European order initiated with Amsterdam, perhaps because like Amsterdam, it entered into force after the failure of the preceding Treaty. There are numerous signs showing that a "new new" Europe is required at present; like when the Amsterdam Treaty was drafted, new institutional reforms appear to be needed. These reforms should, for instance, tackle the issue of the existing asymmetries within the EU, between Eurozone and non-Eurozone Member States for instance, and the related difficulties in ensuring adequate democratic accountability.[23]

Looking back twenty years after the publication of Francisco Lucas Pires' analysis, it thus appears that the Treaty of Amsterdam has indeed marked a crucial change in the European integration process. Undoubtedly, a more democratic and political Union has emerged, but it seems that it has unfortunately not marked the important change Lucas Pires had hoped for in terms of the emergence of a European civil society. In fact, more efforts are currently under consideration to foster the emergence of such a European civil society.[24] Furthermore, the difficulties and the doubts he depicted at the time are strikingly similar to the ones the EU is still facing today.

Actually, his analysis of the structure of EU economic governance contained in the Treaty of Amsterdam is also strikingly still very much up-to-date as will now be shown.

Francisco Lucas Pires' Analysis of the Structure of Economic Governance Contained in Amsterdam

In his postscript, Francisco Lucas Pires also analysed some of the institutional features of the economic governance framework introduced by the Treaty of Amsterdam. He considered in particular the democratic control of the ECB (1), and that of the Council of the EU (2).

The Democratic Control of the ECB

Concerning the ECB specifically, Francisco Lucas Pires underlined the shortcomings of the designation procedure of the President of the ECB. He submits that if the

[23]I refer here for instance to the issues linked to the informality of the Eurogroup, or the inadequacy of the European Parliament as the organ in charge of guaranteeing accountability of Eurozone- or Banking Union-specific issues.

[24]Recent initiatives have included for instance the proposal of an Erasmus programme for civil servants, the delivery of a free Interrail pass to EU citizens when they turn 18 or the *Spitzenkandidaten* procedure in the run-up to the European Parliament elections.

President of the ECB were designated with the assent of the EP and by a qualified majority in the Council, the decision would have the same democratic credentials as the unanimity requirement in place then.[25] This change has since intervened, since the President of the ECB, as well as the members of its Executive Board, are now designated by the Council acting by qualified majority.[26] The EP, however, is still "only" consulted. In the newly established Single Supervisory Mechanism though, the EP has been guaranteed a right of veto on the nomination of the Supervisory Board chair,[27] and some have considered that the increased power guaranteed to the EP in the framework of the Single Supervisory Mechanism could in fact serve as a model to reform the EP's prerogatives vis-à-vis the ECB acting in its capacity as responsible of the monetary policy.[28]

Lucas Pires interestingly already then highlighted the possibility that parliamentary control would go beyond the wording of the Treaties.[29] And indeed, the EP and the ECB regularly exchange, numerous parliamentary questions are being asked etc.[30] Nevertheless, important shortcomings have surfaced, at least at the beginning of the Monetary dialogue between the EP and the ECB. The extent to which this procedure involves the EP, as well as the ECB's limited democratic accountability have been underlined as shortcomings.[31] Furthermore, the ECB President has been found to give the same information to MEPs he already gave to the media during the preceding press conference,[32] thereby limiting media's attention and attractiveness towards the Monetary dialogue sessions.[33] In fact, the Anglo-Saxon model of absolute transparency which Lucas Pires anticipated to become the ECB's model has not fully materialised, i.e. the ECB has arguably not been as transparent as it is independent.[34] Transparency has long been an issue for the ECB, and it is only progressively that some improvements have been made. As a further proof of such insufficient transparency, the use of the Monetary dialogue sessions as an opportunity to advocate for a more transparent ECB can be noted,[35] and it is only in 2015 that the minutes of the ECB Governing Council started to be

[25]Article 11-2 of the Statute of the European System of Central Banks attached to the Treaty of Maastricht.

[26]Article 11-2 of Protocol n°4 on the Statute of the European System of Central Banks and the European Central Bank.

[27]Article 26-3 Council Regulation (EU) No 1024/2013 of 15 October 2013 conferring specific tasks on the European Central Bank concerning policies relating to the prudential supervision of credit institutions.

[28]Fromage and Ibrido 2018.

[29]Lucas Pires 2020, Chap. 5 in the present book.

[30]On the extension of these practices during the crisis especially: Fraccaroli et al. 2018.

[31]Amtenbrink and van Duin 2009, 468.

[32]Claeys et al. 2014, 7.

[33]Heidebrecht 2015, 511.

[34]Lucas Pires 2020, Chap. 5 in the present book.

[35]Amtenbrink and van Duin 2009, 578f.

published.[36] In fact, with the economic crisis and the ECB's participation in the Troika, new difficulties have arisen again as the ECB's role is ever more complex and diverse.[37] Transparency is also a particularly problematic feature of the banking supervision now exercised by the ECB.

Considering in what ways the EP has been interacting with the ECB, it is thus fair to say that (unfortunately) the EP's control did not prove as powerful as it appeared to be,[38] at least when the ECB was first established. While the ECB has published its decision, their justification[39] has not been systematic. New shortcomings have additionally arisen in relation to the ECB's new powers of supervision of credit institutions: the channels of democratic control over the ECB by the EP are now plenty but this multiplication has arguably led to an increased confusion for MEPs who may not always be able to identify in which arena a certain question needs to be asked. Furthermore, the scope of the monetary policy has become increasingly blurred.[40]

The ECB has indeed been "independent but not deaf",[41] as evidenced during the economic crisis in whose context it did "whatever it takes to save the Euro",[42] and the concept of "accountable independence" has been usefully developed to characterize the ECB's status.[43]

The Democratic Control of the Council

Francisco Lucas Pires also examined the democratic credentials of the Council, and more specifically the relationship between the EP and the Council.[44] He noted that this was where the major democratic deficit laid, and that it would only increase once the single currency had entered into circulation. Since the Treaty of Lisbon, the Treaties have arguably limited the EP's role in this framework; it is national parliaments who are responsible for holding their individual ministers to account at national level (Article 12 TEU). Two major difficulties subsist though: even if all national parliaments did adequately hold their representative to account—which not all of them do at present—, the sum of their actions would still fail to guarantee the *collective* responsibility of the Council, and the EP is in no position to fill this

---

[36]Belke 2017, p. 8.
[37]Fromage et al. 2019.
[38]Lucas Pires 2020, Chap. 5 in the present book.
[39]Lucas Pires 2020, Chap. 5 in the present book.
[40]Fromage and Ibrido 2018.
[41]Lucas Pires 2020, Chap. 5 in the present book.
[42]This intention was voiced by then-ECB President Mario Draghi in 2012. Draghi 2012.
[43]Further on this concept: Lastra 1992 and Petit 2019.
[44]Lucas Pires 2020, Chap. 5 in the present book.

gap.[45] Additionally, the flexibility introduced in Amsterdam[46] is certainly beneficial in the sense that it compensates for the increasing difficulty in agreeing to more Treaty reforms as underlined by Francisco Lucas Pires. At the same time however, the *status quo* between Eurozone and non-Eurozone Member States appears to have stabilized, i.e. even Sweden which is formally under the obligation to adopt the single currency does not appear very likely to take this step any time soon. The informal Eurozone-specific executive bodies, i.e. the Eurogroup and Euro Summits, are, to some extent, even less accountable. Some mechanisms have been designed to ensure the Euro Summits' accountability vis-à-vis the EP, but they are not fully satisfactory in practice.[47] And only limited oversight and accountability mechanisms exist vis-à-vis the informal Eurogroup. This has motivated numerous reform proposals, ranging from a parliamentary assembly for the Eurozone to a Eurozone-specific EP sub-committee.[48] The European Commission too has shown commitment towards a more democratic economic governance framework when it presented its "December package" of reforms in December 2017.[49] Yet, not much appears to have changed since the Commission published its proposal. Hence, despite the introduction of the Euro and the transfer of power to the EU level this change has represented, the democratic framework at EU level is still imperfect.

It is interesting to note here that Francisco Lucas Pires envisaged that the EP should counterbalance the transfer of power to neutral administrative institutions.[50] Considering the increased role that the EU has since been attributed in the coordination of national budgetary plans for instance,[51] and considering the long-lasting division between Eurozone and non-Eurozone Member States, it seems that national parliaments should also be involved and that the EP alone cannot play this role in the current context. Some initiatives in the form of the Interparliamentary conference on the Stability, Economic Coordination and Governance in the European Union ("Article 13 Conference") do exist, but they are not fully satisfactory.[52] Some minimum standards for the involvement of individual national parliaments should arguably be defined at EU level; they could, for instance, receive directly the documents exchanged in the framework of the European Semester.

---

[45] Kreilinger 2013, 3. Further on the absence of accountability vis-à-vis the two Councils: Monjal 2016 and Roland 2016.

[46] Lucas Pires 2020, Chap. 2 in the present book.

[47] Fromage 2018.

[48] See on these proposals, *inter alia* Curtin and Fasone 2017.

[49] European Commission, Policy package on 'Completing Europe's Economic and Monetary Union', https://ec.europa.eu/info/publications/economy-finance/completing-europes-economic-and-monetary-union-policy-package_en.

[50] Lucas Pires 2020, Chap. 5 in the present book.

[51] This intervened by means of the introduction of the European Semester for instance.

[52] *Inter alia* Griglio and Lupo 2018.

Conclusion

Several of the positive consequences Francisco Lucas Pires had predicted after the entry into force of the Lisbon Treaty have become reality, in particular with regard to the mechanisms in place to ensure more democracy and with the adoption of a constitution for Europe. Yet, an analysis of the evolution of the EU over the past twenty years shows, in my view, that the single currency has not had the centripetal effect Francisco Lucas Pires had anticipated; rather the centrifugal effects of enlargement appear to have been stronger. Though some important achievements can be observed, a European civil society is yet to emerge.

As far as the structure of the EMU governance is concerned, we notice that the important transfer of powers to the EU level has not been accompanied by the development of a similarly strong accountability framework. Further reforms are thus still needed both for this reason and because the creation of the Banking Union, the ECB's involvement in the Troika and the ECB's resort to unconventional monetary policy during the crisis have made it even more difficult to ensure adequate democratic accountability standards.

The implementation of the necessary reforms will be particularly difficult however because negotiations for Treaty reforms have become even more complex than they were at the time of the negotiations of the Amsterdam Treaty, which already lasted twice as much as a standard gestation period.[53]

References

Amtenbrink F, Van Duin K (2009) The European Central Bank before the European Parliament: Theory and Practice After Ten Years of Monetary Dialogue. European Law Review 34: 561–583.

Belke A (2017) Central Bank Communication: Managing Expectations through the Monetary Dialogue. ROME Discussion Paper Series 17–04.

Claeys G et al. (2014) European Central Bank Accountability: How the Monetary Dialogue Could Evolve. Bruegel Policy Contribution 2014/04.

Committee for the study of Economic and Monetary Union (1989) Report on economic and monetary union in the European Community.

Curtin D, Fasone C (2017) Differentiated representation: is a flexible European Parliament desirable? In: de Witte B et al. (eds) Between flexibility and disintegration. The trajectory of differentiation in the EU. Edward Elgar, Cheltenham, pp. 118–145.

Draghi M (2012) Speech by Mario Draghi at the Global Investment Conference in London, 26.7.2012, https://www.ecb.europa.eu/press/key/date/2012/html/sp120726.en.html (11.11. 2018).

Eurobarometer (2017) Standard Eurobarometer 88, December 2017.

Eurobarometer (2018) Flash Eurobarometer 465, May 2018.

Fraccaroli N et al. (2018) The evolution of the ECB's accountability practices during the crisis. ECB Economic Bulletin.

[53]Lucas Pires 2020, Chap. 2 in the present book.

Fromage D (2015) Les Parlements dans l'Union Européenne après le Traité de Lisbonne. La Participation des Parlements allemands, britanniques, espagnols, français et italiens. L'Harmattan, Paris.

Fromage D (2018) The European Parliament in the post-crisis era: an institution empowered on paper only? In: Fromage D, van den Brink T (eds) Special issue on "National parliaments, the European Parliament and the democratic legitimation of the European Union economic governance". Journal of European Integration. 40: 281–294.

Fromage D, Ibrido R (2018) The 'Banking Dialogue' as a model to improve parliamentary involvement in the Monetary Dialogue? In: Fromage D, van den Brink T (eds) Special issue on "National parliaments, the European Parliament and the democratic legitimation of the European Union economic governance". Journal of European Integration. 40: 295–308.

Fromage D et al. (eds) (2019) Special issue on "The ECB's accountability in a multilevel European order". Maastricht Journal of European and Comparative Law

Griglio E, Lupo N (2018) The conference on stability, economic coordination and governance: filling the gaps of parliamentary oversight in the EU. In: Fromage D, van den Brink T (eds) Special issue on "National parliaments, the European Parliament and the democratic legitimation of the European Union economic governance". Journal of European Integration. 40: 358–373.

Hefftler C et al. (eds) (2015) The Palgrave handbook of national parliaments and the European Union. Palgrave Macmillan, New York.

Heidebrecht S (2015) Wie transparent ist die Europäische Zentralbank? Eine international vergleichende Betrachtung vor dem Hintergrund der weitreichenden Neuerungen zum Januar 2015. Zeitschrift für Politikwissenschaft. 25: 501–525.

Ingravallo I (2017) L'iniziativa dei cittadini europei a dieci anni da Lisbona. Luci e ombre. La Communità internazionale. 72: 241–253.

Jancic D (ed) (2017) National parliaments after the Lisbon treaty and the Euro crisis: resilience or resignation? Oxford University Press, Oxford.

Juncker J-Cl (2017) State of the Union Address 2017.

Karatzia A (2017) The European Citizens' Initiative and the EU institutional balance: On realism and the possibilities of affecting EU lawmaking. Common Market Law Review. 54: 77–208.

Kreilinger V (2013) The new inter-parliamentary conference for economic and financial governance. Notre Europe Policy paper 100.

Lastra R M (1992) The independence of the European System of Central Banks. Harvard International Law Journal. 33: 475–520.

Monjal P-Y (2016) L'Union européenne comme fédéralisme exécutif autocratique par nature irresponsable. La « responsabilité » comme possible clé explicative de la nature juridico-politique de l'Union. In: Geslot Ch et al. (eds) La responsabilité politique des exécutifs des Etats membres. Bruylant, Brussels, pp. 25–40.

Petit C-A (2019) Balancing independence with accountability: A third-metre waltz? Maastricht Journal of European and Comparative Law, pp. 17–34.

Roland S (2016) Un déficit démocratique peut en cacher un autre: la responsabilité politique du Conseil européen et du Conseil en question. In: Geslot Ch et al. (eds) La responsabilité politique des exécutifs des Etats membres. Bruylant, Brussels, pp. 219–239.

Tiburcio T (2015) The right to petition. Study for the PETI Committee of the European Parliament PE519.223.

Chapter 10
Asylum Policy: A Measure of the EU's Fidelity to Its History and Values

Paschalis Paschalidis

Abstract In his last book, entitled 'Amsterdam: From the Market to the European Society', the late Professor Francisco Lucas Pires singled out the EU's asylum law and policy as the measure of its fidelity to its history and values. He also expressed the hope that enlarging the ECJ's jurisdiction in the area of asylum law and policy and elevating the right to request asylum to a constitutional right would remedy the problems arising from the entanglement of law with politics. Although these aspirations subsequently materialized, they were not sufficient to deal with the challenges that the EU and its asylum policy recently faced as a result of the influx of asylum seekers from Syria and other troubled parts of the world. These circumstances ultimately exposed not a legal but a political challenge to transform the European Union in the minds of its citizens from a necessity to a coherent identity.

Keywords Area of Freedom, Security and Justice · Asylum · Refugees · EU-Turkey Statement · Relocation of asylum seekers · Humanitarian visa

Had Francisco Lucas Pires lived to this day, no other chapter of his swansong book 'Amsterdam: From the Market to the European Society' would evoke greater disappointment than the chapter on 'Law and Asylum'. Like many tireless men and women born at the end of the Second World War, Francisco Lucas Pires dedicated his lifetime's work to transforming the Schuman Declaration from words into actions. His book titled 'Amsterdam: From the Market to the European Society' is a testament to the efforts he personally invested in the European project and to his aspirations for Europe's future educated by its own history. This is particularly

---

The author is a senior associate at the International Arbitration Practice of Shearman & Sterling LLP. Prior to that, he was a *référendaire* for First Advocate General Melchior Wathelet at the European Court of Justice from 2012 to 2018. He is also a Lecturer at the Executive Master of European and International Business Law E.M.B.L.-HSG at the University of St. Gallen. Email: paschalis.paschalidis@shearman.com.

P. Paschalidis (✉)
University of St. Gallen, St. Gallen, Switzerland
e-mail: paschalis.paschalidis@shearman.com

M. Lucas Pires and F. Pereira Coutinho (eds.), *What Market, What Society, What Union?* https://doi.org/10.1007/978-94-6265-371-9_10

evident in the Asylum chapter of his last book which is dedicated to the Righteous Amongst the Nations, Aristides de Sousa Mendes, and refers to the millions of displaced people in Europe during the Second World War as well as to the Hungarian exodus of 1956 and the return of millions of Portuguese from the colonies after the Carnation Revolution.

While tracing the history of the EU's asylum policy, Francisco Lucas Pires, a member of the European People's Party (EPP), noted the slow advances that were made since the signature of the Dublin Convention and in particular the gradual Europeanization of the asylum policy through the Treaties of Maastricht and Amsterdam. His criticism focused on two broad areas: the degree of involvement of the European Parliament and the European Court of Justice (ECJ) and the degree of protection, in other words the substantive rights, guaranteed to asylum seekers. It is clear that, to his mind, protection of asylum seekers that would respond to the minimum international standards set in the 1951 Geneva Convention relating to the Status of Refugees[1] and the European Convention on Human Rights[2] could only be achieved through the democratisation of the EU's legislative process, namely by increasing the European Parliament's role.

By today's standards, this is quite remarkable for an EPP member but the EPP of his time was a different creature. Indeed, one of his statements shows the distance that divides the Europe of Francisco Lucas Pires' time and the Europe of today: 'most Member States now claim for an increase of EU authority in terms of asylum and immigration policy'. Such a statement today could not be farther from the truth. A series of events starting with the sovereign debt crisis and continuing with the austerity programmes implemented in many Member States, the rise of populism and of a new alt-right, unknown in Francisco Lucas Pires' era, laid the foundation for reactions very different to the ones that many men and women of his generation would have liked to see. These reactions worsened as the Syrian refugee crisis struck the hardest on those Member States, such as Greece, that were severely affected by the debt crisis and the austerity programmes. One cannot but contrast the humanism of people like Francisco Lucas Pires with the cynicism that other contemporaries and members of his own party displayed more recently. A notable example is that of the German Minister for the Interior, Mr. Seehofer, who rejoiced in the fact that his 69th birthday 'coincided' with the deportation of 69 Afghan nationals from Germany. This is not say that these people had a right to stay in Germany but his joy did not correspond to the Christian values which supposedly constitute the philosophical foundation of his own Bavarian Christian-Social Union (CSU).

In a prophetic statement, placed at the end of his Asylum chapter and nourished by his understanding of Europe's history, Francisco Lucas Pires set out in his own words the standard we can use at present to measure the failure of EU's asylum policy:

[1]Convention relating to the Status of Refugees, opened for signature 28 July 1951, 189 UNTS 137 (entered into force 22 April 1954).

[2]Convention for the Protection of Human Rights and Fundamental Freedoms, opened for signature 4 November 1950, 213 UNTS 221 (entered into force 3 September 1953).

> Most of all, it is necessary to impose the awareness that the right of asylum is the best cornerstone or litmus test of the reality of Europe's desire to be seen by the world as an exemplary defender of fundamental rights. Moreover, no one has a greater interest than Europe in reviewing and being mindful of the painful lessons of its own history in this matter, which show us that whenever and wherever the rights of others were not taken into account, our own also collapsed.[3]

The recent Syrian refugee crisis and its aftermath proved how short the EU fell in attaining this aspiration. Hundreds of people perished trying to cross the sea from the Libyan coast to Italy whilst others drowned in the few kilometres that separate Turkey from the Greek islands. Thousands of people have been packed into squalid conditions on small islands like Lampedusa or Lesbos. Tens of thousands tried to make their way to the north of Europe through Italy or the Balkan route only to find Hungary building fences to keep them out. Member States quarrelled endlessly about the relocation of asylum seekers from Greece and Italy, with several Central and Eastern European Member States resisting relocation to the bitter end. Finally, the EU Member States and Turkey reached some kind of agreement by virtue of which Turkey would be financially rewarded for reducing the migratory fluxes from its Syrian to its Greek border. This agreement was not the end. Asylum and immigration became a hot issue in the period leading up to the October 2018 election in Bavaria and threatened to shatter the coalition between the Christian Democratic Union (CDU) and the CSU.

More recently, a new populist Italian government left numerous immigrants stranded on a vessel as it refused to allow them to disembark on Italian soil. In a fiery exchange with the Luxembourgish Foreign Secretary over immigration, the Italian Deputy Prime Minister and Minister for the Interior, Matteo Salvini, suggested that Italy should be financially assisting Italians to have more children instead of having immigrants from Africa replenish Italy's ageing population.

On 12 September 2018, the European Parliament invited the Council to determine whether there is a clear risk of a serious breach by Hungary of the EU values referred to in Article 2 TEU. According to the Hungarian Helsinki Committee, Hungarian authorities had stopped giving food to adult asylum seekers who were challenging decisions rejecting their asylum applications in court, until the European Court of Human Rights ordered the provision of food to certain applicants as an interim measure.[4] According to the report prepared by the Member of the European Parliament, Judith Sargentini, and adopted by the European Parliament, Ahmed H., a Syrian resident in Cyprus who had tried to help his family flee Syria and cross the Serbian-Hungarian border in September 2015, was sentenced by a Hungarian court to 7 years imprisonment and 10 years expulsion from the country on the basis of charges of 'terrorist acts'.[5]

---

[3]Lucas Pires 2020, Chap. 4 in the present book.

[4]Hungarian Helsinki Committee 2018.

[5]European Parliament, Report on a proposal calling on the Council to determine, pursuant to Article 7 (1) of the Treaty on European Union, the existence of a clear risk of a serious breach by Hungary of the values on which the Union is founded, 4 July 2018, A8-0250/2018, para 67. On 24 January 2019, the

After a period of relative calm and as the book this chapter forms a part of went into production, incidents at the Greek-Turkish land border started to multiply as Turkey intensified its efforts to push hundreds of unfortunate souls into the EU.

In this difficult context, there seems to be growing consensus that the EU rules on asylum and immigration are ripe for reform but any attempt at reform is bound to bring into conflict the Member States that wish to maintain the 'first point of entry' principle under the Dublin regime with the Member States that are first points of entry and cannot bear the entire burden of immigration on their own.

In this respect, it is worth recalling Francisco Lucas Pires' remark according to which 'one of the no less substantial flaws in the situation also continues to be the excessive amalgam of law and politics at the Community level with regard to the matter of asylum'.[6] In his view, things could be different if the ECJ were able to fill in the gaps left by the EU legislature and elevate the right to asylum to a fundamental right of the EU constitutional order.

The Treaty on the Functioning of the European Union put flesh on the bones of this aspiration. Article 18 of the EU Charter of Fundamental Rights recognizes and guarantees the right to asylum. As a matter of policy, asylum is part of Title V of the Treaty on the Functioning of the European Union (TFEU)[7] (Area of Freedom, Security and Justice). Its provisions, especially Article 78 TFEU, grant the European Parliament an enhanced role. Indeed, measures of the common asylum and immigration policies have to be adopted in accordance with the ordinary legislative procedure which guarantees the participation of the European Parliament on an equal footing with the Council. Finally, the jurisdiction of the ECJ and the General Court is not restricted.

Nonetheless, it is doubtful that legal reforms are in themselves sufficient to ensure the decent level of protection that Francisco Lucas Pires envisaged. Indeed, even if its level might be low or unsatisfactory or if its direction may vary depending on the tendencies of the electorate, politics is an essential and indispensable requirement for an asylum policy. In this respect, the law and the courts may not be in a position to make up for a political deficit.

This can be most clearly seen in relation to the so-called EU-Turkey Statement of 18 March 2016[8] concluded between the EU Heads of State and Government and Turkey with a view to regulating the irregular migration flows from Turkey to Greece. The Statement essentially provides that migrants not applying for asylum in Greece or

European Commission announced that it had decided to send a reasoned opinion to Hungary concerning legislation criminalizing activities that support asylum and residence applications and further restricting the right to request asylum (http://europa.eu/rapid/press-release_IP-19-469_en.htm).

[6]Lucas Pires 2020, Chap. 4 in the present book.

[7][2016] OJ C202/47.

[8]The EU-Turkey Statement is available on the European Council's website (http://www.consilium.europa.eu/en/press/press-releases/2016/03/18/eu-turkey-statement/).

whose application is found unfounded or inadmissible following an examination by the Greek authorities in accordance with the Asylum Procedures Directive[9] must be returned to Turkey. In addition, for every Syrian returned to Turkey from the Greek islands, another Syrian will be resettled from Turkey to the EU. In return, Turkey was promised a variety of benefits including visa liberalization for its nationals travelling to the EU and considerable financial assistance in the amount of EUR 3 billion.

The Statement is vulnerable to many criticisms both legal and moral. First, one cannot forget the painstaking efforts made by the EU's legal services not to call this Statement an Agreement, let alone an Agreement between the EU and Turkey. Indeed, calling it an Agreement would be problematic since none of the procedures laid down in Article 218 TFEU for the conclusion of international agreements by the EU were followed. Nonetheless, the press and the public needed to hear of an agreement reached between the EU and Turkey. This is exactly what President Tusk announced at the end of the summit by heralding that '[t]oday, we have finally reached an agreement between the EU and Turkey'. Nonetheless, an action for annulment brought by three immigrants who would fall within the scope of the Statement was dismissed by the General Court of the European Union (GCEU) on the basis that the Statement is not an international agreement concluded by the EU but, in fact, an international agreement concluded between the EU Member States and Turkey. Accordingly, the GCEU lacked jurisdiction to review its lawfulness.[10]

The issue of competence appears to have been completely lost. Even if one were to accept the General Court's thesis that the EU-Turkey Statement is an international agreement concluded by the EU, it is not a foregone conclusion that Member States had competence to conclude such an agreement, especially insofar as the Statement covers areas falling under the EU's asylum and immigration policy. Indeed, although such matters form part of the EU's shared competence in the Area of Freedom, Security and Justice, the EU has exercised its competence by introducing several pieces of secondary legislation in this area, such as the Dublin III Regulation,[11] the Asylum Procedures Directive and the Return Directive,[12] thereby pre-empting its Member States from legislating in this area.[13]

---

[9]Directive 2013/32/EU of the European Parliament and of the Council of 26 June 2013 on common procedures for granting and withdrawing international protection, [2013] OJ L180/60.

[10]See GCEU, *NF v European Council*, Order, 28 February 2017, T-192/16, EU:T:2017:128, para 73; *NG v European* Council, Order, 28 February 2017, T-193/16, EU:T:2017:129, para 74; *NM v European Council*, Order, 28 February 2017, T-257/16, EU:T:2017:130, para 72. The appeals to the ECJ were rejected as manifestly inadmissible (see ECJ, *NF and Others v European Council*, Order, 12 September 2018, C-208/17 P to C–210/17 P, EU:C:2018:705).

[11]Regulation (EU) No 604/2013 of the European Parliament and of the Council of 26 June 2013 establishing the criteria and mechanisms for determining the Member State responsible for examining an application for international protection lodged in one of the Member States by a third-country national or a stateless person (recast), [2013] OJ L180/31.

[12]Directive 2008/115/EC of the European Parliament and of the Council of 16 December 2008 on common standards and procedures in Member States for returning illegally staying third-country nationals, [2008] OJ 2008 L348/98.

[13]See Article 2(2) TFEU and Protocol (No 25) on the exercise of shared competence.

As to the question whether the EU has also external competence to conclude an agreement of this kind, Article 79(3) TFEU confers an explicit competence on the EU to conclude agreements with third countries, such as Turkey, for the readmission of provenance of third country nationals who do not fulfil the conditions for entry, presence or residence in the territory of the EU.

Further to Article 79(3) TFEU, it can also be argued that the EU enjoys exclusive external competence to conclude the EU-Turkey Statement under Article 3(2) TFEU insofar as its content may affect common rules of EU secondary legislation regarding asylum and immigration or alter their scope.[14]

The objections to the EU-Turkey Statement are not only procedural. One of its most contestable aspects is the idea of swapping people as if they were objects. Indeed, the Statement provides for the exchange of a Syrian located in Turkey for every Syrian returned from Greece to Turkey.

Despite all the criticisms, both moral and legal, that could be levied against the Statement and the fact that Turkey is stalling its implementation, the Statement remains a key part of the EU's asylum policy. Indeed, in its conclusions dated 28 June 2018, the European Council stressed the need for additional efforts to fully implement the EU-Turkey Statement, in order to prevent new crossings from Turkey and bring migratory flows to a halt.

At the same summit, the European Council entertained the proposal of setting up migrant processing centres in the territory of third countries in an attempt to deter people from making life-threatening journeys to Europe across the Mediterranean and to break the business model of human traffickers. In its conclusions, it called for the establishment of the so-called 'regional disembarkation centres' which will distinguish individuals worthy of international protection from illegal or economic migrants without, however, creating a 'pull factor'. This means, however, that resettlement possibilities in the EU will not be available to all disembarked persons in need of international protection.

It is perhaps ironic that the ECJ had recently rejected the idea that EU law required Member States to grant a long-term humanitarian visa to people wishing to travel to their territory in order to apply for asylum.[15] This was decided in *X and X*, which involved a Syrian couple with their three young, minor children, Orthodox Christians living in Aleppo, who attempted to escape their besieged hometown by applying for a visa at the Belgian Embassy in Beirut (Lebanon) with a view to applying for asylum in Belgium. This decision was reached despite Advocate General Mengozzi's dramatic call for a radically different approach:

> Before concluding, allow me to draw your attention to how much the whole world, in particular here in Europe, was outraged and profoundly moved to see, two years ago, the lifeless body of the young boy Alan, washed up on a beach, after his family had attempted, by means of smugglers and an overcrowded makeshift vessel full of Syrian refugees, to

[14]For the notion of 'common rules', see ECJ, *EU-Singapore Free Trade Agreement*, Opinion 2/15, 16 May 2017, EU:C:2017:376, paras 231–234.

[15]See ECJ, *X and X*, Judgment, 7 March 2017, C-638/16 PPU, EU:C:2017:173.

reach, via Turkey, the Greek island of Kos. Of the four family members, only his father survived the capsizing. It is commendable and salutary to be outraged. In the present case, the Court nevertheless has the opportunity to go further, as I invite it to, by enshrining the legal access route to international protection which stems from Article 25(1)(a) of the Visa Code. Make no mistake: it is not because emotion dictates this, but because EU law demands it.[16]

The ECJ did not heed the Advocate General's recommendation. It adhered instead to legal orthodoxy, according to which long-term humanitarian visas exceeding 90 days do not fall within the scope of EU law but can only be granted on the basis of national law. At the handing down of the judgment in the *X and X* case, the Belgian State Secretary for Asylum and Migration of the right-wing New Flemish Alliance (N-VA) rejoiced exclaiming on his Twitter account 'Yesss! Gewonnen!' (Yes! We have won!). One is left wondering what exactly had been won, especially in light of the fact that there was little doubt that the Syrian couple and its three children were entitled to asylum. Francisco Lucas Pires' aspiration that increasing the ECJ's jurisdiction would strengthen the right to asylum was not met in this instance.

Similarly, in *AS* and *Jafari* the ECJ did not challenge the orthodoxy of the 'first point of entry' which is entrenched in EU asylum and immigration legislation.[17] These two cases concerned the organization by Croatia of the transit of numerous migrants to other EU Member States through its territory. The ECJ held that despite the existence of a massive influx of migrants, the Member State of first entry remained the Member State responsible for examining the asylum application that those migrants subsequently introduced in other Member States.

One can probably sense a lack of appetite on the ECJ's part for the kind of legal pioneering that it demonstrated in the first decades of European integration. The initiative in this area is left with the EU's legislature and the Member States as is, for example, demonstrated by Council Decision (EU) 2015/1601 of 22 September 2015 establishing provisional measures in the area of international protection for the benefit of Italy and Greece[18] which was the subject of actions for annulment lodged by Hungary and Slovakia. Through this Decision, the Council set up a temporary framework for the relocation of asylum seekers from Italy and Greece with a view to alleviating the pressure that these two Member States suffered as first points of entry. It provided that out of 15,600 asylum seekers to be relocated from Italy, Hungary would receive 306 and out of 50,400 asylum seekers to be relocated from Greece, Hungary would receive 988, namely 1.9% in both instances. Slovakia would receive even less: 190 asylum seekers from Italy and 612 asylum seekers from Greece, namely a mere 1.2%. Being a temporary arrangement, the Council's Decision was scheduled to last until 26 September 2017, the date on which the Decision expired.

---

[16] ECJ, *X and X*, Opinion of Advocate General Megozzi, 7 February 2017, C-638/16 PPU, EU:C:2017:93, para 175.

[17] See ECJ, *A.S.*, Judgment, 26 July 2017, C-490/16, EU:C:2017:585 and *Jafari*, Judgment, 26 July 2017, C-646/16, EU:C:2017:586.

[18] [2015] OJ L248/80.

Hungary and Slovakia nonetheless challenged the validity of the Council's decision. They challenged the Council's Decision on every possible procedural aspect. They argued that:

- the Council's Decision lacked a correct legal basis;
- its period of application was excessive given its provisional nature;
- Greece and Italy as beneficiaries of the provisional measures were not confronted by 'an emergency situation characterised by a sudden inflow of nationals of third countries' and therefore the relevant requirement laid down in Article 78 (3) TFEU was not met;
- the Council infringed Article 68 TFEU and breached essential procedural requirements because the Decision was adopted by qualified majority although it followed from the European Council's conclusions of 25 and 26 June 2015 that the Decision had to be adopted 'by consensus' in a manner 'reflecting the specific situations of Member States';
- the Council failed to comply with its obligation to consult the European Parliament pursuant to Article 78(3) TFEU;
- the Council failed to act unanimously, contrary to Article 293(1) TFEU;
- the Council breached essential procedural requirements, in that the right of the national parliaments to issue an opinion in accordance with Protocols (No 1) and (No 2) was not respected and the Council failed to fulfil the requirement that the deliberations and the vote within the Council be held in public; and
- the Council did not comply with the rules of EU law on the use of languages when adopting the Decision.

On the merits, Hungary and Slovakia argued that the Council's Decision did not respect the principles of proportionality, legal certainty and normative clarity. They also alleged that the idea of relocation was contrary to the 1951 Geneva Convention relating to the Status of Refugees in that asylum seekers have a right to remain in the Member State in which they have lodged their request for international protection pending a decision on that request by the authorities of that country.

Throwing its weight behind the Council's Decision, the ECJ upheld the Council's Decision after examining and dismissing one by one each of Hungary's and Slovakia's arguments. Its judgment is extremely valuable for a variety of issues it resolved such as the status of acts adopted by the Council with the participation of the European Parliament in cases where the TFEU does not use the terms 'according to the ordinary/special legislative procedure'. The ECJ's judgment provides that such acts constitute non-legislative acts.[19] The decision of the ECJ on this matter thus led to the Council's Decision being upheld as valid. It remains,

[19]See ECJ, *Slovakia and Hungary v Council*, Judgment, 6 September 2017, C-643/15 and C-647/15, EU:C:2017:631, paras 58–66.

however, to be seen whether this is a sound decision in terms of the inter-institutional balance of powers between the Council and the European Parliament.[20]

The ECJ's judgment is also noteworthy for another reason. In its intervention in support of Hungary's plea that the imposition of binding quotas on it has disproportionate effects, Poland criticized the allegedly disproportionate effects of those quotas on a number of host Member States which, in order to meet their relocation obligations, have to make far greater efforts and bear far heavier burdens than other host Member States. According to Poland, that is the case of Member States which are 'virtually ethnically homogeneous, like Poland' and whose populations are different, from a cultural and linguistic point of view, from the migrants to be relocated on their territory.[21]

To the author's knowledge, this was the first time that the ECJ was confronted with an argument based on ethnic homogeneity. The ideological foundations of this argument can only cause sadness, especially in light of Poland's own rich history of cultural, linguistic, ethnic and religious diversity. Indeed, Poland emerged onto the global stage as an independent State 100 years ago out of the debris of the German, Russian and Austrian Empires. As such, it was far from being an ethnically homogenous State. On the contrary, it was the multi-ethnic, multi-religious, multi-cultural and multi-linguistic State par excellence to the extent that it signed one of the first minority protection treaties, the so-called Little Versailles Treaty, otherwise known as the Polish Minorities Treaty,[22] which guaranteed total and complete protection of life and freedom to all people regardless of their birth, nationality, language, race or religion. If Poland today can be considered as ethnically homogeneous, this is only the result of major crimes that were committed on its territory during the Second World War.

It is, therefore, unsurprising that Poland's argument based on ethnic homogeneity was rejected outright on the basis that 'considerations relating to the ethnic origin of applicants for international protection cannot be taken into account since they are clearly contrary to EU law and, in particular, to Article 21 of the Charter of Fundamental Rights of the European Union'.[23]

The European Commission considers that, despite the ECJ's validation of the Council's Decision, not all Member States followed through with its implementation. At the end of 2017, the European Commission commenced infringement

[20]Indeed, Advocate General Wathelet had defended the view that every procedure, according to which the Council must obtain the European Parliament's consent, such as in the case of approval of international agreements, is a legislative procedure. See ECJ, *Council v Front Polisario*, Opinion of Advocate General Wathelet, 13 September 2016, C-104/16 P, EU:C:2016:677, paras 151–158.

[21]See *Slovakia and Hungary v Council*, above n 325, para 302.

[22]See Treaty of Peace Between the United States of America, the British Empire, France, Italy and Japan and Poland, 28 June 1919. For a brief description of the treaty and the circumstances that gave rise to it, see Sands 2016, 71–74.

[23]See *Slovakia and Hungary v Council*, above n 325, para 305.

proceedings before the ECJ against three Member States, Poland, Hungary and the Czech Republic, for failing to comply with Council Decisions 2015/1523 and 2015/1601 regarding the relocation of asylum seekers from Italy and Greece.[24]

Interestingly, despite the fact that many of the Treaty reforms sought by Francisco Lucas Pires were met, a 'European necessity',[25] such as the EU asylum policy, failed to meet the quality standards that he set out in his last book.

It is probably fair to suggest that the failures of the EU's asylum policy are not due to the constitutional issues that Francisco Lucas Pires touched upon in his book but stem from the more fundamental challenges to the EU, its policies and even its existence, made by a growing part of the political spectrum in several Member States. These challenges ignore the reasons that led the generation that had lived through and survived the Second World War to create the EU and to seek greater political and economic integration.

Although anti-immigration discourse is generally on the rise across the EU, it is noteworthy that certain Central and Eastern European Member States have taken a particularly strong anti-immigration stand. This is perhaps at odds with the history of that region of Europe which was for centuries ruled by multi-national empires. In this regard, according to the historian Steven Beller, it is no coincidence that the new refuge of Central Europe after the collapse of communism was soon seen to be membership of the European Union, for that was the spiritual political heir of the Habsburg Monarchy, as a supra-national, multi-national polity, only this time with the virtue of being composed of democratic States sharing their sovereignty, rather than a dynastic collection of territories.[26] He notes, however, that the centrality of Brussels and the European bureaucracy in nationalist and populist rhetoric about the EU suggest that from a negative perspective the EU and the Habsburg Monarchy look all too similar:[27] multi-national, multi-cultural polities lacking a clear-cut identity.

Beller's interpretation of the Habsburg Monarchy's eventual collapse in 1918 was that its leadership proved unable to square the circle that would turn a conglomerate of territories into an all-embracing home for all its nations and people(s).[28] Very often, it simply stumbled upon its inability to find and implement compromises

---

[24]See pending proceedings in *Commission v Poland* (C-715/17), *Commission v Hungary* (C-718/17) and *Commission v Czech Republic* (C-719/17).

[25]The term 'European necessity' is borrowed from Steven Beller who used it to describe the Habsburg Monarchy. He argues that the Habsburg Monarchy was seen as a European necessity by other powers as well as its own nations and people due to its ability to play both sides of its dichotomy as a supra-national, multinational, polyglot, quasi-federated refuge for the small nations of Central Europe and a subordinate part of the great power complex of the greater German Empire. See Beller 2018, 241.

[26]Ibid., 283–284.

[27]Ibid., 284.

[28]A similar conclusion is reached in relation to the failure of the ideology of Ottomanism to unite and embrace all the subjects of the Ottoman Empire, regardless of ethnicity, language or faith. See Şükrü Hanioğlu 2010, 106–107, 209.

between the Austrian and Hungarian part of the Monarchy. Over time, it failed to convert the existence of the Habsburg Monarchy from a necessity to a coherent identity.[29] This is the challenge that now lies ahead of the EU at this critical juncture.

References

Beller S (2018) The Habsburg Monarchy 1815–1918. Cambridge University Press, Cambridge

European Commission (2019) Asylum: Commission takes next step in infringement procedure against Hungary for criminalising activities in support of asylum applicants IP/19/469. http://europa.eu/rapid/press-release_IP-19-469_en.htm. Accessed 28 January 2019

European Council (2016) EU-Turkey statement. https://www.consilium.europa.eu/en/press/press-releases/2016/03/18/eu-turkey-statement/. Accessed 25 January 2019

Hungarian Helsinki Committee (2018) Asylum-seekers with Inadmissible Claims are Denied Food in Transit Zones at Border. https://www.helsinki.hu/wp-content/uploads/Denial-of-food-for-inadmissible-claims-HHC-info-update-17August2018.pdf. Accessed 25 January 2019

Sands Ph (2016) East West Street: On the Origins of Genocide and Crimes Against Humanity. Weidenfeld & Nicholson, London

Şükrü Hanioğlu M (2010) A Brief History of the Late Ottoman Empire. Princeton University Press, Princeton/Oxford

[29]Ibid., 286.

Chapter 11
A Sisyphean Struggle: Portugal's Referendum on European Integration

Francisco Pereira Coutinho

Abstract Portugal is one of a handful of Member States which has never held a referendum on European integration. This chapter analyses Francisco Lucas Pires' contribution to the broad political consensus reached in Portugal on the need to hold a referendum legitimizing the shift towards political integration envisioned by the Treaty of Maastricht. One of his last books, "Amsterdam – From the Market to the European Society", is a political and legal manifesto in support of the ratification of the Treaty of Amsterdam in the run-up to what was expected to be the first Portuguese referendum on European integration. However, legal and political constraints blocked this, and every subsequent, attempt to grant the Portuguese people a direct say on Europe. This chapter explains why calling a referendum on Europe in Portugal has transformed itself into a saga that resembles the mythological Sisyphean task.

Keywords Constitutional Treaty · European Union · Francisco Lucas Pires · Portugal · Portuguese Constitution · Referendum · Treaty of Amsterdam

Professor at Nova School of Law (Faculdade de Direito da Universidade Nova de Lisboa) and member of CEDIS—R&D Centre on Law and Society (email: fpereiracoutinho@fd.unl.pt). In the Fall of 1996, while a freshman at Oporto Catholic Law School, I had the opportunity to attend a lecture by Francisco Lucas Pires to the inaugural classes of Political Science under the guidance of Paulo Castro Rangel, which quickly became my favorite course. All direct quotes from doctrinal, legal and judicial sources in Portuguese were translated by the author.

F. P. Coutinho (✉)
Faculdade de Direito da Universidade Nova de Lisboa, Lisbon, Portugal
e-mail: fpereiracoutinho@fd.unl.pt

M. Lucas Pires and F. Pereira Coutinho (eds.), *What Market, What Society, What Union?* https://doi.org/10.1007/978-94-6265-371-9_11

Francisco Lucas Pires' Thoughts on the European Referendum

Francisco Lucas Pires will always be remembered as one of the most prominent Portuguese European constitutional scholars.[1] He was also politically engaged, particularly as a member of the Portuguese (1976–1986) and the European (1987–1998) parliaments, in negotiations of both the Portuguese accession to the European Community and the treaties of Maastricht and Amsterdam.[2]

One of his last books, "Amsterdam – From the Market to the European Society", was written as a political and legal manifesto of support for the ratification of the Amsterdam treaty in the run-up to the first-ever referendum on European integration to be held in Portugal.[3]

Lucas Pires was well aware of the risks of referenda. A "democratic civil war" able to endanger national cohesion is often the result of their "simplistic, bipolar and last resort logic".[4] Nevertheless, he was also convinced that the qualitative leap to political integration initiated by the Treaty of Maastricht required the increased democratic legitimacy that could only be delivered by an instrument of direct democracy.[5]

The need for a referendum on Europe was particularly acute in Portugal. The accession to the European Community was approved in 1985 through a "parliamentary coronation" without meaningful debate.[6] The Portuguese people remained mostly unaware of the implications of a decision which filled the void created by decolonization by dramatically shifting Portugal's geopolitical alignment towards the European continent:

---

[1]Poiares Maduro 2008, 121 ("Francisco Lucas Pires was one of the most creative and original European constitutional scholars").

[2]Alves 2019, 321–324.

[3]Lucas Pires 2020, Chap. 1 in the present book. ("I hope that taking this stance will also serve to go beyond the so-called «community of interpreters» and reach the public debate that will precede the first referendum on Portuguese participation in the construction of Europe" (…). "(…) (R)aising people's awareness along the lines of «Yes, but which Europe?» and doing so in a way that is able to help reach a long-term and certain answer, could well be the most suitable and useful contribution anyone can make"). Lucas Pires 2020, Chap. 1 in the present book.

[4]Lucas Pires 1992.

[5]Teresa de Sousa and José Manuel Fernandes, "Seria um Candidato a meio presidente (entrevista a Francisco Lucas Pires)", *Público*, 20 October 1990, in *A Revolução Europeia por Francisco Lucas Pires*, Parlamento Europeu (Portugal), 2008, 234 ("My position is intermediate: yes to a Europe built bottom-up and (…) (not) by stealth, but only through a referendum in order to get to a second phase, the political Union").

[6]Lucas Pires 1985, 55.

> (…) Europe will represent for us a new paradigm of behaviour and even a deep metamorphosis. After a first historical phase – the independence and its consolidation in the Iberian theatre –, after a second – the discoveries, and the expansion and formation of a Portuguese language world –, our third phase or our contemporary history has a new framework – the European –, and a new motivation – development.[7]

A referendum on the Treaty of Amsterdam would occur in the mist of the liberal *hubris* that emerged at the end of the cold war.[8] Lucas Pires took pride in being a contemporary witness to the Economic and Monetary Union (EMU), which he considers "the victorious apogee of what is both the initial throw of the dice and the biggest milestone in the construction of Europe".[9] He even goes as far as to state that the EMU means "that the Rubicon of irreversibility has now been crossed and a formidable driving force for political union has been created".[10]

The European Union was observed as a panacea for the problems of globalisation,[11] and the Treaty of Amsterdam even criticized for not deepening political integration in order to better tackle such challenges.[12]

In this context, Portugal′s fate is indissolubly linked to European integration. Even traditional Eurosceptic political parties on the extremes of the political landscape were no longer questioning membership to the European Union.[13] Given this unusual political consensus, why then bother with a referendum?

Lucas Pires argued that a referendum would be instrumental in broadening and deepening a sense of European belonging within the Portuguese people. He believed it represented an opportunity to thoroughly discuss the future of European integration and Portuguese idiosyncrasies within it, with the aim of delivering a "contribution as a country to a «new vision» of the construction of Europe".[14] Far more than discussing the virtues and defects of the Amsterdam treaty itself, the

[7]Lucas Pires 1994a, 147–148.

[8]*L'esprit du temps* of the 1990s is reflected in the seminal book by Fukuyama 1992.

[9]Lucas Pires 2020, Chap. 5 in the present book.

[10]Lucas Pires 2020, Chap. 1 in the present book. ("(…) (T)he fact that the threshold of irreversibility and necessity has now been attained, Europe once again appears to be a construct that is consensual and happy (…)").

[11]Lucas Pires 2020, Chap. 5 in the present book. ("(…) (E)ven for the pessimists, the problem is no longer Europeanisation; on the contrary, Europe is once again the solution. Instead of change, it means protection against the fears of a rapid transformation and a sudden immersion in the «problem»—the real one—of globalisation, which, together with digitalisation, increasingly hangs like a Sword of Damocles over middle-class jobs, which are the traditional drivers of liberal modernity and stability").

[12]Lucas Pires 2020, Chap. 2 in the present book. ("At this point in time, the fact is that the large and correct question is whether what is at stake is primarily the enlargement, or rather the model for a Union of a political and enlarged Europe that is capable of unity in the face of the problems of globalisation") or, similarly, Gonzalez 1999, 37 ("We need to define the new form of political representation required by a project capable of meeting the challenges of globalisation").

[13]Lucas Pires 2020, Chap. 5 in the present book. ("(…) (N)ot only the (right wing Popular Party), but also the (Communist Party), recognise that Europe is no longer a choice but a need").

[14]Lucas Pires 2020, Chap. 2 in the present book.

referendum should mobilize a debate on the definition of the Portuguese national interest *vis-à-vis* European political integration, namely "which European model will enable (Portugal) to best defend (its) interests and reflect (its) identity after the enlargement".[15] Lucas Pires identified this interest, first and foremost, with the adoption of federal arrangements—although not a federal State[16]—aimed at protecting small/medium sized Member States against a "Carolingian Europe" or a European Directorate composed of large Member States.[17] Unfortunately, despite a traumatic international bailout, steered by a *troika* that included two European institutions (the European Commission and the European Central Bank) which paid lip-service to the interests of larger (and richer) Member States represented in a non-formalized institution (the Eurogroup), no significant progress has yet been made in formulating a national position concerning a preferred model for the future of Europe.

The 2011–2014 bailout powerfully amplifies another question raised by Lucas Pires: "What has to be done in order to succeed in a much more exposed and competitive situation such as the one that will follow the introduction of the single currency? Are we ready?"[18] We were not. Lucas Pires hoped the referendum debate would clarify "that achieving the single currency (could not) continue to be an excuse for the absence of the necessary structural reforms—on the contrary, it should be the wasp-sting that makes people act now that the conditions for growth are favourable".[19] This foresight is remarkable and revealing of Lucas Pires' deep awareness of the Portuguese collective mind-set, although it is still debatable whether such reforms would have been enough to overcome the flaws of the EMU, which also contributed decisively to the Eurocrisis bailouts.[20]

Having a referendum on European integration without aiming to steer a national debate on these contentious issues would be a fruitless, and even counterproductive, exercise, as it would mean asking people to vote on an *acquis* (European

---

[15]Lucas Pires 2020, Chaps. 1 and 5 in the present book. Increased political integration combined with the federalisation of the European Union's institutional framework would also be instrumental to secure independence from Spain, which is the traditional hegemon in the Iberian peninsula (Lucas Pires 1994a, pp. 145–146). Lucas Pires predicted that the strong Portuguese national identity and cohesion would enable it to cope far better than Spain with the centrifugal forces projected by European integration (ibid.), which is mostly to blame for the rampant nationalism observed in Catalonia (Connolly 2014, 51–105).

[16]Lucas Pires 1994b ("Europe will not be a federal State as there is neither a European people nor a European territory. But I accept the word «federate», as Europe is very much a cooperative federation"). Lucas Pires proposed the creation of a "federation of States" instead of a "federal State" (Lucas Pires 1995, 77).

[17]Lucas Pires 2020, Chap. 2 in the present book ("The question at point is thus whether, in the absence of another alternative, the time has come for the small countries to prefer a more federalist model which, although reducing their power as states, would also decrease the power of the big countries. Unlike the alternative offered so far, such a solution would also continue to guarantee the smaller nations a formal principle of equality").

[18]Lucas Pires 2020, Chap. 5 in the present book.

[19]Lucas Pires 2020, Chap. 5 in the present book.

[20]Bento 2013, 41–59.

membership) or on "obscure" and "complex" normative provisions, which would most likely "end up not even mobilising the fifty per cent of voters needed to legitimise it".[21]

Contrary to Lucas Pires' expectations, no referendum was held on the Treaty of Amsterdam nor on any other European treaty. Alongside Belgium, Bulgaria, Germany and Romania, Portugal stands as the only Member State never to have held a referendum on European integration.[22] Notwithstanding multiple political pledges to the contrary, legal and political constraints blocked every attempt to allow the Portuguese people to have a direct say on Europe. Calling a referendum in Portugal transformed itself into a saga that resembles the mythological Sisyphean ordeal, in which Sisyphus is eternally condemned to the exhausting and fruitless task of rolling a heavy rock up to the top of mountain only, at the summit, to have it roll back to the bottom, and for this cycle to repeat in perpetuity.[23]

The European Referendum Saga

The 1976 Portuguese Constitution was, and to some extent still is, a by-product of the revolutionary years that followed the military coup that overthrew the authoritarian right-wing regime of the "Estado Novo" (1926–1974).[24] The democratic euphoria that followed the "Carnation Revolution" was reflected in proposals that foresaw the inclusion of referenda in the constitution, including from Francisco Lucas Pires himself,[25] but the original version of the Portuguese constitution neglected this instrument of popular sovereignty. Two reasons may have contributed to this absence. One was historical and related to the stigma which was then still associated with referenda after the Estado Novo's use of a plebiscite in 1933 as a proxy for democratic constituent power.[26] The other was political; being a "highly democratic instrument", referenda only work without substantial risks within mature liberal (representative) democracies, which definitely did not describe Portugal in 1976.[27]

---

[21]Lucas Pires 2020, Chap. 2 in the present book.

[22]Ziller 2012, 246 (Table 11.1). The table does not include the 2012 Croatian referendum on the accession to the EU and the 2015 Greek bailout referendum.

[23]Homer 2016, 154. ("(…) I saw Sisyphus, suffering cruel agonies, using both his hands to heave at a monstrous boulder. Time after time he would brace himself with hands and feet to push the stone upwards towards a hill's crest, but when he was about to shove it over the top, its mass turned it back, and at once the pitiless stone bounded back to the plain").

[24]Pereira Coutinho and Piçarra 2019, 592.

[25]Lucas Pires 1975, 109.

[26]Canotilho and Moreira 2007, 98.

[27]Miranda 1978, 397.

Local referenda were included in the Portuguese constitution in 1982.[28] Calling a referendum on the accession of Portugal to the European Community was thus not an option at the time of the accession to the European Community in 1986.

The 1989 constitutional amendments introduced referenda on matters of relevant national interest, but excluded popular consultations related to international treaties.[29] The ratification of the Maastricht treaty precipitated an extraordinary revision of the constitution in 1992, where proposals aimed at bypassing this limitation were rejected.[30] The outcry against the parliamentary approval of the Treaty of the European Union prompted mainstream political parties to propose constitutional amendments aimed at allowing a referendum on European integration.[31] After a first failed attempt in 1994, referenda on matters of relevant national interest within international treaties were finally introduced in 1997,[32] just in time for the ratification of the Treaty of Amsterdam.

"Do you agree to the continuation of Portugal's participation in the construction of the European Union within the framework of the Treaty of Amsterdam?". This was the question approved by the Portuguese parliament on 29 June 1998.[33] The drafting of the question was constrained by the Constitution, which only authorizes referenda on political matters included in a legal act.[34] This meant that the referendum could not directly seek approval of the treaty itself,[35] but could only pose questions related to the latter.[36] Moreover, the question had to be "objectively, clearly and precisely formulated".[37]

The Portuguese Constitutional Court, which the President of the Republic is obliged to request a review of the constitutionality and legality of referendum

[28]Article 167(l) of the Constitution (1982).

[29]Article 118(3) of the Constitution (1989).

[30]Pereira Coutinho 2006, 90.

[31]Ibid., 90–91.

[32]Article 115(5) of the Constitution (1997).

[33]Resolution of the Assembly of the Republic 36-A/98, of 29 June (Proposal on the organization of a referendum on Portugal's participation in the construction of the European Union).

[34]Article 115(3) of the Constitution ("Only important issues concerning the national interest which the Assembly of the Republic or the Government must decide by approving an international convention or passing a legislative act may be the object of a referendum").

[35]Canotilho and Moreira 2007, 101 ("The referendum cannot be on the direct approval of the text of a law proposal or a negotiated or signed treaty"). See also concurring vote of judge Guilherme da Fonseca in the Constitutional Court, case 531/98, of 29 July 1998, para 3. Constitutional Court judgments are available in Portuguese at the website of the Portuguese Constitutional Court (www.tribunalconstitucional.pt).

[36]Portuguese Constitutional Court, 29 July 1998, Case 531/98, para 10.4. ("(…) the object of popular consultation may be (…) questions which stem from Portugal's participation in international organizations"). Article 7(1) of Law 15-A/98 (Organic Law of the Referendum Legal Framework) establishes a maximum of three questions per referendum.

[37]Article 115(5) of the Constitution.

proposals,[38] rejected the question approved by the parliament, arguing that it was misleading:

> (the question) could be interpreted by voters in the sense that a «no» answer would entail Portugal's withdrawal from the European Union.
>
> According to the current constitutional framework, a referendum on the «European question» cannot jeopardise either the approval of Portugal's previous participation in the European Union or its future membership of the latter.[39]

The Treaty of Amsterdam was ultimately approved by parliament without popular intervention.[40] The same happened with the Treaty of Nice.[41] Only with the ratification of the Constitutional Treaty did the parliament decide once more to attempt to call a referendum on the "European question". On 18 November 2004, it approved the following question: "Do you agree with the Charter of Fundamental Rights, the qualified majority voting rule and the European Union's new institutional framework as established in the Constitution for Europe?"[42]

The thematic plurality and length of the question stems from the Constitutional Court's Amsterdam referendum ruling, according to which the conditions of clarity and precision are fulfilled only when the referendum questions "shortly state the general direction or the key aspects of the treaty which is the object of the referendum".[43]

Once again, however, the Constitutional Court declared that the referendum question was misleading because it included three autonomous questions whose answer did not allow the voter "to express a global opinion on the content of the Constitution for Europe".[44]

These two failed referenda attempts reveal that the European treaties' complexity makes it extremely difficult, if not impossible, to draft referendum questions that express their main features while simultaneously meeting the constitutional requirements of objectivity, clarity and precision.[45] The Portuguese parliament seems to have reached this same conclusion. On 22 June 2005, in an extraordinary

---

[38]Article 115(8) of the Constitution ("The President of the Republic shall submit all draft referenda submitted to him by the Assembly of the Republic or the Government to compulsory prior review of their constitutionality and legality").

[39]Case 531/98, above n. 36, 29 July 1998, para 14.

[40]Resolution of the Assembly of the Republic 7/99, of 6 January 1999 (Approving, for ratification, the Treaty of Amsterdam).

[41]Resolution of the Assembly of the Republic, 79/2001, of 25 October 2001 (Approving, for ratification, the Treaty of Nice).

[42]Resolution of the Assembly of the Republic 74-A/2004, of November 18 (Proposal to hold a referendum on the Constitution for Europe).

[43]Case 531/98, above n. 36, July 29, 1998, para 14.

[44]Portuguese Constitutional Court, 17 December 2004, case 704/2004, para 8.

[45]Pereira Coutinho 2013, 325.

revision procedure,[46] it approved a constitutional amendment which allowed the people to have a direct say on the approval of European treaties.[47] The amendment was backed by a cross-party consensus on the need to hold a referendum on the Constitutional Treaty,[48] which reflected the electoral programs submitted to the parliamentary elections of February 2005.[49]

Ironically, no referendum was ever called on the Constitutional Treaty because the Member States postponed its ratification in the European Council on 17 June 2015, after popular rejections in France (29 May 2005) and in the Netherlands (1 June 2005).[50] This was much to the dismay of the Portuguese Prime Minister, who, a week earlier, stated that the "(Portuguese) government (was) absolutely determined to have a referendum on Europe", and that a European Council decision "should only be taken after all the people, including the Portuguese, had a say (on the Constitutional Treaty)".[51]

The European referendum impetus of the Portuguese Prime Minister did not last for long. On 9 January 2008, he announced in parliament that the Lisbon Treaty would not be submitted to a referendum. It is worth analysing the three arguments that supported this decision.

First, a referendum was not necessary when there was "a broad consensus in Portuguese society on the European project and on the Lisbon Treaty itself", which had the backing "of 90% of the Members of Parliament".[52] However, as Lucas Pires explains in his book on the Amsterdam Treaty, this consensus existed even

---

[46]Amendments to the Portuguese constitution may be introduced after five years have elapsed since the date of publication of the last ordinary constitutional revision law. However, by a majority of at least four fifths of all the Members in full exercise of their office, the Assembly of the Republic may take extraordinary revision powers at any time (Article 284 of the Constitution).

[47]Article 295 of the Constitution ("The provisions of Article 115(3) do not prejudice the possibility of calling and holding referenda on the approval of treaties concerning the construction and deepening of the European Union").

[48]The amendment was approved with 180 votes in favour and 13 abstentions (*Diário da Assembleia da República*, 1 Series, 32/X/1, 23 June 2005, p. 1327). This was the seventh (and last) constitutional revision procedure, and the first in which there was no votes against.

[49]Lusa, 12 December 2007 "Referendo em Portugal a Tratado de Lisboa "nas mãos" de Cavaco Silva, que é contra", *RTP Notícias*, available at http://rtp.pt/noticias/presidencia-uniao-europeia/referendo-em-portugal-a-tratado-de-lisboa-nas-maos-de-cavaco-silva-que-e-contra_n53937 (accessed on 23 August 2019).

[50]Officially, the Member States decided to take a one-year "period for reflection, clarification and discussion" on the future of the Constitutional Treaty. See European Council Press Release, 17 June 2005, "Jean-Claude Juncker states that there will be a period for reflection and discussion but the process to ratify the Constitutional Treaty will continue with no renegotiation", available at http://www.eu2005.lu/en/actualites/communiques/2005/06/16jclj-ratif/index.html (accessed on 23 August 2019).

[51]Lusa, 10 June 2015 "José Sóctrates garante que PR e Governo querem referendo europeu", available at http://rtp.pt/noticias/pais/jose-socrates-garante-que-pr-e-governo-querem-referendo-europeu_n11741 (accessed on 23 August 2019).

[52]*Diário da Assembleia da República*, 10 January 2008, 1st Series, 32, 2008, 7.

before the accession and only broadened afterwards,[53] and did not preclude almost unanimous political support—which included the Prime Minister himself—for a referendum on European integration.

Second, the Prime Minister argued that a referendum could be used to question the "legitimacy of parliamentary approval (of the Lisbon Treaty) in other Member States", increasing "the risk that the Treaty would never enter into force".[54] But how could the support of the Portuguese people in a referendum, which reflected the abovementioned consensus, be a liability for the entry into force of the Lisbon Treaty? Moreover, the Prime Minister was well aware that at least one Member State was going to held a referendum: Ireland held a mandatory referendum that approved the Lisbon Treaty only on a second try after receiving guarantees from the European Council that answered some of the concerns of the Irish people.[55] Popular rejections of European treaties in small/medium size Member States were never detrimental to their entry into force and were arguably beneficial to those Member States.[56]

Third, the Prime Minister contended that the Government's pledge to the Portuguese people was to have a referendum on the Constitutional Treaty and not on the Lisbon Treaty, which is "substantially different" from the treaty signed in Rome on 29 October 2004.[57] This argument does not hold when "most, if not all, (of) the substantive reforms envisaged in Constitutional Treaty have been preserved (in the Lisbon Treaty)".[58] The argument is based on the idea that the Lisbon Treaty is "just another international treaty without a constitutional nature",[59] thereby ignoring the autonomy of the EU legal order, proclaimed by the Court of Justice in *Van Gend en Loos*. In the latter, the Luxembourg court declared that the Treaty of Rome (Treaty of the European Economic Community) is not merely an agreement between States, but an agreement between the peoples of

[53]Lucas Pires 2020, Chaps. 2 and 5 in the present book.

[54]*Diário da Assembleia da República*, 10 January 2008, 1st Series, 32, 2008, 7–9.

[55]Council of the European Union, "Brussels European Council, 18–19 June 2009, Presidency Conclusions", 11225/2/09, Brussels, 10 July 2009.

[56]In 1992, after popular rejection of the Treaty of Maastricht, Denmark was offered the Edinburgh Agreement which proved decisive for the change of mind of Danish voters in a second referendum (European Council, "Denmark and the European Union", 92/C 348/01, *Official Journal* C 348, 31 December 1992, p. 1). In 2002, the Seville declaration was enough to persuade Irish voters who had just rejected the Nice Treaty (Presidency Conclusion of the Seville European Council, 21 and 22 June 2002, Doc/02/123, 22 June 2002, p. 3). See Atikcan 2015, 937–956.

[57]*Diário da Assembleia da República*, 10 January 2008, 1st Series, 32, 2008, 9.

[58]Piris 2010, 48–50.

[59]Parliamentary discourse of the Portuguese Prime Minister (José Sócrates) on 27 June 2007, *Diário da Assembleia da República*, 28 June 2007, 1st Series, 99, 6.

Europe,[60] which "created a municipal legal order of trans-national dimensions, of which it forms the «basic constitutional charter»".[61]

In the first real opportunity it had to finally submit a European treaty to a referendum, and symbolically one that bear the name of its capital, the Portuguese Parliament succumbed to *realpolitik*. Similar reasoning was decisive for the rejection of proposals for a referendum on the "Fiscal Compact Treaty"[62] in 2012,[63] although it was likely that the Constitutional Court would have blocked these proposals, as the Constitution does not allow for referendums that concern budgetary or financial issues.[64]

Final Remarks

European integration was the guiding light of Portuguese elites of Francisco Lucas Pires' generation, who came of age during the demise of the Portuguese Empire. Sharing this enthusiasm with the layman was going to be a challenge because "traditionally, and even culturally, the (Portuguese) were often eccentric towards Europe, up to a point where European Portuguese were considered in Portugal to be «estrangeirados» (foreigners)".[65] Lucas Pires thought that a referendum could help bridge this gap if it spearheaded a meaningful discussion on the country's priorities regarding European integration. The absence of this discussion may well explain why Portuguese turnout in the European elections is one of the lowest in the European Union,[66] and why Portuguese people rank poorly in Eurobarometer queries regarding knowledge of how the European Union works.[67] More than thirty years after accession, the European Union is still not truly part of Portuguese public space and identity.

---

[60]Court of Justice of the European Union, *Van Gend en Loos*, 5 February 1963, 26/62, ECLI:EU:C:1963:1, 210.

[61]Advocate-General Miguel Poiares Maduro, *Kadi*, C-402/05 P e C-415/05 P, ECLI:EU:C:2008:30, para 21. The "specific nature" of the European Union is also mentioned in the Opinion of the Council legal service of 22 June 2007, 11197/07 (JUR 260), which was attached by the Member States to Declaration 17 to the Treaty of Lisbon concerning supremacy.

[62]The Treaty on Stability, Coordination and Governance in the Economic and Monetary Union was signed on 2 March 2012 by all member states of the European Union, with the exception of the Czech Republic and the United Kingdom. Its adoption was precipitated by the Czech and United Kingdom's veto to the approval of a treaty amending the EU treaties (Tuori and Tuori 2014, 110).

[63]Draft Resolution No. 268/XII/1 and No. 95/XII/1, *Diário da Assembleia da República*, 1st Series, 96/XII/1, 14 April 2002, pp. 32; Draft Resolution No. 1007/XII/3, *Diário da Assembleia da República*, 1st Series, 94/XII/3, 14 June 2002, 40.

[64]Article 115(4)(b) of the Constitution.

[65]Lucas Pires 1985, 53.

[66]In the 2019 European elections, turnout in Portugal (30.75%) was only superior to Slovakia (22.74%), Czech Republic (28.72%), Slovenia (28.89%) and Croatia (29.86%). Data retrieved from https://election-results.eu/turnout/ (accessed on 25 August 2019).

[67]McCormick 2015, p. 281, Fig. 17.5, which shows that only Germans, Italians and Danes rank below the Portuguese in agreeing with the statement "I understand how the EU works" (Eurobarometer 79, Spring 2013).

References

Alves E (2019) Lucas Pires, Francisco. In: Baltazar I and Cunha A (eds) Dicionário das Grandes Figuras Europeias. Assembleia da República, pp. 312–325.
Atikcan Ö (2015) The Puzzle of Double Referendums in the European Union. Journal of Common Market Studies 53, 5, pp. 937–956.
Bento V (2013) Euro forte, euro fraco – duas culturas, uma moeda: um convívio (im)possível? Bnomics.
Canotilho G and Moreira V (2007) Constituição da República Anotada, 4th rev. edn. Vol II. Coimbra Editora, Coimbra.
Connolly C K (2014) Independence in Europe: Secession, Sovereignty, and the European Union. Duke Journal of Comparative and International Law, 24, pp. 51–105.
Fukuyama F (1992) The End of History and the Last Man. Free Press.
Gonzalez F (1999) European Union and Globalization. Foreign Policy, 115, pp. 34–43.
Homer (2016) The Odyssey (transl. Verity A). Oxford University Press.
Lucas Pires F (1975) Uma Constituição para Portugal. Imprensa de Coimbra.
Lucas Pires F (1985) Na fronteira da Europa: uma política para a integração europeia de Portugal. Democracia e Liberdade, 34, pp. 51–65.
Lucas Pires F (1990) "Seria um candidato a meio presidente". Público, 20 October 1990.
Lucas Pires F (1992) Referendo ou Guerra civil democrática. Expresso, 26 September 1992.
Lucas Pires F (1994a) Europa. (O QUE É), 4th edn. Difusão Cultural.
Lucas Pires F (1994b) A Europa não será um Estado federal. Expresso, 4 June 1994.
Lucas Pires F (1995) Portugal e o Futuro da União Europeia: sobre a revisão dos Tratados. Difusão Cultural.
McCormick J (2015) European Union Politics. Palgrave.
Miranda J (1978) A Constituição de 1976 – Formação, estrutura e princípios fundamentais. Petrony.
Pereira Coutinho F (2006) O Referendo Político Nacional em Portugal. In: Leão A, Pereira Coutinho F et al. (eds) Estudos de Direito Público. Âncora, pp. 11–146.
Pereira Coutinho F (2013) Referendo. In: Enciclopédia da Constituição Portuguesa. Quid Juris, pp. 323–325.
Pereira Coutinho F and Piçarra N (2019) Portugal: The Impact of European Integration and the Economic Crisis on the Identity of the Constitution. In: Albi A and Bardutzky S (eds) National Constitutions in European and Global Governance: Democracy, Rights, the Rule of Law. T.M. C. Asser Press, pp. 591–639.
Piris J C (2010) The Lisbon Treaty: A Legal and Political Analysis. Cambridge University Press.
Poiares Maduro M (2008) Um constitucionalismo para várias constituições: o pensamento constitucional europeu de Francisco Lucas Pires. In: A Revolução Europeia por Francisco Lucas Pires. Parlamento Europeu, pp. 121–123.
Tuori K and Tuori K (2014) The Eurozone Crisis. A Constitutional Analysis. Cambridge University Press.
Ziller J (2012) The Treaty of Lisbon: Constitutional Treaty, Episode II. In: Laursen F (ed) Designing the European Union: From Paris to Lisbon. Palgrave Macmillan, pp. 244–268.

The manufacturer's authorised representative in the EU is Springer Nature Customer Service Centre GmbH, Europaplatz 3, 69115 Heidelberg, Germany. If you have any concerns regarding our products, please contact ProductSafety@springernature.com

Printed and bound by CPI Group (UK) Ltd, Croydon, CR0 4YY
05/10/2026
02228154-0008